D0271125

# without a word

# without a word

## teaching beyond women's silence

### magda gere lewis

Routledge
New York • London

Published in 1993 by

Routledge
29 West 35th Street
New York, NY 10001

Published in Great Britain by

Routledge
11 New Fetter Lane
London EC4P 4EE

Copyright © 1993 by Routledge

Printed in the United States of America on acid free paper

All rights reserved. No part of this book may be reprinted or reproduced or utilized in any form or by any electronic, mechanical or other means, now known or hereafter invented, including photocopying and recording, or in any information storage or retrieval system, without permission in writing from the publisher.

Library of Congress Cataloging-in-Publication Data

Lewis, Magda Gere.
Without a word : teaching beyond women's silence / Magda Gere Lewis.
p.—cm.—
Includes bibliographical references (p.—) and index.
ISBN 0-415-90593-1.—ISBN 0-415-90594-X (pbk.)
1.Feminism and education—United States. I Title.
LC197.L48 1993                                    93-2318
305.42—dc20                                       CIP

British Library Cataloguing-in-Publication Data also available

She writes on sand or weaves cloth for the reader who can see something other than the printed page as text.

—Marcus,
*Art and Anger: Reading Like a Woman*

I have before me the image of a weaver sitting at her loom. Scattered about her on the bench and at her feet are balls and cones of yarn. Some are brilliantly colored of high intensity and interestingly unusual hues that draw the eyes. Others are more subtle and subdued—some would say even boring and nondescript. Some snap or fray easily and these she handles with care. Others are firm and strong withstanding more rigorous handling. While to the uninitiated onlooker the weaving is just now about to begin, the weaver has in fact been at work for a long time. The loom has been painstakingly dressed and now the warp is taut. Yet the loom sits inanimate, inarticulate about its potential as a tool of production/creation until the weaver throws the shuttle and, with a throwing in motion of the beater, secures the weft in place.

—Lewis,
(unpublished prose)

When we look closely, or when we become weavers, we learn of the tiny multiple threads unseen in the overall pattern, the knots on the underside of the carpet.

—Rich,
*On Lies, Secrets and Silence*

# CONTENTS

# ACKNOWLEDGEMENTS

THIS WORK HAS COME A LONG WAY SINCE THE TENTATIVE COMPLETION OF its first draft some many months ago. On that occasion, a friend offered to read and critique it. Hoping for and, simultaneously, fearing her honesty, I was grateful for the time she was willing to give to it. I was also anxious that my text bear up to her scrutiny. My fears and anxieties arose from my need to shelter this ultimately public text, to hold it in my hands for the remaining time I had it to myself. Yet these trepidations were contradicted by my desire to share and have confirmed as legitimate this text which had so much consumed and isolated me during its writing. Writing is always an exercise in contradictions and no more so than in the writing of a book. We do not work in a vacuum. The image of the solitary, independent, "objective" intellectual worker is a myth perpetrated by those who wish to keep others from speaking/writing their words/their lives. In my experience, forefronting the solitary work of writing and the singularity of authorship not only belie the many hours of discussion, shared discourse, critique and debate but as well hide the support of those who have cared enough to stay around while I struggled with both the joys and the pains of this text.

When I arrived at her home, both late for and apprehensive about our pre-arranged discussion, I found my friend crying. Her explanation both moved and disturbed me. Like her, I—and many women—go about our daily work repressing our pain and hiding our open wounds even (or perhaps especially) from ourselves. Ignoring or covering up the raw scars of oppression we manage to achieve a level of active engagement most of the time. We raise children, do work both inside and outside our homes, go to school, and engage in social and political movements aimed at making real the rhetoric that claims concern for human dignity. At the same time, we know that we do not set and enforce social policy, we do not benefit, proportionately to men, from our work and education, and we do not set the terms of the social and political agenda of the relations in which we are engaged.

Were it not for our ability to hold these contradictory realities in our heads at the same time, were it not for our ability to mediate the conflicting nature of our subordinate and violated social position, we would, as my friend suggested in the graphic way she has with language, be "bleeding all over the place all of the time." And yet we all know the pain when the tenuous scabs of feigned sanity are scraped off. The silence of the oppressed is not all of a piece. As an experience it is neither totalizing nor without its contradictions which allow us the spaces to transcend and transform our possibilities. Rubbing against the coarse realities of our subordination measured in both big and small ways, we cannot escape the terror of our wounds. The stories of other women are often the precipitating moments that force us to acknowledge our own pain and to hear the crescendo of the trembling of our collective silence.

Over the many months of writing it, I have come to care deeply about this work, about the way its writing has touched me and those around me and about the possibilities it promises for how I understand my own teaching. I care, also, about those whose reading of this text might move them to feel safe enough to share their own silences. Finally, as I now leave it behind me, I am encouraged to find a brief moment of tranquility when I might once again touch my world the way it should be touched when one's mind is not burdened by the pressures of writing this painful text of the body.

There are many who have contributed, often without their even knowing how much, to the richness and challenges of my intellectual, political, and personal life. "An honorable human relationship," writes Adrienne Rich (1979, p. 188), "that is one in which two people have the right to use the word 'love'—is a process, delicate, violent, often terrifying to both persons involved, a process of refining the truths we can tell each other. It is important to do this because it breaks down human self-delusion and isolation. It is important to do this because in so doing we do justice to our own complexity. It is important to do this because we can count on so few people to go that hard way with us." For "going that hard way" with me I am greatly indebted to all those students, colleagues, friends and family who have shared with me their stories, who have risked speaking the meanings they have made of their lives in order that I might measure, and keep in perspective, the meanings I have made of my own.

Some of these individuals enter my life daily in intimate ways. Others have touched me more distantly but no less profoundly through their writings and their own professional and personal commitment to healing and mending a scarred world. To each one of them I am truly grateful. I thank the many students who have entered my classrooms and have risked the challenges that a transformative pedagogy required of them, in particular: Megan Aston, Marie

Barton, Sonja Boyce, Jennifer Cann, Irene Chisholm, Deborah Collins, Michele Corbiel, Jennifer Cunningham, Susan Fowler, Karen Grossman, Hanna Kaufman, Felica Kelso, Esther Lee, Leslie Lewis, Morna Mathie-Nelson, Sharon Mohamdee, Andrea Moffat, Mutindi Ndunda, Judith Popiel, Andrew Postma, Laurel Schilling, Alison Taylor, Tina Tom, and Sharon Wohlgemut. I thank Pat Deir who, by keeping my working life organized, created the space I needed to devote to this work. I am grateful for the friendship of Lyse Ward who over many years has helped bring humor and perspective to difficult times. I thank those who, through their own work and a commitment to inclusionary practices, have provided me, over many years, with an intellectual and collegial environment without which I could not have proceeded, specifically: Deborah Britzman, Linda Brodkey, Anne-Louise Brookes, Glenn Eastabrook, Elizabeth Ellsworth, Jane Gaskell, Kathleen Herman, Patti Lather, Nancy Lesko, Kathleen Martindale, Mimi Orner, Ruth Pierson, Kathleen Rockhill, Amy Rossiter, and Barbara Schlafer. I shall always be indebted to Philip Corrigan and Dale Spender who were the first to suggest that this work might be a book. Not only their openness to sharing freely their exceptional insights but also their mentorship has meant more to me than they could possibly know. I thank Janet Miller and Jayne Fargnoli, who, through their support of this work turned the possible into the real. I thank Valerie Walkerdine with whom, while I have shared only sporadic conversations on those occasions when we have found ourselves on the same continent, I have never been able to find that moment when I could tell her how deeply her work has always touched me. I thank Roger Simon, who, through his own commitments to teaching with integrity and honor clarified the politics of self-reflection as a radical act and thereby laid the foundations for my pedagogical practices. As well, I thank him for sharing with me his intellectual rigor and willingness to listen and challenge in ways that over a number of years of my graduate studies made it possible for me to explore and reemerge from worlds in which I might otherwise have perished. I acknowledge Dorothy Kirkby in her life committed to teaching, learning and sharing her creative energy. I am deeply indebted to my mother and father, Erzsebet and Lajos Gere, whose lives have taught me about caring and taking a stand. I thank and dedicate this book to my children, Christine, Geoffrey and Cameron whose lives speak to the future even as they strive to create their own meanings out of our shared past. And finally I thank Barbara McDonald with whom I share the words/worlds of this text and a life intertwined with commitment to struggling for a better world. There are no parts of this text that have not in some way been touched by ongoing conversations in which we never have to explain ourselves.

# 1 | BEGINNINGS

Stories and narrative, whether personal or fictional, provide meaning and belonging in our lives. They attach us to others and to our own histories by providing a tapestry rich with threads of time, place, character, and even advice on what we might do with our lives. The story fabric offers us images, myths, and metaphors that are morally resonant and contribute both to our knowing and our being known.

The narrator too has a story, one that is embedded in his or her culture, language, gender, beliefs, and life history. This embeddedness lies at the core of the teaching-learning experience.

—Witherell and Noddings,
*Stories Lives Tell: Narrative and Dialogue in Education*

Writing always requires some measure of disassociation from the tumble of daily life. Because, historically, women could not easily "achieve" such disassociation, our access to intellectual production has always been problematic and invisible. Indeed, were it not for the fact, in this age of technology and the rush of the postmodern struggle for meaning, that the computer has become the representational image for those who write, my writing this work might never have caught anyone's attention. However, in the last stretches of this work, and because the solitude required to complete it continued to elude me, I had taken to carrying my computer back and forth between my office and my study. Even though it is just a very little computer—small enough to be carried easily under the arm—its presence was enough to make the doing of my work rather more visible than it would otherwise have been. It is, therefore and ironically, this visible and burdensome coding of my work—for however little it is, my computer will never achieve the subtlety and sheer grace of my fountain pen tucked safely and invisibly into its case in my bag—that has generated more questions about my writing than might otherwise have come my way.

Despite the often anxiously lived moments that such questions cause me to feel, the requirement to tell what this book is about is, I believe, a useful undertaking in the service of clarity and focus. This book is about feminist pedagogy: It is about the issue of women and silence as a social, cultural, and historical artifact; It is about the implications for education of the politics of women seeking autonomy and self-determination (Pierson, 1987); It is about speaking of experiences which I know make women vulnerable in institutional environments built on repressing the personal—even where such "personal" *is* the substance of what happens to us in the political; It is about speaking out at a historical point when the backlash against women seeking autonomy, whether inside or outside the academy, is visible, real, and frightening; And, in the end, this book is about *the lived contradiction between silence as oppression and silence as revolt.*

In distinct ways, this book is highly *academic* and *theoretical.* Coming as it does directly from my teaching and work in the university, the questions I raise in this book are questions that have, in one way or another, been with me for a long time: What does it mean to be a feminist teacher? What are the significant aspects of feminist scholarship? What is feminist about Feminist Pedagogy?

In other ways, this book is quite *personal,* even, perhaps *intimate.* The personal claims regarding what this book is about sound much more pedestrian, yet much more impassioned than what is expected of me as an academic. The book is about my experiences as a feminist in the classroom. It is about the realities of women's lives told through what I know about the world. And it is about women's experience of silence as the grounding of my pedagogic practice.

Finally, fusing content with form, the intent of this book is to articulate the politics of the personal as the basis for thinking about teaching and learning in ways that do not reproduce the status quo. By embracing the politics of the personal—as this is lived through the concrete mandates of gender even as we contest them—this work signals the stepping into a dialogue about the frustrations and questions I have about teaching and learning as a woman and a feminist in the academy.

## PEDAGOGY AND THE "QUESTION OF SILENCE"

As a woman who teaches women, I am among those feminist teachers and scholars who have worried about the way women's silence has been coded in the academy. I have worried, as well, about how I might look anew at the practices and possible meanings associated with women's silence as a function of our multiple and complex social location. More specifically, as I contemplate pedagogical strategies in classrooms heterogeneous in gender, class, race, ethnicity, sexual desire, and age, I ask myself how it might be possible to formulate a conceptual understanding of women's silence not, as has been traditionally the case, as a lack that concretely reaffirms women's nonexistence, but rather as the source of an active transformative practice.

Our need as feminist teachers is to find a pedagogic practice that can address women in terms other than through the patriarchic symbolic order. Just as this requires more than offering women spaces within which to speak but which foreclose serious challenges to those phallocentric discourses which have limited and violated us, it requires more than "including women" in the curriculum. I question what sort of understanding of women's silence is required in order to see in it women's concrete and active engagement of the world as social, political, and economic agents in the face of massively phallocentric discursive and symbolic practices that support the governing order in patriarchic institutional structures and ideological formations.

As a pedagogical "problem," women's silence has most often been articulated and framed within an ideology of deficiency—as a consciousness drugged into stupor by the opium of male power. Hence, the interventions envisioned are most often directed toward compensating for this presumed lack. Yet, all around me I see women from all social, cultural, ethnic, racial, and economic backgrounds contesting the myth of our nonexistence even as we articulate the limits of our possibilities. From my own experience, I know that not all of what appears to be women's silence is the absence of discourse. Infused with the context of my own lived realities, the text of this book gives integrity and political meaning to my own silences grown, as I know they are, not out of inadequacy and deficiency, but of a deeply felt rage at those who live their unexamined privilege as entitlement.

By fusing an examination of that silence which cannot be spoken with an understanding of that silence which offers the possibility of a transformative politics—silence born of dissent—I come to the writing of this text with my feminist double vision (Kelly, 1984) simultaneously looking inward and outward in search of the locus of domination/subordination; in search of the practice that might free all of us from both; in search of a pedagogical practice that might address women's silence not as an absence but as a political act; and in search of a practice that can hear women's silence as I hear my own and make out of it a discourse directed toward change.

There are no recipe answers to these concerns—and in this book none will be offered. However, it is possible to generate a set of propositions about the potential of a feminist pedagogy as a transformative practice in the context of institutional settings. I believe that it must be possible for women to speak as women and to be heard within the social context to which we are and have always been central as the subordinate. Locating the barriers we need to speak beyond is the first step in dismantling them.

If we are to generate an educational project out of this process we need to develop our own methods, articulated through theories and discourses which as Audre Lorde has suggested:

> enable us to descend into the chaos of knowledge and return with true visions of our future, along with the concomitant power to effect those changes which can bring that future into being. (1984, p. 111–112)

### EXPERIENCE AS A FEMINIST ISSUE

Without question, this is a feminist text. Feminism is a politics of active social transformation achieved, as Sheila Radford-Hill (1986) suggests, through the shared conceptualizations and meanings of our exploitation as women. This can no more be accomplished at a purely theoretical level than it can be without a clear articulation of the transformation toward which practice is directed. Hence, as is suggested by Kathleen Weiler:

> for feminists, the ultimate test of knowledge is not whether it is 'true' according to an abstract criterion, but whether or not it leads to progressive change. (1988, p. 63)

Feminism is a political practice whereby we:

> move from the ideal, the archetypal in our portrayals of women's experiences, to the real, the concrete, the particulars of our lives—those daily activities that may distinguish us from one another and yet also unite us. (DeShazer, 1986, p. 296)

It is possible to see the common features of phallocentric oppressive forms only by expressing explicitly their variations reflected through the prism of racism, or class subordination, or homophobia, and so on. Working for change in terms aimed at staying attentive to our own best interests requires that we make specific both the ways we share common oppressions and alienations as well as the ways in which our oppressions and alienations differentiate us by virtue of our race, ethnicity, social class, and sexual desires.

What sets feminism apart from other forms of transformative practice is its explicit focus on generating suggestions for practice based on experience. I take de Lauretis' (1984) meaning of experience by which she means:

> a process by which, for all social beings, subjectivity is constructed. Through that process one places oneself or is placed in social reality, and so perceives and comprehends as subjective (referring to, even originating in, oneself) those relations—material, economic and interpersonal—which are in fact social and, in a larger perspective, historical. (p. 159)

Designating experience as the ground for social transformation is central to a feminist politics because it is here—in our experience, not some abstraction of it—that we find both our subordination as well as our strength. Politicizing the personal through the articulation of experience is supportive of this process. With Adrienne Rich I believe that:

> only the willingness to share private and sometimes painful experience can enable women to create a collective description of the world which will be truly ours. (1986a, p. 16)

It is precisely because of the power of the personal that, traditionally, the academy has encouraged us to believe that knowledge is possible only if we set our looking outside of the context of our lived realities. Contained by the blinders of "objectivity" our peripheral vision has been limited by those restrictive codes which forbid personal discourse. In this context, telling the "truths" we have lived is both difficult and risky; more so for those in positions of subordination—as women are.

On the one hand, women's experience in the academy, whether as students or teachers, serves to confirm how far we have yet to go as feminists in being thought legitimate. And yet, even as I say this, I realize that perhaps the reality is even more perverse: It is precisely because our concerns are known to be legitimate that such violence is directed toward our political analyses; analyses which threaten the foundations of Western intellectual thought and political power, but analyses which, as well, are wholly dependent on that which the academy has excluded from its practice—the acknowledgment that knowledge is a function of personal experience.

It is precisely the denial of the legitimacy of such expression that forms the locus of phallocentric power. Pushed into the private, the politics of the personal is made invisible. Personal institutional dilemmas become private burdens unspeakable except to make their speaker inadequate. By trivializing our experience as mundanely personal and hence insignificant, we live out oppressions and subordination with eyes cast to the ground limiting the horizons of our own visions.

With Patricia Williams, I believe that:

> the personal is not the same as [the] "private": the personal is often merely the highly particular. I think the personal has fallen into disrepute as sloppy because we have lost the courage and the vocabulary to describe it in the face of the enormous social pressure to "keep it to ourselves"—but this is where our most idealistic and our deadliest politics are lodged, and are revealed. (1991, p. 93)

Even as we are encouraged to keep our secrets to ourselves, we know that withholding the truths we have chosen not to tell frames not our liberation but our need to survive intellectually, emotionally, psychologically, socially, and economically both in the realm of the private and in that of the public. For women in a phallocentric world culture this bears particular relevance.

As Catharine MacKinnon defines it, "the personal is political" means:

> that women's distinctive experience as women occurs within that sphere that has been socially lived as the personal—private, emotional, interiorized, particular, individual, intimate—so that, what is to *know* the *politics* of women's situation is to know women's personal lives. (1983, p. 247)

The exploration of the political effect of the distinction between the public and the private is key to the analyses in this book. The stories I tell here are offered as a tapestry, the woven texture of which emerges as a particular kind of telling. This text is one which fuses concrete experience with the abstractions of theory in the service of understanding. It is offered as a way of traversing the distance between the private/personal and the public/political. In this respect, the experiences of which I speak in this book are both private and public matters in that I explore both individual/personal as well as collective/political relations and the conjunction between them.

Clearly, as a political practice, I embrace the emancipatory fusing of the personal and the political in women's lives. However, as a textual form, holding that fusion in place was a struggle. I did not want to negate those experiences and desires in the realm of the personal which are lived through the concrete dynamics of family, friends, students, colleagues, commitments, obligations, work, social, moral and ethical imperatives. But I also did not want to subordinate the analytical rigor required to formulate new and politically effective notions of women's silence. This challenged me in particular ways. To begin with the telling of my own story seemed self indulgent; of interest even to myself only vaguely. I wanted to guard against that potential "explosion" as Kristeva puts it so reverberantly, "of an ego lacking narcissistic gratification" (1986, p. 200). Yet, to begin with the political seemed redundant. It seemed violating of exactly that personal position from which an understanding of the political could arise.

I was aware that the struggles to legitimize the private/personal places from which we speak are validated by most feminist theorists. Yet, it seemed to me that the actual textual practice that would support these politics are—with only a few exceptions and with good reason—mostly avoided. Fully aware of the attendant risks, in this text I wanted to make that practice part of my agenda.

Interestingly, reflecting on my own dilemmas about these beginnings served only to confirm the very realities about which I proposed to write: that is, women's contradictory situation in which we are positioned in such a way so as to be simultaneously the object of phallic discourse while we are non participants in its articulation:

> locked into the determinations of an order in which there are no limits, no outside, (woman) . . . exists only in the space between signs, radically exterior to any given meaning system. (Longfellow, 1986/87, p. 29)

## "MEMORY WORK" IS A DANGEROUS AND UNCERTAIN TERRAIN

While I embrace the idea of this politics as emancipatory, the actual doing of it is not an easy prospect. As I made the decision to attempt the, as it turned out, difficult yet necessary project of drawing on my own experience as the ground of my analysis, I continually weighed the personal impact against the political possibilities of this text. I wondered how I might confirm through my own words the power of the feminist political position as a lived condition. Telling our stories is not a simple act abstracted and objectified from the social/political contexts within which they are lived. The theoretical forms presented by the "stories" we tell are embodied in individual and concrete lives, lives lived close to the bone at the level of the everyday and lived in the interstices between the public and the private. While I support the political/ intellectual practice that takes seriously experience as the source of knowledge, for me, the challenge of this text lay in the question of how to articulate the politics of the personal with sufficient self-reflection to satisfy the politically transformative power of feminism and simultaneously survive the potential (self-)violations of such an analysis. This is neither a trivial nor an easy task to face up to.

Reclaiming the centrality of women's contribution to history, to social and economic development, and to culture is the context within which women can begin to legitimate our own experiences. It is also the context within which we might transcend the split between personal experience and social form. And finally, it is what is necessary in order to bridge the gap between hysteria—"the conflict between instinctual impulses and their repression"—and legitimate discourse. For many women, this bridging is dangerous indeed as we are caught between moments of re/examination, re/evaluation, re/appropriation and re/affirmation on the one hand and experiences of pain and loss on the other.

The double meaning of the notion of "danger" signifies the contradictory condition of women's subordination and exploitation—a condition which frames how women come to know (Brookes, 1992).

Sharon Welch is suggestive of this when she says that:

> dangerous memory . . . is not only a memory of conflict and exclusion as in Foucault's genealogies. It is also a memory of hope, a memory of freedom and resistance. . . . In order for there to be resistance and affirmation that is implied in the presentation of the memory of suffering, there must be an experience that includes some degree of liberation from the devaluation of human life by the dominant apparatus of power/knowledge. (1985, p. 39)

Yet, the difficulty posed by a textual practice committed to making public the private struggle over meaning is, as suggested by Chris Weedon, the extent to which:

> it involves personal, psychic and emotional investment on the part of the individual. (1987, p. 79)

As women, we know the lived effects that the speaking of our "dangerous memories"—telling the stories of the realities we have lived—requires us to negotiate. Contradictorily the speaking of our "dangerous memories" have both conservative and revolutionary moments. On the one hand, recalling our "dangerous memories" encourages only tentative speaking as we remember those times when we had assumed particular interpretations of social relations/possibilities and then found that those interpretations turned against us because we had (in the joy of speaking) forgotten the context.

We know from experience, that the contest against the inscription of our own domination is often met with brutality and violence—the very violence against which we try to speak our words. Turned back on us as deviance and inadequacy, our difference is used to justify a vast range of interventions intended to "normalize" (Griffin, 1981/82). Or, by turn, it is used to justify a vast range of exclusionary practices at the most fundamental level. Yet we know that the subordinate condition of our difference is not a function of our biology. Rather it arises from the propositions for normality put forward by those who have the power to enforce it. As a consequence, our desire to expose the "dangerous memories" of our social and cultural realities brings us to a place from which we can speak only very quietly—often tentatively—always with a fragile trembling like china on an insecure wall mount. Having several times crashed to the ground and now holding together with "crazy glue", the seams are still, and perhaps forever, visible against the ornamentation designed in the first instance to adorn but now functioning to draw our eyes away from the markings which continually remind us that there are such seams which mark profoundly.

Similarly, as women, we cannot hide all of the insecurities that come from the recall of those moments of violation that forever after the event relocate all of our seeing, all of our speaking—relocate our very desires. As a consequence, our memories of violation and subordination are dangerous for their potential to serve as conservative moments, requiring us to measure our words and to weigh their impact always within and against the phallocentrism which marks us as being outside it; making us wish to turn away from the possibilities for transformative praxis; making us "wish we didn't know what we know"; and making us deny our visibility as the Other in order to embrace invisibility and silence as a strategy of survival.

On the other hand, our "dangerous memories" are the basis of our collective consciousness of resistance, subversion, and political action. For this reason, our memories are dangerous to the culture within which we experience our violation and subordination. As Paulo Freire (1972) has suggested, memories of violation and exploitation are pedagogically powerful because of the possibilities such memories afford for learning and action for change (Lewis, 1977). In this context, our rememberings/retellings are dangerous not because they are interesting cameos of people's lives—providing a voyeuristic access to deeply private life stories—but precisely because they stand as a critique of the ways our social relations are organized. As critique, their neutrality is denied as they are repositioned within a transformative discourse.

To be politically effective, our "dangerous memories" require that we hold the past in the present. This connectedness to the past is important, as Adrienne Rich has said, not in order "to pass on a tradition but to break its hold over us" (1979, p. 35). Feminist practice requires the holding of our "dangerous memories" in tension with the transformations necessary to bring about a new reality. What does this mean?

## UNDERSTANDING THINGS MAKES IT EASIER TO CHANGE THEM

The importance of the feminist focus on "the story" born of experience is not the vacuous and gratuitous telling of our private stories as a cathartic moment, but, indeed, to emphasize that subordinate groups live subordination and marginality through our subjectivity, that we live it through social relations which are inscribed in personal practices which are, in turn, reflective and constitutive of our social organization. It is to emphasize that our subordinations are lived precisely in the context of the details of our individual experiences which, to the extent that they can be made to seem to be private, cannot then offer the ground for a collective political practice.

Linda Brodkey (1987) has said that:

> the story generated by theory can be evaluated in the discourse that recalls experience. (p. 74)

Conversely, not only is "experience" that through which our subjectivity is constituted, but it is also the substance of theory—that on which we hang the meanings we make of the world. The fact that experience is the substance of theory has particular meanings for women. Much of what we experience of the world is the dichotomous and contradictory realities that, on the one hand, overdefine our social status through our bodies and, on the other hand, require our consent to be absent from the spheres of social and political interchange.

As an example, I often think of the difficulty women have in reconciling this contradiction whenever I observe a young adolescent woman displaying the peculiarly North American version of this struggle: hidden under the multiple layers of clothing all several sizes too big for their developing female bodies, young women seem, justifiably, to be unwilling to concede childhood any sooner than is required of them. Popular images of women reflected through the visual media of television, magazines, billboards and the cinema all work to collude in presenting the acceptable body forms which women are encouraged to embrace—bodies that are often underclothed and unnaturally posed in invitational postures. However, as women, we also know that when we embody such prescriptions of ourselves, particularly dire consequences follow. We know that to live out the body forms as displayed, is to agree that women are by our own design (pun intended) the objects of ridicule, verbal, emotional, psychological, and intellectual abuse, sexual assault, physical violence, and rape. The *good girl* who does as she is told, is, by the transpositions of the phallocentric "double-cross-reversal" (See: After the Words, this volume) transformed into the *bad girl* who should have known better.

Clearly, how we experience our lives as girls and women is not arbitrary. Nor is our subordination a function of our difference but rather of the discursive forms and relations that delimit its meanings. In short, it is women's experience, not the elaboration of women's and men's difference, that is the bedrock of what is possible for us. The discourse about women's separate sphere is dangerous precisely because it hides women's centrality within phallocentric social relations as subordinate. It conceals the fact that it is precisely women's central, though subordinate position, that is so essential to the power of phallocentrism; a position that "supports our social institutions at the same time that it serves and services men" (Kelly, 1984, p. 57). Yet, as women, we know that we find ourselves subordinate not because our biology rooted in difference puts us there, but because our biology defined through politics denies us (Delphy, 1987). In other words, we know that the subordination of women does not arise out of our biology but out of a particular "interpretation of biology" (Eisenstein, 1983, p. 22).

We do not need experts to tell us that our experiences in the world, marked by the structural relations of patriarchy/phallocentrism, are massively different from those of men and that these different experiences generate profound inequalities between us. Phallocentrism always inscribes us (and here I include both women and men) in the masculine in relation to which we (but especially women and those men who refuse its inscriptions—which is, I note, different from not embodying it), can only be deviant (McDonald, 1993). Such inscriptions are deeply felt, lived, and concretely experienced, yet our struggle against them are not always spoken.

Women's and men's divergent social experiences, as is the case with all differentially empowered social groups, form a pattern that becomes the foundation of how our social world is organized not just across gender, but across a whole range of disjunctions between dominant and subordinant groups. None of these stand independently, but instead form a web of mutually supportive social structures and relations that continually turn back on themselves. As social, political, and economic relations, these disjunctions always appear as a landscape on three canvases which, while they exist independently, can only be made sense of as an interdependent and interconnected whole. It is a pattern that is reflected through the content and process of educational provision, through the kinds of work women and men do inside and outside the home, through the way family life is organized and idealized, and through the way the social agenda is set, who sets it and for what purpose.

For the majority of the population—women, racial and ethnic minorities, the working classes, the young and the old, and for those whose erotic desires do not conform to the requirements of heterosexuality—these inequalities become profound daily experiences, marked fundamentally by disempowerment, the struggle to survive, and silencing. This is the power of phallocentrism: the modal form of subordination.

The notion of subjectivity as a social position constructed in discourse is central to the theory of feminism. It is also central, I believe, to how we might transform feminist notions of women's subject formation into a pedagogic practice. For me, the burden of this text lies in bringing into coherence practice and theory through a clarification of my understanding of the relationship between experience and meaning-making as the basis of subject formation.

How we understand language and subjectivity is central to this project. In her book *In Other Worlds: Essays in Culture and Politics*, Gayatri Spivak makes the following statement:

> The problem of human discourse is generally seen as articulating itself in the play of, in terms of, three shifting "concepts": language, world, and consciousness. We know no world that is not organized as language, we operate with no other consciousness but one structured as a language—languages that we cannot possess, for we are operated by those languages as well. The category of language, then, embraces the categories of world and consciousness even as it is determined by them. (1987, p. 77–78)

Language, as Spivak explains it, is the tool of a political practice. It brings together the lived realities of our experience with the meanings we apply to that experience through the stories we tell ourselves of what we know about the world. However, understanding experience—and, therefore, understanding where and how one might begin the critique of gendered social/pedagogical practices—is no simple matter. Experience does not speak for itself; it is not the site of uncontested meanings. "Experience," says Chris Weedon (1987), "has no inherent meaning" (p. 34). Rather, we are able to uncover the politics of our subordination as we interrogate our experiences for how they delimit what is possible for us. The agenda of a feminist politics directed toward transformation is not to validate the telling of our stories and, thereby, hold them up as the irrefutable source of our knowledge. Rather, the political efficacy of a transformative pedagogy based on feminist principles arises from the extent to which it can broaden the understanding of our experience (Weedon, 1987, p. 79).

As de Lauretis explains it:

> the notion of experience . . . is crucial to feminist theory in that it bears directly on the major issues that have emerged from the women's movement—subjectivity, sexuality, the body, and feminist political practice. (1984, p. 159)

This is not intended to totalize all experiences of all women and all men for all time. Certainly there are specific individuals who have been able to work out personal relations in their own and collective lives which are not founded on the enactment of oppression, subordination, and the appropriation of women's labor and words. It is, in fact, this possibility which makes feminism a politics and not proselytization. While it is important not to reduce every particular individual to the collective of which they happen to be a part, at the same time, however, we cannot shrink away from uncovering those forms of social relations that mark and brutalize, both individually and collectively, those who carry the weighted baggage of their gender, class, race, and sexual desires—forms that continue to perpetuate oppressive and hurtful experiences. Social, political, and economic disparities are the foreground of the oppressions/repressions that are the very texture of phallocentric social forms. To be sure, we live these oppressive/repressive social forms differently both within cultures and across cultures (See: Silvera, 1983, 1991; Jayawardena, 1986; Moraga and Anzaldua, 1981/83; Hull, Scott, and Smith, 1982; hooks, 1981, 1984, 1989, 1990, 1992; Silman, 1987; Brookes, 1992). As Anne Phillips has said:

> class and race and gender are *not* parallel oppressions. . . . No one, is 'just' a worker, 'just' a woman, 'just' black. (1987, p. 10–11)

These are all converging/intersecting as well as diverging/contradictory social realities. There is no doubt that much of the absence from history, from culture, and from participating in setting the terms of the social agenda is accomplished by the discursive absence of all disregarded and exploited peoples even as they remain physically central to the oppressive practices that stage their silence. However, as Gerda Lerner points out:

> The point is that men and women have suffered exclusion and discrimination because of their class, [race, cultural and sexual identity], yet no man has been excluded from the historical record because of his sex while . . . all women were. (1986, p. 5)

Like Patricia Williams:

> I [am] not concerned with ranking degrees of pain into some kind of hierarchy, although of course degree is vital to the maintenance of perspective. (1991, p. 72)

What does concern me is addressing women's collective consciousness (Keohane, Rosaldo and Gelpi, 1981/82; Bartky, 1985), the central feature of which is the experience of silence: being silenced/choosing silence. Naming the silence or articulating the experience of it is not easy.

## ISSUES CONCERNING FORM AND PRESENTATION

How to proceed textually was a challenge. As I stated at the beginning, my intention in this book is to explore through content and form the meaning of women's speaking and silence in the context of a system of signs, significations, and discourses that privilege phallocentric interests. In the act of taking up this text, I was constantly struck by the enormity of the contradiction which its production required me to overcome. It has been suggested that as academic women:

> We must continually ask ourselves why we write. What do we hope to achieve through writing? This is an especially important question for academic feminists since there are so many pressures to write without regard for audience or purpose, and to privilege our conversations with men and their traditions. (Sawicki, 1991, p. 2)

In this work, I wanted to write beyond the restrictive boundaries that make the concept of the writing woman an oxymoronic category. Madeleine Grumet (1988) has suggested that there is, in "esthetic practice":

> a dialectic of withdrawal and extension, isolation and submission . . . that requires both the studio where the artist harvests silence and the gallery where she serves the fruit of her inquiry to others. (p. 94)

To the extent that "esthetic practice" requires the nonlinear spiraling of this dialectic in a mutual exchange between the public and the private, women's access to intellectual production is problematic. As I believe is the case for many women, for me the dialectic between the "studio" and the "gallery" not only holds open the possibility for creative work, but, as well, articulates those moments of closure that define me through the terms of my participation in the social construct "woman." Despite Grumet's tenacious and politically burdened resolve to identify the "artist" by the use of the feminine pronoun, women can claim for ourselves neither a safe public space of intellectual exchange, nor take as given the possibilities for solitude in the private sphere (Wear, 1993). For women, both the public and the private aspects of intellectual work present a particular dilemma. Laced with contradictions and what I have called the "double-cross-reversal" of phallocentric language regimes [See: After the Words, this volume], the discursive legitimation of our subordination hides the lived realities both of our public and of our private lives.

Breaking the silence is difficult enough. To talk/write about it seemed sometimes to be impossible. In the first place, the difficulty for me in this process was the need to reconcile the way I know it makes me—as it does all women—vulnerable to those very processes of marginalization toward which the uncovering of our experiences are directed. And second, textual beginnings implied a linearity that continually collapsed in my head as I attempted to fuse together words that at the very least could be accessible to my reader. Yet the layers of meanings and the language through which to articulate these meanings continually seeped into one another in ways that wanted to defy this traditionally linear mode. The linearity of this writing could only do violence to those realities about which I wished to speak and write.

In "Curriculum as Form" Madeleine Grumet talks about the gap wherein lies the critically educational moment—between:

> the axiomatic world of science (which) describes space and time as connected, relative and cyclical, (and) the lived world of space and time (which) disassociates them. (1985, p.11)

Teaching and learning can have effective human outcomes only so long as we acknowledge that experience itself is not linear. Our moments of experience transform our ways of seeing not only what is to follow, but as well what has gone before. They re/form our consciousness at the moment of their generation, uncover understandings, and generate constantly new visions of past events and future possibilities. In writing these words it was hard to know where to begin precisely because beginnings not only transform what has not yet been written, but themselves are continually transformed by what is to follow, which, in turn, prompts ways of re/thinking these beginnings.

In the end linearity had to find a comfortable coexistence with the spirals of lived experience. Similarly the fusing of the private with the public, at times mediated through metaphor, while at other times brought into view by the direct retelling of old stories, helped to uncover the politics of personal experience and to give these personal experiences social meaning.

In general, the stories I share here are intended as an exploration of my understanding of the nature and import of how our social relations are organized through the specific discourses which assign to each of us our particular social position. Understood as metaphor, the creative potential of these stories lies in the possibilities they create for making concrete the abstractions of ideology. A metaphorical writing/reading allows, as Kristeva suggests, that we: "break the code . . . shatter language . . . find a specific discourse closer to the body and emotions, to the unnameable repressed by the social contract" (1986, p 200). With Kristeva, "I am not speaking here of a 'woman's language', whose (at least syntactical) existence is highly problematic and whose apparent lexical specificity is perhaps more the product of social marginality than of a sexual-symbolic difference."

Rather metaphor allows a moving back and forth between theory and practice in such a way that it makes problematic those everyday, common social practices which otherwise appear to be devoid of political meaning. It also allows the possibility of uncovering the subtly yet deeply embedded nature of our social relations that, in the name of freedom, justice, and democracy, in the name of love, vision, and hope threatens to destroy us. And in the end it allows us to:

> forge a collective voice, construct representations that could authenticate women's experience without lapsing back into the old models, the old gestures, the circular movement by which resistance is undermined and returned as the same, as the mirror image of the status quo. (Longfellow, 1986/87, p. 27)

The accounts which comprise the stories in this book are not intended as demonstrations of women's silencing. Nor is it the case that my interest in these accounts is to present the exemplary nature of the incidents described. Rather, they are to be read as narratives that serve as the lens through which might be articulated a possible pedagogic practice. The stories I offer are intended as concrete moments of transformative possibilities that do not presume to offer teaching strategies, but rather suggest analytical context from within which such strategies may be developed. The question posed by these accounts are intended to help locate those necessary epistemological shifts required to achieve possibilities for pedagogic intervention. In this sense then, these accounts serve as disruptions of that discourse that would wish to limit women's desires within a phallocentric text. They are intended to raise to view questions of how the contradictions of women's speaking and silence might present spaces and strategies for teaching and learning.

These stories are an invitation to the reader to bring a creative reading to what we are encouraged to see as common and unremarkable/unremarked in the everyday details of our everyday lives that we have learned to live—learned to live so well, in fact, that their political intent is no longer obvious to us.

Like every story we tell, the telling of my stories is not arbitrary: these are not just any stories, told anytime, anywhere. The specificity of these narratives, my telling them here, and my claiming them as *my* stories makes this text an act of political intervention consciously chosen by me to enact a moment of transformation. In the simplest sense, the chapters of this book reflect a private struggle over meaning as much as they constitute political stories and reflect political struggles.

What makes storytelling political—and, therefore, potentially transformative—is the fact that other stories may also be told. I want to affirm that the possibility of telling a multiplicity of stories exists. Indeed, such different tellings are useful as a way of possibly telling another story altogether—one that might focus on the ground of our difference, not so that we might finally decide who is right and who is wrong but so that we might:

> learn about the terms on which others make sense of their lives: what they take into account and what they do not; what they consider worth contemplating and what they do not; what they are and are not willing to raise and discuss as problematic and unresolved in life. (Brodkey, 1987, p. 47)

To be sure, the stories I tell here are not the only stories to be told. Others may have altogether different stories to tell. This is not an attempt to silence those voices. Indeed, the story we would tell "differently" would not lack the seam of our social difference. Being women and men within multiple social/cultural environments renders not only our experiences but, as well, our understandings of our experience different. The voices of my social difference will be heard in this text. However, this is not a theoretical liability. Rather, it is the basis for political action. I believe that achieving solidarity across our difference—however these may be marked in gender, class, race, ethnicity, desires of the body, body proficiency, and presentation, or any other socially divisive category of our human be/ing—is the challenge of feminist practice. And transforming the terms of our difference toward the possibility for social equality is the potential achievement of feminist politics.

# 2 FRAMING WOMEN AND SILENCE
## DISRUPTING THE HIERARCHY OF DISCURSIVE PRACTICES

Understanding things makes it possible to change them. Coming to see things differently, we are able to make out possibilities for liberating collective action as well as for unprecedented personal growth—possibilities that a deceptive sexist social reality has heretofore concealed.
—Bartkey
"Toward a Phenomenology of Feminist Consciousness"

It is in looking at the nightmare that the dream is found.
—Moraga and Anzaldua
*This Bridge Called My Back:*
*Writings by Radical Women of Color*

There will be a time when our silence will be more powerful than the voices you strangle today.
—August Spies

I HARDLY EVER HAVE OR FIND THE TIME TO READ FICTION. MY life's work has taken me variously into the sphere of student, teacher, mother, political activist, and researcher—sometimes all of them at once. While in the main, the political struggles toward which I direct my work seem mostly to be hopeful and surely making a difference, the work itself is also often difficult and exhausting. Before beginning to write the manuscript for this book, and noting my need to put aside the work that had so engaged me all year, I determined that I would spend my two-week vacation by the lake reading only fictional novels—books I had been "meaning to read" for a long time. Included on my list was *The Handmaid's Tale* by Margaret Atwood.

Because I had always regarded the reading of fiction as, at best, a leisurely activity meant for those who have time on their hands, not work on their minds, I approached the reading of this book as sanguinely as it is possible to do knowing one is about to engage Margaret Atwood. Cocooned in my hammock with cooling drink in hand, I eagerly anticipated her firm, powerful, unambiguous words which I hoped would be tempered by the warm sun, the relentless breaking of the waves pushed by the somnolent summer breezes and the vague and distant sounds of my children's voices as they cavorted unencumbered by the constraints that imprison them during most of our Canadian winter—school and snow suits.

Such peace, however much needed, was not to be mine. With Margaret Atwood I entered a world that overnight, without prior warning, and with the aid of a simple technological process—the computerized obliteration of women as autonomous and self-determining human beings—had shut women down/out/in. Denied access to financial resources, to jobs and positions of political decision making, to education and control of their own sexuality and reproduction, the women in Atwood's book were rendered once and for all silent.

Atwood's words left me angry. She did not offer the emotional and intellectual peace for which I longed under those most idyllic leisurely circumstances. She did not deliver the promise of fiction to match the much needed tranquility of my summer afternoons and evenings by kerosene lamp. Instead, her book transformed me into the "mad woman" (Gilbert and Gubar, 1979) on the beach made hysterical by my rage—a profoundly concrete human emotion often denied to women through a "sleight of word" which, by equivocating on the double meaning of madness, transforms women's anger into hysteria (Daly, 1978; Spender, 1980; Gilman, 1973).

Yet, even as I repeatedly heaved into the sand Atwood's unsettling words, I knew, as one knows at those deep levels of body response to a text that causes disquiet, that the rage washing over me was not born of my impatience with the fabrications of another's whimsical and unlikely imaginings. Atwood's words had flung me to the outer limits of my objectivity not because I had, by suspending disbelief too uncritically, allowed myself to be happily cajoled away from the rigors of everyday life. Rather, my anger came from the realization that in some ways, ways I already knew about, the brutal yet simple reality of the world Atwood laid before me was already with us.

Much as a biologist might present an organism under a microscope, in *The Handmaid's Tale* Atwood presents a world which, because distorted through magnification, displays an oversized image that repels us by making its aspects seem unreal, disproportionate and grotesque. Yet, despite our repulsion at an image that, unlike our commonplace reality, may make us wish to take our eyes from the microscope to look with the naked eye and, in our search for comfort, reassure ourselves that the world is still as we had always known it, not the overwhelming monster into which the magnifying lens had transformed it, we know that we can never quite forget what we had seen. My resistance to the disquiet Atwood's text forced upon me achieved little success. Returning again and again to Atwood's book I searched for those connections that would allow me to understand why its reading caused me such pain.

The Handmaid's Tale uncovers the logic of phallocentrism as no theoretical account ever could and exposes, through metaphor, the simple brutality with which women's voices are battered into silence.

In this explanation, I use the concept "phallocentrism" instead of the more commonly used term "patriarchy" because I want to signal an expanded notion of the system within which women have been subordinated worldwide. While the term "patriarchy" has come to mean a total system of entitlements and privileges accrued through specific acts of domination, oppression, and exploitation in the social, political, and economic realm, I believe, with Gerda Lerner (1986), that the common usage of the term "patriarchy":

> distorts historical reality. . . . It can be argued that in the nineteenth century (and onward) male dominance in the family simply takes new forms and is not ended. Thus, the narrow definition of the term "patriarchy" tends to foreclose accurate definition and analysis of its continued presence in today's world. (p. 239)

As is suggested by Toril Moi, male domination is not only a concrete political and economic organization but, as well, a linguistic and social organization which "defines women and (simultaneously) oppresses them accordingly" (1985, p. 163). For this reason, my preference is to use a term that, as a symbolic discursive system, includes not only the material constraints of women's lives, but also the namings, meanings, and referents through which these constraints are given social connotations.

In other words, by choosing to use the term "phallocentric" I wish to expand our understanding of male dominance beyond its operations in the economic and legal spheres of our social organization to its functions within a deeper, more fundamental systemic set of relations of inequality. The term signals the inclusion not only of traditional ways in which women have been subordinated to the "male head of household" (the father or husband or lacking either of these, the son/brother—young or old so long as male), but also of the symbolic system through which our social relations are organized and maintained, extending beyond but still including immediate familial forms of patriarchic dominance.

The force of this social process requires a discursive system that prioritizes, not only concretely in terms of social practice, but as well symbolically in terms of assigned meaning, men's words over the words of women. Phallocentrism is that sort of discursive system.

Not only particular topics but particular modes of expression become acceptable not because they are so for obvious reasons of logic or because they are more expressive of particular truths, but because they are:

> grounded in the working worlds and relations of men, whose experience and interests arise in the course of and in relation to participation in the ruling apparatus of this society. (Smith, 1979, p. 148)

Understanding this created for me a transformational moment, one that gave words and images to my growing dis/ease about ideological practices that hinted at the increasing backlash to a collective feminist social consciousness (Faludi, 1991). Simultaneously, Atwood's text raised difficult and important questions for me about the sources, meanings, and import of women's silence. I needed to make sense of my resistance to the brutalizations Atwood described in her text as simply/terrifyingly an extension of the social, political, and economic realities that form women's daily experiences in the present.

With Chris Weedon, I believe that:

> the wish to give expression to women's subjectivity is a key motivation behind the current feminist emphasis on the importance of speaking out as women. (1987, p. 81)

Indeed, as has been suggested by Angela Miles, within the frames of phallic discourse, speaking the stories of our abuse, violation, poverty, marginalization, and powerlessness—and these in their varied cadences across different cultural, historical, class, race, and sexual identities—requires not the voice of a victim but that of a powerful sense of a self refusing to be subordinated (personal communication, 1987; see also Chernin, 1987; MacKinnon, 1987).

This makes me think that women's silence has not been adequately theorized. Feminist literature notes it, describes it, and locates it historically and culturally. To be sure, this is an important place from which to begin our understanding of the conditions of women's silence. Yet, if our understanding only takes us as far as pinpointing women's psycho/social construction as deficient on the one hand or as indicating women's weak political/material conditions defined through absence on the other, we risk losing its political significance and potential. It is, furthermore, inadequate to spotlight specific political and pedagogical strategies designed to redirect our attention and practice away from addressing our presumed deficiencies and toward engaging our active presence.

This chapter is an exploration of this dynamic from the point of view of women in the context of a pedagogical response to the diverging constraints and possibilities posed by our lived realities.

Spurred by the practical questions raised by teaching from a feminist perspective in mostly mixed gender classrooms and the offer of a theory of women's subordination provided by Margaret Atwood, the urgency of finding the limits and possibilities of my own teaching is imperative. The questions I need to ask and probe in order to clarify the political intent and efficacy of my teaching converges with the theoretically infused narrative of Atwood's text in a way that illuminates for me the profound implications of male power and privilege.

I begin by analyzing two feminist texts presented through the medium of film. My intention is to present two specific moments of analysis, to capture them in the lens of my feminist "double vision" in order to make sense of how it might be possible to generate a pedagogy out of women's double-edged discourse of speaking and silence.

## FIRST CASE IN POINT: A JURY OF HER PEERS

The short film *A Jury of Her Peers* (Heckle, 1980) is based on the story of the same title written in 1927 by Susan Glaspell. It is a succinctly articulate expression of the possibilities for understanding the discourse of women's silence as a subversive politics. In it Mrs. Peters, a woman who is "married to the law" by virtue of being the wife of the local sheriff, accompanies Mrs. Hale, a neighbor of the woman, Mrs. Wright, who is being held on suspicion of murder in the death of her husband who was strangled as he slept.

The sheriff Mr. Peters, the neighbor Mr. Hale, and a third man, the county attorney Mr. Henderson, have come to the isolated farm house in order to try to piece together sufficiently firm evidence of Mrs. Wright's guilt that would hold up in court. The men have come to investigate the site of the murder. Mrs. Peters and Mrs. Hale are brought along to gather up some of Mrs. Wright's personal belongings to take to prison for her as she awaits the laying of charges—personal belongings which, importantly, Mrs. Wright had specified and requested them to bring to her. While it is clear that the men believe Mrs. Wright to be guilty of her husband's murder, they also know that, given the circumstantial nature of the "crime," without evidence for the motive the woman might never be charged: "Mr. Henderson said, coming out, that what was needed for the case was a motive. Something to show anger—or sudden feeling," said the sheriff's wife in conversation with Mrs. Hale.

During the course of the short film which focuses mostly on the interaction between the two women in the kitchen, Mrs. Peters and Mrs. Hale piece together a story of violent emotional, psychological, and quite likely physical brutality and abuse on the part of the murdered husband toward his wife.

The source of all of the evidence required to judge Mrs. Wright's guilt or innocence is yielded by the kitchen, the place assessed by the men as least likely to suggest anything important and, therefore, not worthy of their attention. "Nothing here but kitchen things," says the sheriff in response to the county attorney's question as to whether the kitchen should be investigated for clues.

Indeed, as the men search the house, the yard, and the barn for significant signs of violence, they overlook the ways in which the evidence they seek is visible in the mundanities of everyday life made palimpsestic as the "trivial" superimposes on the "important"—stories inscribed on the surface of the ordinary yet hidden to those made blind by the brilliance of their own self-regard: a bag of sugar abandoned in a hurry and left half emptied into the sugar bin; a table only half wiped—work left quickly and unfinished; a fallen-over broom; the broken leg of a rocking chair left unrepaired; shabby clothes folded neatly in a chest; fragments of quilting squares on some of which the stitching had been pulled too tightly; a broken bird cage ("looks as if someone must have been rough with it" says Mrs. Hale) carefully put away under the sink; and finally, at the bottom of a small box containing fragments of colorful quilting fabric, the decomposing body of a bright yellow canary whose neck had been wrung ("No," says Mrs. Hale with growing insight, "Wright wouldn't like the bird—a thing that sang. She used to sing. He killed that too.")

The men do not believe that leaving the women alone in the kitchen could result in any significant risk to the discovery of evidence for the motive to the murder. The irony of Mr. Hale's words will eventually become evident: "Would the women know a clue if they did come upon it?" The men's judgement that the women would not be capable of identifying significant clues is magnified in its violation by their mocking laughter. Nor do they assume, should Mrs. Peters and Mrs. Hale find anything, that the women might make different sense out of their findings and therefore have reasons for declaring solidarity with the woman in jail rather than with the interests of the men who wish to accuse and punish the woman for murdering her husband:

> I suppose anything Mrs. Peters does'll be all right? She was to take in some clothes for her, you know—and a few little things. *Of course Mrs. Peters is*

*one of us.* And keep your eye out, Mrs. Peters, for anything that might be of use. No telling; you women might come upon a clue to the motive—and that's the thing *we* need. (emphasis added)

The men do not question their own prejudiced interpretation of life in the isolated farmhouse and, in particular, of the events that might have taken place the previous night. That Mrs. Wright might be guilty, not of self-defense but of murder, seems to be, for the men, a foregone conclusion reflected in the attorney's words: "I guess before we're through with her she may have something more serious than preserves to worry about."

Initially, the women, Mrs. Peters and Mrs. Hale, whose differential social positions in the community make them unlikely social companions, engage in rather benign exchanges intended to fill the discomfort of the social moment. Indeed, Mrs. Peters seems somewhat ill at ease in the home of the imprisoned woman whose social status is more closely akin to that of her neighbor Mrs. Hale than to her own as the socially and quite likely economically advantaged wife of the sheriff. In contrast, rather than discomfort at being in the home of her neighbor in her absence, Mrs. Hale feels anger at the investigators for requiring that the women join the men in trying to "turn her own house against her." She also feels a deep and culpable regret in not having been more supportive of her neighbor whom she knew was obviously experiencing considerable difficulties in her life with a man whose assumed privilege to violate seemed without question. She admonishes herself:

Oh, I *wish* I'd come once in a while! That was a crime! That was a crime! Who's going to punish *that*? . . . I might 'a' *known* she needed help! I tell you, it's *queer*, Mrs. Peters. We live close together, and we live far apart. We all go through the same things—it's all just a different kind of the same thing! If it weren't—why do you and I *know*—what we know this minute?

This story might suggest a variety of analytical approaches, not the least of which is how it might contribute to the debate surrounding the definition of "family violence" across a range of violations from physical to emotional abuse. The question of whether the specific version of women's self-defense— often done when the attacker is incapacitated in some way—should be admissible as justified given the context of male provocation in the patriarchic family marked by the uneven physical strengths of the combatants is another issue that might be considered in a legal response to particular enactments of women's violence. And finally we might reflect, with Mrs. Hale, on the social definition of crime: whose meanings are invoked, who has the power to judge, and who determines the punishment? These are all important questions the debates around which articulate the tensions between the rhetoric of equality and the reality of the violations of power.

All of this aside, what I find interesting is how, as the women come closer to understanding the truth of the details that led to the death of the husband of the imprisoned woman, their verbal interchanges become more indirect. The dialogue, from the start fragmented and coded, becomes even more so as the drama unfolds.

The two women evaluate the circumstance of their neighbor's life as revealed by the kitchen things, socially insignificant yet providing all the women's understanding. In their conversation with the women, the men never fail to demean the life sustaining and comforting work of women from which they themselves benefit. In contrast, Mrs. Peters and Mrs. Hale register both the details and the significance of the condition of the kitchen.

Indeed, perhaps because they wish to prepare the case that justifies her husband's brutality against her, the men search for signs of moral weakness in Mrs. Wright's apparent inability and/or unwillingness—in the end it comes to the same thing—to keep an "acceptable" house (Showalter, 1985; Steedman, 1982, 1986). Based on the state of the kitchen roller towel, the attorney judges that Mrs. Wright's housekeeping skills were inadequate. "I wouldn't say she had the homemaking instinct," he says to the "ladies"—a term used often throughout the film with a contemptuous tone aimed at diminishing and belittling the women and the work required of them. In opposition, Mrs. Hale defends her neighbor by suggesting that life lived with a man whose presence would not make a place any "the cheerfuller for [his] being in it" is neither easy nor conducive to a lighthearted disposition.

Mrs. Hale transposes what the men have assumed to be Mrs. Wright's guilt in the death of her husband and instead holds the dead man, as she does all men, responsible for the condition of women's lives. In this her words are heavy with metaphor. Offering an explanation for the dirty roller towel Mrs. Hale says: "Those towels get dirty awful quick. Men's hands are not always as clean as they might be." To this Mr. Henderson responds with a laugh, a keen look and perhaps some insight laced with a faint sense of worry—a concern he deflects by his diminishing of her and the possibilities for solidarity among women: "Ah, loyal to your sex, I see." We might wonder if men's fear of women's insights regarding the politics of gender arises because of the potential for oppositional practice such understanding makes possible.

The imprisoned woman is aware that her only chance at a fair "trial" is if, in her absence, she can make a case for herself to the other two women. Through a series of requests for personal items, Mrs. Wright leads Mrs. Peters

and Mrs. Hale to the evidence of her brutalized life and the motive and ratio-
nale for her act of self-defense in a moment of rage culminating in the death
of her husband by strangulation. Claiming her competence in "women's
work," Mrs. Wright expresses concern about her preserves. This leads the
women to examine the preserve cupboard where they discover that her hard
work had gone to naught as the bottles broke for lack of heat in the house.
Mrs. Peters speaks:

> Oh—her fruit. She worried about that when it turned so cold last night. She
> said the fire would go out and her jars might burst.

In her absence, Mrs. Wright develops a coded discourse between herself
and the other two women—a discourse of shared experience and understanding out of which sense and meaning might be made in her defense. By
drawing their attention to the preserve cupboard, Mrs. Wright offers it to the
two women as evidence in support of her case. Her meaning is not lost on
Mrs. Peters or Mrs. Hale:

> It's a shame about her fruit. I wonder if it's all gone? Here's one that's all
> right. This is cherries, too. I declare I believe that's the only one. She'll feel
> awful bad, after all her hard work in the hot weather. I remember the after-
> noon I put up my cherries last summer.

Later, seeing the only surviving jar of fruit on the table, Mrs. Hale suggests
using it as a way of communicating to Mrs. Wright that the understanding she
required of them to bring to her situation had been accomplished. She says:

> If I was you I wouldn't *tell* her her fruit was gone! Tell her it *ain't*. Tell her
> it's all right—all of it. Here—take this in to prove it to her!

Then, because she also knows that Mrs. Wright is in the hands of "the law"
and all that that implies, she says: "She—she may never know whether it was
broke or not."

In contrast to the women's shared knowledge, the men remain unaware of
the significance the women draw from this moment: "Well, can you beat the
women! Held for murder, and worrying about her preserves!"

The condition of Mrs. Wright's life is further articulated through the
mean and drab state of the house itself, amplified by the disheveled kitchen
juxtaposed against the view from the kitchen window of a brand-new and
well constructed barn. The search for her nightgown leads the women to a
picture of Mrs. Wright in happier days when, as Minnie Foster, "she used to
wear pretty clothes and be lively—when she was . . . one of the town girls,

singing in the choir. But that—oh, that was twenty years ago," says Mrs. Hale regretfully.

Finally Mrs. Peters and Mrs. Hale look in the pine chest in the kitchen. They are in search of a clean apron which Mrs. Wright asked them to bring to her. Initially this request perplexes the women: "Funny thing to want . . . for there's not much to get you dirty in jail, goodness knows." However, subsequently its significance is revealed. In the chest they find the colorful box filled with quilting squares and at the bottom the dead canary with the twisted neck.

Quilting is a central metaphor throughout the text: the active process of piecing together colorful/expressive bits of cloth/information which, while each in itself seems insignificant and without value, becomes meaningful, useful, and articulate when the pieces come together into a coherent whole through the painstaking attention to detail and the collective work of women. Quilting as a metaphor for consciousness-raising is both a useful abstraction and historically a concrete reality of women's lives (Barton, 1991).

The conversation between Mrs. Peters and Mrs. Hale is significant:

> Mrs. Hale:  She liked the bird. She was going to bury it in that pretty box.
> Mrs. Peters:  When I was a girl my kitten—there was a boy took a hatchet, and before my eyes—before I could get there. (She takes a long, reflective, and revealing pause, then continues.) If they hadn't held me back I would have *hurt* him.

Through observation, careful consideration, and knowledge born of shared experience, Mrs. Peters and Mrs. Hale weave their way to the motive for the "crime" and find their own reflection in it.

With all of the evidence in, the stage is set for the judgement. In her absence, Mrs. Wright has led the two women through the evidence of her abuse and makes the case for her own defense.

In the end Mrs. Hale acting as "counsel" representing the accused and Mrs. Peters acting as "judge" assessing validity find the woman not guilty of murder on the ground of just provocation. However, in the final moment of determination the women also know that the body of the dead canary—the condensed site of Mrs. Wright's own life of abuse—could be used equally to indict her as well as it could to exonerate her. The women act on their judgement: Mrs. Peters attempts to stuff the small box containing the dead bird into the pocket of her bag. Her bag being too small, however, precipitates the moment of active collaboration/solidarity among the two women as Mrs. Hale takes the box and puts it into the pocket of her loose coat just as the men—whose voices first invade the women's silence—reenter the room having failed to find anything definitive by way of evidence of the woman's guilt or innocence.

In closing the story, I quote at length from the written text:

> Again, for one final moment, the two women were alone in that kitchen.
>
> Martha Hale sprang up, her hands tight together, looking at that other woman, with whom it rested. At first she could not see her eyes, for the sheriff's wife had not turned back since she turned away at the suggestion of being married to the law. Slowly, unwillingly, Mrs. Peters turned her head until her eyes met the eyes of the other woman. There was a moment when they held each other in a steady, burning look in which there was no evasion nor flinching. Then Martha Hale's eyes pointed the way to the basket in which was hidden the thing that would convict the third woman—that woman who was not there, and yet who had been there with them through that hour.
>
> For a moment Mrs. Peters did not move. And then she did it. Threw back the quilt pieces, got the box, tried to put it in her hand-bag. It was too big. Desperately she opened it, started to take the bird out. But there she broke— she could not touch the bird. She stood there helpless, foolish.
>
> There was a sound at the door. Martha Hale snatched the box from the sheriff's wife and got it in the pocket of her big coat just as the sheriff and the county attorney came back into the kitchen.
>
> "Well, Henry," said the county attorney facetiously, "at least we found out that she was not going to quilt it"[referring to an earlier conversation between the two women when they were examining Mrs. Wright's quilting—when Mrs. Hale removed the evidence of Mrs. Wright's stressful state coded through the tightness of her stitching on some of the quilting squares]. "She was going to—what is it you call it, ladies?"
>
> Mrs. Hale's hand was against the pocket of her coat.
>
> "We call it—knot it," was her answer.

The irony of Mrs. Hale's words is powerful. As the film closes Mrs. Peters and Mrs. Hale depart with their husbands, leaving the attorney to "poke around a bit more" to see if he can turn up anything. The evidence he might have found with which to incriminate the woman, however, slips away in Mrs. Hale's pocket having instead already vindicated her.

The purpose of this example is not to valorize women's silence. Nor is it to fabricate it as a language of difference and thereby transform it into a form of mystical communication governed by intuition and emotion. Women's language seen exclusively as a function of women's biology deprives both women and men of the possibility of envisioning a future free of gender inequalities. Rather it is important to note the social and political context within which the women's discourse of silence was constructed. It is precisely these social and historical relations which:

while marking their speakers as "Other" . . . also give expression to "other" experiences, permit coded discourse, and the expression of anger and protest. (Smith-Rosenberg, 1986, p. 35)

Were it not the case that control over women's intellectual, emotional, and physical labor is the unproblematized social norm supported by an edifice of policy, legal, and ideological structures justifying (encoding) violence against women, Mrs. Peters and Mrs. Hale might have thought it appropriate and safe to use quite "common" language in which to expose the evidence of the emotional, psychological, and physical abuse to which their neighbor was subjected, confident that unequal power relations and the discursive forms through which such relations are articulated would not be the guiding principles on which their neighbor's guilt or innocence would be determined.

Contrary to Sheila Rowbotham's suggestion that women's "version of the world has always been fragile and opaque" (1973, p. 34) the version of the world the women in this drama understand is quite clear. With Sonia Johnson, I believe that:

tearing the scrims away from our eyes is necessary, that it is essential to look clearly at women's lives, and without flinching to see the truth about men and women. (1987, p. 262)

Our subjectivity as women is not confused or poorly developed—as is often suggested by educational theorists who, by focusing on notions of false consciousness, would wish to dismiss the real and lived contradictions of our everyday experiences and choices. Rather, embedded in our historically specific social structure, our subjectivities are constructed within those conditions made available by the constraints and possibilities offered by this structure.

Nor is it the case that our voices are fragile and opaque. Stripped of its political context and therefore of its potential to stand as a powerfully subversive social form, the signifying practice that is often identified as women's problem, lack, deviance, and proof of our deficiency, is women's silence. Yet, what is at issue is not women's silence, but men's appropriation of women's words for the purpose of advancing their own interests. The following is a case in point.

I recall some time ago, a radio review of the film version of Alice Walker's *The Color Purple*, produced by Steven Spielberg. The reviewer spoke about the strong character development in the film, its well developed story line, and its well balanced humor and pain. He spoke about (and seemed surprised by) the incredibly complex female characters around whose lives the action of the film revolved. And he talked about Spielberg's genius! It astonished me to realize that as the review ended not a single mention was made of the fact that the film, with only a couple of omissions of substance, was based almost verbatim on Alice Walker's book. Alice Walker's name never came up once. For those listeners unaware of the written text or of the fact that at the time of the film review the book was listed as number one in *The New York Review of Books* had no way of knowing that the movie was not a single-handed creation of Steven Spielberg's genius.

Such appropriation always carries the burden of sexism and is not discursively benign. Women know that the consequences of our speaking are various and often severe since our words may be reinterpreted for us within those frames inscribed by the masculine that give our words meanings other than, short of, or beyond those which we intended for them. This reinterpretation leaves us forever and without end *explaining ourselves* only to find that every explanation suffers the same fate leaving us ultimately with no explanation at all and therefore mercifully silent, yet still suffering the brunt and pain of having our words mistaken for male words, inscribed within the signifiers of the masculine, subscribing to and fulfilling the needs of masculine desire. And sometimes we lose nerve altogether, and our practice fails as our words are co-opted, sucked into the dominant discourse as if into a "black hole," and then released anew clothed as a whore might be in the company of her pimp, he enticing us loudly to believe that our words have not undergone brutal transformations for the experience. Patricia Williams is insightful in her analysis of the situation of women caught in the discursive lacunae of speaking and silence:

> split at the seams and returned to the womb . . . lay huddled in a wilderness of meaning, lost, a speechless child again, her accommodative language heard as babble. (1991, p. 197)

Our concern is not with women's discursive lack but rather about a cultural, political, and ultimately historical discourse of the everyday, the present, and the immediate. Mrs. Peters and Mrs. Hale know that their words may be used against them. Hence, they do not simply refuse dominant discourse but act in opposition to it. To do so requires new namings and new meanings not free of the history out of which they have sprung, but precisely connected to it and explicitly expressed.

By way of an oppositional analysis, I want to reappropriate, for the purposes of re-examination from a feminist/pedagogical standpoint the social meanings ascribed to women's silence. Furthermore, I want to disrupt the understanding that seems able only to support the dominant images of women as both silent and by our silence simultaneously consenting to and absent from a discursive arrangement of male privilege to name the world.

Our subjectivities are constructed within those conditions made available by the constraints and possibilities offered by the historically specific social structure. To the extent that our voices carry the weight of our collective history, these formations of our subjectivity are not unconsciously appropriated or uncontested even as we may discursively reinforce them.

The case I want to make here is that there is an active discourse of silence which is politically grounded as well as politically contained. To the extent that women's social/economic survival is structurally connected to our relations with men, severing our selves from it is a potentially dangerous prospect. Yet not to challenge its conceptualizations leaves us equally annihilated. Understanding this dynamic is one aspect of the feminist political project. The other is the will to want to change it.

## SECOND CASE IN POINT: A QUESTION OF SILENCE

In *A Question of Silence,* the central plot revolves around what I would call the coming-into-silence of the psychiatrist who has been assigned to assess the psychological stability of three women: an at-home housewife with a husband and a young child, a waitress who lives on her own and who is the mother of grown children with children of their own, and a young, fashionable, corporate executive secretary. The women, strangers to one another, are on trial for the execution of a male boutique owner.

I use the word "execution" rather than the word "murder" because in the highly metaphorical text of the film this act is depicted as a formally ritualistic act, a reading which is supported by the actions of the women immediately following the event. Afterward, the young mother takes a symbolic Ferris Wheel ride with her child. In a moment of exuberance and obvious freedom, they go around several turns. The secretary begins by buying herself an ice cream cone as she strolls down the street. When she is propositioned by a strange man, she accepts. However, by remaining clothed against his nakedness, speechless against his attempts at verbal interchange and "on top" during the entire encounter (which she leaves as she entered it—disengaged, and non-speaking), she reverses and, therefore, makes perverse the social codes that mark women's bodies and sexuality as the object of male fiction. And finally, in opposition to her daily life, the older woman, the waitress, prepares for herself an exquisite gourmet dinner complemented with flowers, candles, and fine wine. She proceeds to eat it by herself as she reflects on a life which had been, in the past, abusive (her husband) and disrespectful (her children and the customers at the grill where she works).

The story begins when the three women find themselves, along with three other women—none of whom know one another—browsing in a small, shopping-mall boutique store. Christine, the young mother, who would be the most economically dependent of the three, had not spoken a single word at this point and will continue not to speak throughout the entire film. Pushing her child's stroller she wanders distractedly through the racks of women's fashions guarded by the male boutique owner. None of the details of this moment are arbitrary. That the scene takes place in a fashion boutique, that the boutique owner is a man, that all of the patrons in the shop are women come together to serve as the coded text for patriarchy. This is not lost on Christine. Her decision to act on her own behalf creates a moment of opposition against her situation. Pulling items of clothing off the hangers and stuffing them into her large shopping bag signals her resistance to the mandate that women acquiesce to the priorities of male interests defined through the confines and social prescriptions of femininity.

When the boutique owner confronts Christine, she forces her way past him and with increased determination continues to grab handfuls of items off the racks and push them defiantly into her bag to the befuddlement and amazement of the clothing shop owner who glares at her. Christine's eyes never leave the man's face. He again confronts her, this time by grabbing her bag and forcefully imploring her to put the items back. She refuses. Clutching the items tightly in her hands she holds his eye with hers in a stance of self-determination.

The other women notice the encounter and two of them, the secretary and the waitress, join Christine in her defiance. They surround the man and, without speaking, simultaneously encircle and confine him. The boutique owner is visibly shaken and pleads with his eyes that the women let him go. The remaining three women present in the boutique stand off to the side and become "witnesses" to the act that is to follow: the boutique owner is bludgeoned to death with the props that hold his merchandise. Throughout this entire episode no one but the man speaks. The act complete, the six women leave the shop still without speaking. The shared knowledge is clear between them: patriarchy, symbolically embodied in "the man," had been destroyed.

Following their various acts of celebration, in the next scene we see the three women being picked up by the police. None of them refuse to go. None of them protest. It is clear to them that patriarchic retribution is the consequence of their actions. It is what they had been anticipating. While their arrests are uneventful, they are a source of extreme disbelief to those with whom they work and live. In the case of the waitress, the moment is made more poignant by the jeering of the regular male customers of the grill where she works. The women's confinements within the terms of patriarchy had been assumed to be so complete that an act of rebellion had not seemed possible.

For the men they leave behind, the husband, the corporate boss, and the patrons and owner of the grill, the most inconvenient aspect of the women's arrests is the loss of their labor on which, while never acknowledged, the men had come to depend. The young woman's husband is outraged that he will now have to take responsibility for making arrangements for the care of his child—a responsibility of which he had assumed himself to be absolved. The corporate executive, despite his treating his secretary as incompetent and childlike, has to acknowledge that she carries knowledge about the operations of his company in ways no one else, including himself, does. And for the men at the restaurant, their jeering and taunting of the older woman signals their feelings of loss of the object of their harassment.

It is our common experience as women that we are often the butt of male joking. Indeed, this is a significant aspect of men's claim to power through their assumed right to abuse in what has traditionally been passed off as an insignificant social encounter. Even in the closest of intimate and caring relations, such as the family, women are expected to absorb such violation, in the name of joking. Yet, as is the case with other socially violated groups, women know that the encouragement to "laugh off" the lived effect of our violation is an invitation to laugh against ourselves. It is to participate in the staging of our own humiliation (Williams, 1991, p. 167). When women identify such practices as premeditated acts of abuse and when we resist this violation by challenging its perpetrators to take responsibility for their acts we are often accused of being "man hating." The power of patriarchy is such that the "refusal of the designated other to be dominated is felt as a personal assault" (Williams, 1991, p. 66) by those who, from their position of power, initiate the violence. It seems that not the violation but our acts of self-defense come to be read as "antisocial" behavior and are thus used to reposition us on the disadvantaged side of the gender binary. In this case the power of the oppressor is such that it can create social support for acts of violence, a support that in turn justifies the use of more violence to counter challenges to the oppressor's power to violate. This is a classic example of the double-cross-reversal where words are used to reverse the order of experience and hence to discursively create victims out of violators and violators out of victims.

The refusal of Christine, the young mother, to speak during the entire pretrial investigation is a mystery to the court and eventually to the psychiatrist brought in to assess the sanity of the three women and in particular that of Christine. Both the court and the psychiatrist would wish Christine to speak and thereby validate their judgement regarding her emotional state. In particular, by way of support, the psychiatrist would like to convince the women to plead insanity in order to receive leniency from the court.

The women refuse the plea of insanity, and Christine continues to refuse to speak. Her silence is initially pathologized by the psychiatrist by being named catatonic behavior. However, as the psychiatrist begins to uncover the events surrounding the act; as the condition of the lives of the women become apparent to her through her realization of the parallels with her own life; as she begins to recognize the power of patriarchy to create meaning only in its own interest defined by its own terms; as she sees in the actions of men their collusion in this project, exemplified by her husband in particular who insists, throughout the film, on making judgements against the women in a situation where he is mostly ignorant about the details; and finally as the investigation moves into the courtroom and the meaning of the demands made on the women to comply with the interpretations of the court become clear to her, the psychiatrist's understanding shifts dramatically.

As is the case for the women on trial, the psychiatrist's own embodied knowledge is confronted by the rising chorus, displayed in the ever increasing crescendo imploring the woman (Christine) to speak, *speak*, SPEAK. In this demand, the situation of women is highlighted: by what imperative is it required that the women speak *now*? What might the women say that would not turn their justified anger into a liability? What might the psychiatrist say that would not diminish the women's actions as insane? The requirement to speak affirms for the psychiatrist that what Christine is being invited to do— and, thereby, what Christine, through her silence, refuses to do—is to engage in a discourse directed toward the legitimation of her own subordination.

The social codes through which women are invited to demonstrate our compliance with our own subordination take numerous forms; demands for our silence and, conversely, requirements for only particular forms of discursive engagement, are but two examples. As a concrete social text, women's compliance with displays of femininity is another. Importantly, the ideology which requires overt and embodied demonstrations of femininity, variously, the requirement that we *not* speak, or that we speak only in very specific ways (Spender, 1980), act as forms of social control by requiring us to demonstrate our willingness to participate in the covering over of the scars of our lived subordination. As women, our subjectivity is inscribed materially in our body—a body heavy with the ideological constructs that prescribe and limit possibilities.

By way of example the "blush" of innocence, our "wide-eyed" wonderment, and the "unsteady" and "tentative" gait of elevated heels are meant to signal our agreement to cover over the realities we know we have lived. The hyper-demonstration of our vulnerability encoded through feminine fashion and the practice of "painting" women's faces is used to justify the violence directed towards us. Conversely our refusal to participate in displays of our compliance names us uncooperative, insubordinate, and no less, even if differently, the objects of violation (Lees, 1986).

Similarly, in the case of Christine, were she to agree to speak, while restricted to using words that could not describe the social/political meaning and intent of the women's actions, she would be agreeing to participate in the greater exclusion of women from a discursive space that never allows the speaking of our history, our present, or our future; she would be agreeing to participate in creating the illusion of speaking. By being *required* to speak, Christine is being "invited" to take up discussion in terms not of her own making. By refusing to speak, Christine's silence becomes a political discourse, which, as an oppositional form, transgresses and defies the power of phallocentrism. Philip Corrigan is suggestive:

> Phallocentric discursive regimes, forms and practices are constructed around masculine experience, generalized both as the norm or ideal *and* as natural, universal, neutral, and Obvious. The world thus consists, in this system of ruling, of proper men and varieties of un- or non-men, who in *the infinite hospitality of the regime* and its forms have only to learn the rules to become proper. They thus also learn to be outside their bodies and speak in voices and vocabularies not their own. Silence is thus both enforced (only rulers have the choice of hearing or not hearing, subordinates always have to listen carefully) but can also be chosen. Significantly in the most masculinized regime possible, the English Army, "dumb insolence" is still an offence under Queen's Regulation. Refusing to speak—a subset of refusing to yield—has a long history with feminism; as also does speaking out and cursing against (witchcraft exhibits both). (Corrigan, personal communication, June 1988, emphasis added)

The judge and the prosecuting attorney press first Christine and then the psychiatrist on Christine's behalf to explain to them the murder of the man. Isn't it so that Christine's refusal to speak is a sign of her mental imbalance, they query. How could it be that the women, unfamiliar to one another, could act with such shared purpose, they wonder. Isn't it so that the women were engaged in a shared conspiracy of murder, they accuse. Why is it significant that the boutique owner was a man, they question. Isn't it a fact that Christine was simply committing an illegal act by shoplifting, they charge. Isn't it the case that the boutique owner could just as easily have been a woman, and these crazy women would have murdered her too, they implore.

The psychiatrist tries to explain. The judge and attorney are confused, befuddled, incapable of understanding the explanations. The psychiatrist struggles again with their questions and their inability to understand. The judge and prosecuting attorney cannot understand why the psychiatrist refuses to put forward a simple plea of insanity. In her desperation to be understood, the psychiatrist's eyes catch the eyes of the women in the prisoner's dock and then those of the women who had been witness to the event and who have sat quietly in the courtroom throughout the entire trial proceedings.

It is relevant to say that on the occasion of my watching this film in a large movie theatre with a gender-mixed audience, almost as if in anticipation of the film's conclusion, the sporadic laughter of women could be heard rising and then escalating throughout this scene in the courtroom. First Christine, then the secretary and the waitress, and then finally the three other women and the psychiatrist seemed to join in laughter with the women watching in the movie theater. Why were the three women on trial laughing? Why were the other women in the courtroom laughing? Why were we all laughing? What knowledge did we share? What consequences did we know were ours for the knowledge we carried? What was the social/political meaning of our shared laughter?

As much as there are real risks associated with breaking this silence, there are real joys in finding a community in such oppositional discursive practices.

In the end, the three women, their insubordination encoded in silence and punctuated by our shared laughter, are removed from the courtroom. Subsequently, they are led off handcuffed down the stairs into the basement and removed through the darkened door at the bottom of the stairs. The other three women, sitting in the gallery, are also taken out of the room. Everyone goes peacefully, laughing.

Having regained control of the courtroom, the judge and prosecuting attorney turn to the psychiatrist and once again implore *her* to speak and thereby, through speaking, confirm Christine's silence as devoid of meaning. The seriousness of the moment is compelling. After a moment of reflection the psychiatrist moves as if to begin. Then with a wave of her hand gives up, turns, and walks out of the courtroom. As the judge speaks his final words (before the camera follows the psychiatrist through the door into the street) his voice cracks. The discursive seams of phallocentric power are dislodged. The words, "this trial will now continue in the absence of the accused," are left desperately trying to find meaning.

## PEDAGOGICAL IMPLICATIONS

> Silence is precisely the sum of the voices of everyone, the equivalent of the sum of our collective breathing. . . . And this collective silence [is] necessary because it [is] . . . through this silence that a new mode of being [is] fostered; it [is] from common obscurity that collective action springs into being and finds direction. (Duras, 1981, p. 111–112)

What are the implications for teaching and learning? I begin by reflecting on my experience earlier in the summer of teaching a graduate seminar entitled "Feminist Theories in Education." For me and for the students with whom I shared the seminar, this was a high pitched experience, one with which I am increasingly familiar. The immediate and enthusiastic response of many of the women students who comprised three-quarters of the class set a pace over the term that constantly left the male minority behind. While to some extent both the women and the men struggled to overcome their resistance to the feminist theoretical frames which articulated the course agenda this seemed to be more difficult for the men, I believe, because, unlike the women, the men could not draw on specific life experiences which could give body to our conceptual work.

At one level, questions about how the class might have taken different form had it been a male instructor teaching it, had most of the women not been significantly older than the men, had the course title not specifically named it a "feminist" course, and so on, are interesting to contemplate. However, such musings do not offer a way into the pedagogical issues I wish to take up.

Using the films analyzed above as the backdrop, the experience of this course left me wondering about the practices and politics of a feminist pedagogy: its limits and its possibilities. My own experiences as a woman in the academy, first as student and then as a teacher, left no doubt that women are not coherently integrated into the processes and intentions of the schooling agenda. Like other feminist academics, I have struggled to formulate the frames of my teaching practice within educational institutions relatively newly and grudgingly open to women (Murch, 1991, Cann, Cunningham, Fowler, Kelso, Mohamdee and Postma, 1993). Progress seems slow, gains are countered by losses, and despair lies always just on the underside of hope. Despite over twenty years of the second wave of the feminist movement, it continues to be the case that as a society we know almost nothing about women's contribution to literature, women's significant involvement in history, women's social and economic lives in the workplace and in the home, women's contribution to scientific and mathematical fields, women's work in politics and the influence we have had there, women's contribution to social policy through decision making, and the diversity of women's experiences in different cultures, geographic locations, and historical times.

As an issue of feminist pedagogy, the question of how to create access for girls and women to the sites of policy and decision making and to the sources of economic viability has been central in generating a vast range of curricular and classroom practices. The following example is a case in point.

During a recent visit of Dale Spender to the Education Faculty where I teach, approximately 120 young women between thirteen and eighteen years of age were invited to share with her in a forum entitled "Young Women in Education: What Happens to Girls in Classrooms." One of the discussion sessions raised the issue of women's and girl's experience of non-participation and non-inclusion in much of traditional classroom dynamics and curriculum organized by and around male interests.

As do many women, the young women present at this particular session struggled with the contradictions between making explicit their own understandings of their past experiences of exclusion and simultaneously wishing to spare themselves the pain of "outsiderness"; some attempted to disassociate themselves from the lived realities of social and intellectual marginalization. Disagreements raged between those who acknowledged their experiences of exclusion and those for whom such experiences represented social moments too threatening and too painful to admit. At a moment when the tension in the room was intense, one young woman, sitting at the back of the lecture room spoke out forcefully. Her tone carried both frustration and irritation with what she perceived to be her peers' personal shortcomings. Caught between the particular prescriptions that articulate "speaking out" as a feminist politic, on the one hand, and the tendency toward victim blaming, on the other, she said:

> If you don't speak up in class it's your own fault, and you're just looking to blame someone else for it. If you have something to say just open your face.

For a split second the room fell into a stunned silence. Then, by way of support, the young woman's teacher (a member of the local school district's status of women committee) who was sitting directly in front of her, turned around and, with a pat on the young woman's knee, signalled her approval of her student's comments.

I do not want to dismiss such efforts by teachers whose practices are derived from their genuine interest in and concern for the lives of their students. Women's struggles to achieve discursive space within the overwhelmingly masculinized forms of social/political/economic relations has historically dominated most feminist practical and theoretical work. Traditionally, the issue of women's silence—particularly in relation to pedagogical strategies—has focused on "making space" for women, on "encouraging" women to speak and on finding ways in which women might be included in the curriculum. I too have engaged such strategies directed toward making women "visible," to making our voices "heard" and to making women's experiences central to our examination.

To be sure, a consideration of what women might do in order to intervene politically is crucial and necessary. With Audre Lorde (1980) and Kathleen Rockhill (1987b), I believe that silence, no matter how deeply it goes or how quietly it is borne, has not prevented women from standing as objects of that violence which the ideology of phallocentrism assumes as its prerogative. Audre Lorde writes:

> My silence has not protected me. Your silence will not protect you. . . . In the case of silence, each of us draws the face of her own fear—fear of contempt, fear of censure, of some judgment, of recognition, of challenge, of annihilation. But most of all I think, we fear for the very visibility without which we cannot truly live. (1980, pp. 20–21)

Practically, this means that, as teachers, we need to be willing to share (indeed become conscious of the need to share) not only the nuts and bolts of academic strategies but also the details of our concrete, non-academic lives that support and limit these possibilities. As a pedagogical project, how we negotiate and accomplish the daily work of child and home care is as relevant for women's education as how we theorize the political economy of housework. For women students—particularly those with young children—what I can teach them about how to theorize language or ideology is as important as knowing who does the laundry at my house, what negotiations were required to accomplish this particular division of household labor, and how I feel about it. Equally important is what they can teach one another about the strategies required for them to get from one day to the next within the variety of life contexts of which being a student is just one aspect.

A feminist analysis of familial forms opens the way for women to legitimately explore, at the seam between theory and practice, the implications of their unequal responsibility for home and child care as they have experienced it—or have observed their mothers experience it—so that suddenly what had appeared to be natural begins to lose its "of course-ness." The "home-as-haven" begins to lose its ideological seamlessness as the deeply contradictory reality of this social form begins to find expression.

Similarly, as feminist politics elaborates the gender specificities of women's and men's sexuality, women's experiences of direct or embedded (systemic) violence provides the possibility for articulating women's experiences in their everyday lives. As the connections between pornography, rape, and world violence begin to be made, women find the discursive space within which to acknowledge and make legitimate their fear that violence is not something that happens just to other women: the indiscreet, the careless, or those who are looking/asking for it. Rather they begin to understand that violence is a fundamental expression of phallocentric power and as such is essential to its legitimation and perpetuation. Naming gender as specifically relevant to modes of production and consumption likewise contributes to feeling that having something to say is a legitimate activity for women.

Lifting the taboos and legitimating discussion regarding the mundane yet profoundly relevant aspects of everyday life frees us to recognize precisely those social forms that have limited women's access to political and economic viability.

Yet, while all of this is important, simply including women in the curriculum is not enough. Despite good intentions in the attempts of feminist teachers and educational theorists to counter the prevailing educational/institutional modes identified as blocks to women's full participation in education and schooling outcomes, women have achieved only tenuous gains both inside the academy and out. Despite our commitments bound by hard work, our attempts have achieved only equivocal success. As a project that has engaged us explicitly as feminist educators for well over twenty years—a formal status to which I admit to being a relative newcomer—in comparison to the effort the gains seem minimal.

I am convinced that the struggle over pedagogy is not to fit women into the phallocentric model for social relations and work and family life, a project that will always "leave us on the short end of life" (words from a song by Arlo Guthrie). Feminist pedagogical practices are more than critique, just as they are more than making women historically and currently visible in the curriculum. Clearly, as a pedagogical problem the issue of women's silence is not a simple case of how we might make women feel "comfortable" enough in the mixed-gender classroom that they might find their place in the discourse. These strategies are not unimportant. Yet, there is a level at which such propositions do not reach deep enough into the sources and political potential of women's silence and cannot, therefore, offer the necessary perspective on pedagogical interventions that we may utilize toward social change. Under conditions of constraint, choosing not to speak, choosing not to engage the language of the dominant, can be seen as an act of subversion. The pedagogical challenge is in how we identify and make sense of the politics of silence.

If we are to propose pedagogical strategies that might really make a difference for women, we need to find a way of understanding the discursive meaning of women's silence and not dismiss it as an example of women's lack and absence out of which we need to be recovered. Similarly if we seek to include women in the curriculum and schooling experience as agents of social change our task as feminist teachers is not only to make the representation of women the object of our discourse; not only to "donate" (Lewis and Simon, 1986) those spaces in which women might speak and then implore them to do so. But we need, as well, to hear both the voices *and* the silence through which women engage our social world; to make meaning not only out of what woman say, but also out of what women refuse to say and to understand why we might refuse to speak.

This is not to say that "the world as it is constituted by men in authority over that of women" (Smith, 1987, p. 86) does not often and concretely silence us against our will. To be sure, women have been historically and discursively absent from cultures to which we have been materially central. By our experience we know the political economy that has created women's work simultaneously indispensable and without social value—work without which the nature of men's work would change dramatically.

Yet, as women, our lived realities are experienced as contradictory and complex because the sources of their generation are neither reducible to strictly economic circumstances, nor entirely to psycho/social parameters. While in Western economies our social, political, and economic condition is obviously heavily contained within the capitalist mode of production, it is neither reducible to it nor untouched by the psycho/social meanings generated by phallocentric discourse. Under conditions of patriarchic meaning making, women's discursive authority is not guaranteed even as our gendered subjectivities are constituted through specific discursive forms of self-presentation (Weedon, 1987, p. 98).

As I begin each new term of teaching, I do so always from the ground of my own self-reflexive practice. I examine not only what worked and what did not, but more fundamentally, try to understand the meaning and import of what I consider to have been successes in bringing a feminist perspective to teaching. Grounded in a variety of classroom and personal experiences, I am increasingly uneasy about the victim-blaming aspects of most discussion concerning women's silence. Coded as women's oppression and imposed by the strictures of phallocentric meaning making, women's non-participation in social and discursive practices is often used to suggest seductively simple pedagogical strategies in the form of validative and supplementary models of education. As a way of rectifying imbalances and injustices, such proposals are aimed at *getting women to speak*—the curricular equivalent to "if you have something to say just open your face." The compelling power of this formulation as a political/pedagogical strategy is apparent in the practices of teachers, like the one described above, committed to feminist political principles aimed at supporting their women students in engaging the available terms of social interaction by speaking out.

Yet we cannot bring about social change from within those concepts and practices that have limited our possibilities. Phallocentric discourse, inside the academy or out, will not cease to be a violent affront to women's knowledge until our silence ceases to be used against us as the justification for intrusive, corrective procedures demanding that we speak, using words already prepared for us. Questioning the silence of the students I teach—as I question my own—probing for the details of its generation, has brought me to an extended understanding of such silence as, among other things, a form of active resistance displayed under conditions of women's socially untenable position within the governing forms of patriarchy and phallocentric discursive forms that require that women speak and remain silent at the same time. For me the salient question has to do with the implications for education of the notion of women's historically arbitrated silence across social and cultural forms that have left us disadvantaged and outside the terms of the dominant discourse.

As feminist teachers in the academy, we need to engage a deeper and more complex examination of the conditions and contexts of women's learning and the significance of a social/cultural/political world environment that consistently subordinates the interests of all women to that of men. Leaving women with the weight of the burden of bringing about the social changes we seek, without uncovering the complexity of the inequalities within which social space is negotiated across gender, seems, contradictorily, only to reassert our deficiencies.

I question where might intellectual women committed to social change begin to effect what we see as necessary transformations? To be sure, the connections at the political level between women's lives and the course content contributes to a possibility for the expression of women's voices which women embrace. Feminist politics would mean nothing if we did not feel profoundly the painful contradictions of our lives: the "choices" we have had to make and the "choices" that were/are clearly not available to us. It is as a pedagogic practice that we want to locate our experience within academic discourse. Simultaneously we want to claim a space within the discourse of feminist practice that brings into congruence the analytic and the poetic—

"praxis by a feminist consciousness" (Bersianik, 1986, p. 45)—where each finds its clarity of meaning within the other—not in the sense of standing side by side and finding meaning in the gaze that each casts to the other all the while falling victim to false hierarchies that judge the efficacy, the very possibility, of the existence of the other—but rather in the sense of each finding lodging and comfort within those hidden crevices that define each as the other to the other and thereby obliterate that division:

> At this point in time, I believe that women carry within ourselves the possibility for fusion of these two approaches so necessary for survival. (Lorde, 1984, p. 37)

To the extent that feminism is not an exclusionary practice but a transformative political discourse, the specificity of its perspective is as much a fusion of the poetic with the analytic as it is the articulation of the relationship between the personal and the political.

In this way feminist politics becomes a challenge, at the level of practice, to a male-defined, male-described social world lived, as it is, not in theory but in practice within the discourse of the masculine that always assumes itself to be all there is to say and hear; that actively de/forms discourse in such a way that huge chunks of women's words, ways of being in the world, and experience are not merely discarded but not even noticed as needing inscription, both in the concrete and the symbolic sense.

Yet, the history of the spiralling recurrence of women's struggles has taught us that the dominance of the masculine voice will be dislodged not by our speaking it louder or more forcefully than men do themselves, but by refusing the criteria of its significance (Pierson, 1987). If education is to play a major role in bringing about the changes for which we are looking, then we need new ways of envisioning the possibilities for teaching and learning. The answer to the question of women's education lies, I believe, in how we find and draw out new and politically effective meanings from women's experiences and practices. One place where we might begin to look for pedagogical strategies for change is through an examination of the terms of women's silence. Immediately issues arise that require us to rethink the ways in which women's silence has been theorized in educational literature and critical discourse.

## CONCLUSION

> We cannot revision the world with the tools we have been given. The unspoken and the repressed, as Wittig says, must become part of our social discourse and social reality or there will be no one left to speak at all. (Flax, 1980, p 38)

The purpose of this chapter has not been to prove that social discourse, supported by an edifice of political and economic disadvantage, indeed renders women's voices mute and irrelevant within the frames of phallic discourse. For women, exclusion from social discourse is a daily reality lived as a feature of our regular and "normal" encounters within patriarchy. Women do not need to be taught what we already know. The power of phallocentrism may undermine our initiative, it may shake the foundations of our self-respect and self-worth, it may even force us into complicity with its violence. But it cannot prevent us from knowing.

Nor was it my purpose to provide examples of how this silencing is done. A great deal of feminist literature and theoretical analysis has already done much of this very important historical, empirical, and analytical work. The explosion of volumes written by women concerning all of these aspects of women's lives is, in 1993, impossible to list. Women do not lack the words needed to speak what we know. However, the fact remains that a deep silence shrouds women's work and words in educational institutions articulated by a curriculum that systematically withholds knowledge.

Under such conditions, speaking—those discursive acts that might attend to our interests and desires as women—are clearly to be seen as both radical and massively disruptive of the status quo. Without doubt, much of what we hope our students will embrace through feminist teaching and learning is the political potential of speaking out on their/our own behalf.

Yet the central question is not only that of how we might envision positive alternatives. A vision of the future that is not yet is no guarantee that it ever will be: dreams of possibility can only wreak despair and hopelessness—death of the spirit if not of the body—if our looking is not simultaneously inwardly as well as outwardly directed. The vision is both moral and prescriptive, but moral and prescriptive from a deep sense of knowing that how we experience the world matters; our experiences are never individualized moments of our singular being but arise from economic, political, and social constructs that have a history and that work in concert—moments both of constraint and possibility—that have both material and psychological/emotional consequences.

It was my intention on this occasion to revisit the question of women's silence, not so that it might be affirmed, once and for all, as the fundamental condition of women in a patriarchic culture, but so that we might, by understanding the social limits/power of women's speaking and silence, generate suggestions for a transformed pedagogic practice. It is in this context that I explore the pedagogical possibilities of the complex ways women might use silence as a politically intended intervention. In this regard, Virginia Woolf is exceptionally helpful.

In Woolf's astoundingly poignant and brilliantly metaphorical text, *A Room of One's Own* (1929/1977), we are invited to join her protagonist in search of the answer to the question of "women and fiction." But what about "women and fiction"? Does it mean women and "what they are like"; or "women and the fiction that they write"; or "women and the fiction that is written about them" (p. 5)? In the end, Woolf weaves all three into a tapestry piercingly articulate about the condition of women in a world culture that depends on the subordination of women for its survival. Dorothy Smith is informative:

> Marx's concept of alienation is applicable here in modified form. The simplest formulation of alienation posits a relation between the work an individual does and an external order which oppresses her, such that the harder she works the more she strengthens the order which oppresses her. This is the situation for women in this relation. The more successful women are in mediating the world of concrete particulars so that men do not have to become engaged with (and therefore conscious of) that world as a condition of their abstract activities, the more complete man's absorption in it, the more effective the authority of that world and the more total women's subservience to it. (1987, p. 90)

In *A Room of One's Own*, having crossed the quad, taking care not to step on the grass more often than what would result in her being heaved onto the street once and for all by a "horrified" and "indignant" Beadle entrusted with "the protection of the turf" for "the Fellows and Scholars" of "Oxbridge," the woman—a thinly disguised Woolf—finds herself at the door of the "Library" in search of "the word" Milton might have, much to the dismay of Charles Lamb, changed in his poem *Lycidas*. Lost in her musings, she opens the door to enter. Woolf continues:

> Instantly there issued, like a guardian angel barring the way with a flutter of black gown instead of white wings, a deprecating, silvery, kindly gentleman, who regretted in a low voice as he waved me back that ladies are only admitted to the library if accompanied by a Fellow of the College or furnished with a letter of introduction. (Woolf, [1929]1977, p. 9)

Like Woolf, we too find ourselves at the door of phallocentric knowledge—Woolf's metaphorical library—guarded by the power of patriarchy to exclude. Absentmindedly preoccupied with the desire to know, we too have opened the door only to be confronted, not by the brash young man (The Beadle) of earlier times but this time by that "deprecating" old gentleman who "regrets" the need to "wave" us back.

As the woman in Woolf's narrative turns from the man and the door that bars her way to the knowledge she seeks, the anger of Woolf's words are clear. Together with Mrs. Wright, Mrs. Peters, and Mrs. Hale, with Christine, the secretary, the waitress, and the psychiatrist, Woolf knows what we all know:

> That a famous library has been cursed by a woman is a matter of complete indifference to a famous library. (p. 9)

Yet she does not stop here. Woolf is decisive in what she proposes:

> Venerable and calm, with all its treasures safe locked within its breast, it sleeps complacently and will, so far as I am concerned so sleep for ever. Never will I wake those echoes, never will I ask for that hospitality again, I vowed as I descended the steps in anger. (p. 9)

Curiously, in the presence of the genteel, kindly gentleman, Woolf's feminist anger, which earlier in the presence of the naively presumptuous younger man seemed merely confrontational, now appears hysterical, rude, and poignantly ungrateful for being turned away kindly.

Reflecting on the terms of my teaching and fueled by my anger at the backlash to a feminist presence in the academy that marginalizes me and the work I do with my students (McDonald, 1990; Grossman, 1992) my entry into this discussion arises from my desire to understand and make pedagogically significant that moment when women no longer wish to stand banging on the door; when our desires, limited by our possibilities, bring us to discover what we already know—knowledge available to us as we stand on our side of the door.

Without doubt, the silence of this moment is complex and contradictory. Yet it seems to me, it is not without its political import. Who speaks and the political determination of that speaking is, in relations of unequal power, always in the hands of those who govern. Unchecked privilege and entitlement mandate the perverse requirement that the oppressed confirm the power of the oppressor by engaging—always by definition inadequately—the discourse of their own subordination. As Chris Weedon says:

> To speak is to assume a subject position within discourse and to become *subjected* to the power and regulation of the discourse. (1987, p. 119)

When the governed are required to speak, but only in terms that affirm their acquiescence to name the world against themselves, the act of not speaking might be seen as an act of insubordination and, therefore, as an act potentially disruptive of the power of the powerful to force agreement for such self violation. Given the particularities of phallocentric discursive forms which constantly require that the centrality of their own reality be legitimated even as they display fear of their own silence, women choosing silence might offer a discursive form on women's own terms rather than on terms prescribed by phallocentric imperatives. Where our speaking is confined within the terms of patriarchy, not speaking might claim a space for women's interpretations and epistemology. Luce Irigaray elaborates:

> What is important is to disconcert the staging of representation according to a phallocratic order. It is not a matter of toppling that order so as to replace it—that amounts to the same thing in the end—but of disrupting and modifying it, starting from an 'outside' that is exempt, in part, from phallocratic law. (1985, p. 68)

How might this be done? To speak from outside the frames of phallocentric discourse means that women must disrupt both its content and its form. For women, taking up the word can only be a political act. To write/speak with political meaning necessitates taking up the personal as the cutting edge of the political. It necessitates that we not only engage the political project as a personal commitment, but that we find ways of transforming our personal experience into the basis for political action. Yet silence too disrupts this phallocentric "staging." Might we not equally see women's silence as a practice directed toward social transformation?

I began this writing from a desire to explore the efficacy of feminist pedagogy to transform social relations, and to envision a pedagogy which, by taking the risk of transgressing allowable discourse, might paint a transformative possibility which having once been glimpsed can never be abandoned.

If this project is to be successful, it cannot be attempted on the terms presently available to us. To be liberated to work/speak on men's behalf is not enough. It is, therefore, imperative that we look anew not only at the possibilities of women's speaking, but as well at the potential meanings of women's silence.

To be sure, silence is not a simple linguistic device free of contradictions. Nor do I advocate it as the end toward which feminist transformative politics/pedagogy ought to aim—quite the contrary.

I began this chapter by reflecting on Margaret Atwood and her unflinching feminist critique of a culture that has to date refused to acknowledge the indignities of inequality. The reality Atwood speaks about is inscribed in language/discourse no less so than in how we experience our everyday lives. For women, the notion of a social discourse is marked by such contradictory possibilities that all of the places we inhabit—our family life, institutions and organizations in and with which we work, the political projects we undertake, and the social relations which we engage—are sites both of struggle and of possibility. These sites evidence the concrete manifestation in practice of the tension between morally viable utopian dreams and material realities (Radway, 1984).

With her words Atwood pushes us beyond the margins, to the margins of the margins and demands of us that we find the common ground of our experience. But she does more than this. We need also to find the terms of our difference from which to create an emancipatory pedagogic practice. With Atwood, I want to cut away the loose and fraying edges of our everyday lives and uncover those social forms upon which all of the bits and pieces of our contradictions are hung. Yet, I want to take care that I not cut away too much. For all of us, our reality:

> has two edges, one of laughter, one of anguish, cutting the heart asunder. (Woolf, [1929]1977, p. 17)

On one side of this reality is the concrete materiality of our everyday experiences as these are mapped in real relations of power that shut us down/out/in as a function of our social place defined through our gender, our social class, our race, our ethnic identity/identification (Young, 1987), our age, and our sexual desires. These are social forms and contexts that stand over and above whatever it is that we may want to envision as possible for ourselves, marked by the constraints and possibilities of the social world.

On the other side is our own appropriation of moments either of possibility or of self-denial—responses which, although concrete in their manifestation, have a psychological basis often marked by contradictory and conflicting moments of desire; possibilities assessed in the very moment of their presentation as being either closed or open to us. But in these moments, despite our inward focus, we also look for confirmation in our relation with the social other. Roger Simon (1987) offers a useful explanation when he says that these social forms are:

> modes of organizing, regulating and legitimating the way the structuring of practice is accomplished; hence practices are not arbitrary but subject to both objective and subjective determinations. (p. 158)

When you wish upon a star *it makes a difference* who you are!

My point here is that as feminist teachers we need to be clear not only about the political goals toward which we strive, but as well about the social context within which we wish our students to join us in the struggle. We need to formulate pedagogical practices which address not only the political issues that define silence as absence, but as well those active practices which arise out of the notion of silence as a discourse aimed at telling a different story.

Yet I propose this thesis with the caution befitting the complexity of the relation between women's socially imposed silence, our erasure from history, the violence that has stilled our voices for centuries—what Anne-Louise Brookes has called "women's learned way of silence" (1992)—on the one hand, and, on the other, that silence which women have appropriated as an act of resistance and transformation.

We need to understand women's silence—the silence of all oppressed, exploited, and subordinate people—as in Bonnie Smith's words "a counter language" (1981), a language carrying the full force of our opposition to what has been said before—those words that have created the world in their own image and which now can no longer, if ever they could, sustain our desires for possibility, freedom, and integrity. Silence in this case is a political practice that challenges how social meaning is made. It is a site of struggle not because it juxtaposes masculine discourse, infused with its particular phallocentric meanings, against women's silence, devoid of any meaning at all, but rather precisely because it opens the possibility for drawing competing meanings and competing discourses out of social relations.

Understanding the social complexity of discursive practices is central to this. Transformations toward a morally viable politics are not, after all, won through violent revolution—the history of the world is testament to this. Sometimes, seduced into shouting our words, we are left desperate/despairing to hear that the sounds of our shouting echo back into our ears as if bounced off granite, seemingly having touched no one's inner ear or the soft tissue of their body/mind. At such times I know that no amount of noise will be heard if there is no one who cares to listen—while even silence will be heard if there is. The potential power of a pedagogical practice, whether in the realm of the personal or that of the political, whether inside the academy or out, is its ability to bring people to a point where they care to listen. "This listening is one way of finding out how to get to the new place where we all can live and speak to each other for more than a fragile moment" (Pratt, 1991, p. 30–31). The pedagogical implications are profound. Feminist teaching/political practices are like that silence heard above the patriarchic thunder disrupting the hierarchy of discursive practices. And silence, no longer absence, turns listening into pedagogy.

# 3 | TAKING (OUR) PLACE IN THE ACADEMY

As women share stories of their own lives, a common experience of oppression and of resistance is recognized. This politicizing gives women the courage to persist in resistance, recognizing that their difficulties have not only an individual basis but also a social and political basis as well. Fear of moving beyond accepted definitions of behaviour is not definitively allayed, but the experience of self-affirmation and hope that comes from the affirmation and community of sisterhood gives courage and enables creative resistance.

—Welch,
*Communities of Resistance and Solidarity:*
*A Feminist Theology of Liberation*

Those involved in my own life are as likely to take issue with my construction of our story as are those whose stories I tell to dissent from my versions of their stories.

—Hamilton,
"Feminism and Motherhood, 1970–1990: Reinventing the Wheel?"

I WAS SITTING WITH MY COMPUTER LATE ONE AFTERNOON HOPING to finish this chapter, when a knock at my door interrupted my thoughts. Had I known that opening the door would mean giving over what remained of my afternoon to the young woman who stood on the other side, I might have decided not to answer the knock . . . the pressure was on to finish this work and package the manuscript off to the publisher. I did, however, open the door and was greeted by one of the over 650 preservice teachers who form the undergraduate student body at my faculty. She asked if she could speak with me and, because she appeared to be distressed, I set this work aside and agreed. We closed the door, she sat in the chair opposite me and cried.

Two-and-a-half months into the teacher education program into which she had struggled hard to enter (at my faculty only about one in three applicants to the program succeed in entering it) and following her first round of practice teaching, she could no longer absorb what she called her "persistent, low-level rage" at the sexism, misogyny, racism, homophobia, exclusion, and marginalization she perceived to permeate the entire spectrum of schooling. She talked; I listened.

She told me no stories I had not heard before; she shared no feelings of frustration and anger I had not myself felt. Such stories get repeated again and again by both graduate and undergraduate students. They get repeated by mature students picking up the fragments of their educational lives after raising families (because, for women, the attempt to do both at the same time is often profoundly exhausting), or by those who are returning to their education, after having cut their studies short precisely because of such experiences. They get repeated by both students and teachers alike. And they get repeated by women who often experience their first gender-inclusive course as an "oasis" they had not realized was possible. The voices we hear through the "wall" of alienation, silence, and "death" tell neither new nor unique stories. The hidden boundaries of women's experiences in the academy are the source of my disquieting thoughts and words in this chapter.

Over the more than two decades of the most recent wave of the feminist movement we've gone the round with gender-inclusive language; with the vetting of the curriculum for gender bias, gender misrepresentation, and gender exclusion; and with the struggle against the alienation many women and minority students feel in classrooms where they can speak only in the whispered nuances of their marginalized social location. The apparent spaces opened up by feminist publishing, feminist presses, women's studies programs, and the seemingly open discourse in feminist politics on many university campuses are significantly countered by limited job opportunities, denials of tenure and promotion, and open harassment, which taken in their entirety indicate:

> not the random prejudices of particular individuals; [rather] they are evidence of institutionalized sexism in academe. (McCormack, 1987, p. 289; Hamilton, 1987)

This is not to say that a feminist presence on campus is in any way unimportant. Our desire to articulate our understanding of the relationship between the deep rooted social relations of inequality and feminist politics often translates, at the institutional level, into such things as: the production of booklets on the desirability and suggestions for gender inclusive language;

the monitoring of the number of women and men interviewed for potential academic and administrative positions and promotions; the gauging of women's exclusion from committees fundamental to the policy-making apparatuses of the academy; and the supporting of one another so that we not be disproportionately overburdened with meeting student needs—a scenario feminist faculty often share with those male faculty who also bring a critical, transformative perspective to their work.

While simply holding ground on such fundamental and basic issues often takes all the energy we have, the result is that sometimes blatant misogynist practices go somewhat less unnoticed than they did perhaps ten years ago. The presence of women students in larger numbers and the sporadic and uneven institutional support of women in positions which clearly articulate a feminist perspective in women's studies programs and courses in feminist research and theory sometimes create a broadening, even if still somewhat limited, level of institutional consciousness.

Yet in this period of closure and back-to-basics rhetoric, in this period of postmorality that justifies human suffering by a turn to efficiency and "generic" thinking skills, the dent these efforts might have made are vigorously being worked back into conformity by the self-proclaimed ideological police of the socially myopic "standards" movement. The closing decade of the twentieth century is gripped by the atomizing effects of such status-quo politics inscribed in the backlash attitude of the present historical moment. Speaking as a feminist in the academy this makes all the difference in the world. Despite our efforts, for women, the experience of institutional education continues to have profound consequences: by our experience we know that in the intellectual community *patriarchy lives, feminism is under siege, and the accomplishment of feminist pedagogy* (those teaching practices aimed at creating the conditions for understanding the possibilities for and restrictions on women's autonomy and self-determination) *is a struggle.*

I know by my own experience that for feminist intellectual workers—whether they be students or teachers—the academy is, for the most part, an uncomfortable and unwelcoming home. I know that educational institutions are a primary site where, for women, the possibilities for achieving meaning and resistance come into conflict with those forms of knowledge production which limit women's chances. I know that, as feminist academics in socially and culturally elite institutions mostly resistant to social critique unsupportive of the status quo, feminist courses are derided for being too political, too subjective, too personal. I know that such derision has come from colleagues who have not troubled themselves to become knowledgeable about the work we and our students do. I know that the work of students who embrace a feminist perspective has been excessively scrutinized from outside the intellectual frames from within which it was proposed while that of students doing more "traditional" work has been waved on with a genteel nod of a fatherly head (Grossman, 1992). I know that my office door has been vandalized on several occasions. I know that there are those who do not think about taking responsibility for the politics of their teaching and learning even as they require me to take responsibility for mine. I know that there are those who, in the name of standards, continue to cling tenaciously to the power of their privilege to limit others' possibilities. I know that as women speak the experiences of the brutalizations of sexism the flood of stories that fill my seminar rooms and the privacy of my office are emotionally and intellectually draining.

My interest in the issues of feminist pedagogy arises specifically out of such everyday practices, experiences, and relationships as these are constituted precisely within the context of my political perspective, yet given space within the academy under the umbrella of institutional authority. This academic legitimacy is neither secure in the long run nor unchallenged in concrete, daily expressions of the marginalizations we experience.

As women in the academy, the terms under which we are required to speak and the conditions under which we cannot speak must become a focus for analysis as to how the academy might be used to disrupt the project of its own agenda. For me, the problem posed by this reality is twofold. First, no gathering of women directed toward an articulation of these experiences can escape the retelling of the brutalizations as an aspect of their schooling. The consequence is that, as a woman, I carry with me my own versions of the stories other women relate to me that, while differently detailed, carry the same social intent. Their words connect with my own, beneath the surface, in the deep crevices of my woman's body. The barely perceptible trembling of their bodies catches the rhythms of my own creating the compounded resonations of a shared knowledge spoken often for the first time. In addition, as a teacher, I seek to find an analytical framework within which these resonations can be used not only to help my students and myself understand the source and import of our experiences, but also as the basis for social transformations through teaching and learning.

What can we learn from the stories we know we have lived? I have for a long time felt uneasy with a characterization of feminist methodology as a process of empowerment achieved through the practice of personal confessionals (Beck, 1983, p. 285). Locating our experiences in the materiality of our everyday lives is not the same as "telling all" (p. 290). As much as they serve a clearly articulated political agenda, theoretical frames are crucially important to how we assign meanings to the specificities of personal experience across all of the social disjunctures that divide us. Yet, the politics of "story telling," like the politics of teaching and learning, must be directed toward a particular and explicit project.

What distinguishes feminism as a method and a practice is the way in which it insists on making explicit our historical and social place as a concretely lived reality that touches us, like the wind, imperceptibly and yet unmistakably. Conversely, it is also the belief that theoretical discourses that cannot or will not do this are profoundly impoverished even as they are passed off as objective and beyond collective self-interest. Hence feminism and pedagogy converge at the point of intersection between personal experience and commitment to transformative politics. As the instrument of social change, a truly transformative pedagogy requires the embodiment of a subjectivity conscious of her own subordination. It requires the concrete articulation of a body knowledge—that fusion of the mind and body—as the primary site of our oppression through which our subjectivities are formed (Rockhill, 1987a). In the case of feminist teaching this project is directed toward social transformation which names the social construction of gender identities explicitly as one of its concerns.

In contrast, valorized academic practices have long depended on the separation between experience and the stories we tell ourselves about what we know about the world. Devalued as anecdotal, the academy has made illegitimate the sharing of that knowledge which we live most closely, that by which we are violated, and that by which we are silenced. As it stands, curriculum is the discursive representation of the dominant male experience as it is reflected back onto us not only in classroom experience and content, but in the ways we speak to one another, in the ways we organize our social and professional life, in the ways we encode representations of power and inequality concretely in our surrounding architecture, in the ways we establish and maintain family forms, and in the ways we organize work and leisure activities. In this context, telling the stories of women's experience in the academy, speaking the realities we know we have lived, whether we are students or teachers, requires that we transcend the subtleties of taboo and the limits of discretion.

## WOMEN IN THE ACADEMY: THE DIFFERENCE IT MAKES

Much has been made recently of the fact that over the last twenty years, the numbers of women on university campuses has been steadily increasing to the point that women now constitute more than one-half of full-time undergraduate students. While such statistics are comforting, our presence in higher education should not be taken as proof that we partake of social relations free of the male-dominated phallocentric discursive forms which pertain in society at large (Gaskell, McLaren, and Novogrodsky, 1989). On the one hand, in Ontario, for example, provincially funded equal opportunity officers at many universities have, at least at the level of policy, had the effect of making visible the real discrepancies between women and men in higher education. Yet, on the other hand, the perplexing outcome of recent affirmative action plans indicates that practice often does not reflect policy. Over the past ten to fifteen years, when affirmative action programs should have begun to redress the imbalances of women and men in the academy, women in full-time tenured and tenure-track positions have not increased to any significant measure. Statistics show that women's participation remains below twenty percent of all teaching faculty and hovers at a low of six percent at the level of full professor (Bellamy and Guppy, 1991, pp. 163–192). The situation of women *and* men of color is even more outrageous as their presence continues to be "insignificant" in statistical terms.

To be sure, the relatively few women who hold full academic positions do enjoy economic and social positions which accrue them privileges not available to those in menial, poorly paid, and hazardous work environments populated in disproportionate numbers by women from economically and socially disadvantaged race, ethnic, and class groups. However, the reality for many academic women is that they do not hold full-time, fully funded academic positions, but are granted only a tenuous and underfunded existence (McCormack, 1987).

There are concrete ways in which our work in the academy has been hindered: our qualifications have been judged with prejudice; our research and course proposals have been evaluated from an overtly anti-feminist/anti-woman bias that leaves open the question of "academic freedom"; and there has been unequal distribution of material and financial resources. The reality for many academic women is that they often enter the academy at low levels of authority and remuneration and generally stay there with only limited promotional possibilities. Or they constitute a loose, part-time, migrant, and easily replaced group of intellectual workers who lack long-term institutional support and whose poor pay and lack of job security undermines their self-respect and drains them of emotional and physical energy. And finally, many are underemployed in jobs not related to their intellectual interests or they are not employed at all. "The feminization of poverty" (O'Connell, 1983), or what Maria Mies (1986) refers to as the "rapid process of pauperization of women in the Western economies" (p. 16) is now a well known social phenomenon which carries a lifelong legacy, and which is not absent from the academy.

Seeking to tell the stories of our experience, we find only words weak with meaning, and we struggle to capture the complexity of how we live our lives as women. We have achieved some levels of engagement in paid work, but not the power to decide what the processes and content of that work will be. We have achieved greater access to education, but not to articulating what will be taught, by whom, and how. We have struggled for and gained the right to participate in the political process, yet the presence of women in even low-level political positions is still an anomaly, recent events in Canadian provincial and federal politics not withstanding. Women's apparent gains for the most part are undone by the continued brutalization of women economically, emotionally, psychologically, intellectually, and physically.

The results for women have been chronic: the apparently public discussion often engaging an overtly co-opted feminist discourse has not resulted in women's generally improved economic status relative to men; the gap between women's and men's economic viability has increased worldwide; pornography is an ever-growing industry seeping more and more overtly into everyday social discourse and cultural images; and the statistics on violence against women and children of both sexes are continually and steadily rising. Worldwide, women are discursively absent from social formations to which we are physically central. Our presence is made irrelevant in the social discourse even as our labor is made indispensable for the maintenance of life on this planet. By requiring our consent to be absent, we continue to be colonized even as we struggle for autonomy and self-determination for women and all subordinate, violated, and dismissed peoples. And in the end, despite the odds, it is left to us to mediate the lacunae created by these contradictions.

What is important about women's accounts is that they do not represent some deviation from an otherwise sane context of equality and possibility. By and large women's accounts of our experience are not expressions of unusually brutalizing moments identifiable in opposition to otherwise "normal," "commonplace," "everyday" experiences. The power of these experiences to effect women's notions of self and identity is precisely that they *are* normal, commonplace, and everyday. Placed within the dominant phallocentric social world with its specific classed and raced version of male privilege and entitlement, however, the articulation of women's experiences, as is the case with the experiences of other subordinate class and race groups, is often viewed as profoundly disruptive of this discourse. Like a vulgar voice against the harmonious chorus of the dominant refined through countless centuries of practice, the telling of the experiences of the disempowered and the subordinate seem inharmonious, abrupt, impolite, and out-of-place.

What does this mean for me as a feminist teacher? Reflecting on the words of one of my colleagues who described feminism as "an invasion on the corpus of academic offerings" feminist intellectual workers are left to negotiate an academic work environment that takes male prerogative and expertise for granted.

In contrast, it is required of us that we constantly demonstrate in concrete and self-conscious ways that we are also deserving of being granted yet only feeble prerogatives for which we are then required to demonstrate concrete and self-consciously articulated gratefulness. Feminist courses come to be derided for their "high profile" and for their potential to "take students away from other faculty" and course offerings, jeopardizing, so we are told, the "core" courses.

I hear these words as accusations and am astonished to discover that, in my teaching practice and relations with students, that which is considered desirable and indeed coveted under "normal" circumstances is suddenly transformed into a liability when it is associated with pedagogies arising from radical social perspectives—pedagogies aimed at disrupting rather then preserving the status quo.

"Corpus" and "corps" both derive from the same Latin root for "body." The body of knowledge upon which we are fed, the Corpus Christi of Western civilization, the feast of the Father, Son, and Holy Ghost, is a fraternal banquet that systematically excludes vast numbers of women as well as men who do not conform to its prescribed "etiquette."

For women who embrace the politics of feminism—defined as the political struggle for autonomy and self-determination for women—our work in the academy is risky. Veiled threats permeate my work environment forcing upon me an attitude of defensiveness: "Professor Lewis teaches from a feminist perspective!" I stand accused. With these words I feel myself invited to defend myself or, by turn, I feel invited to apologize and to promise never, ever to do it again.

These are not words with which the academy is comfortable. Our words, however tentatively they might enter trembling into our collective space, for "it is with fear and trembling that one crosses the threshold of street space strictly forbidden by the fathers" (Marcus, 1988, p. 78), offered in the studied ease and physical comforts of the university laid heavy with the ideological draperies of intellectual discussion, stand as a challenge to an academy deeply indebted to the patriarchic symbolic order. Impassioned and lacking "objectivity" our words offend while simultaneously they reinforce the perception of the embodied persona of the strong woman—itself a socially burdened signifier that has a long history of violence against us—and so construct the double-edged contradiction of the politics of feminism.

I intend neither offense nor reinforcement. Given the strong phallocentric bias of the academy, any acknowledgment that our words might offend academic sensibilities is to concede the power to enforce this bias as legitimate. Simultaneously, to give into the seductively intended compliment of being different from other women by virtue of being "strong" is to participate in constructing women as weak, and therefore, collectively deserving of our subordinate social position.

Women's participation in higher education is a relatively recent phenomenon in the history of formalized institutional educational systems. Despite the fact that such participation has only been allowed grudgingly, after struggle, the spaces thus achieved are made available by the extremely slow, albeit steady, growth—the "transition from 'a precarious to a permanent marginality'" (Thompson, 1983, p. 128)—of women's studies programs in some universities as a response to the changing demography of higher education. While we might be encouraged to celebrate this intrusion, at the same time, I want to be cautious not to overstate these apparent changes. As Somer Brodribb has said:

> One interdisciplinary course, complemented with a scattering of courses in various disciplines, does not meet [the] needs [of a feminist pedagogy]. What is essential is the presence of a common ground for feminist intellectual discourse, debate and exchange, and autonomous thinking and expression. (1987, p. 5)

The existence of such "common ground," except in a few highly unusual cases, is still a long way in the future (Aiken et al, 1988). Adequately funded women's studies programs enjoying long-term commitment are few indeed. More often what exists is a loosely affiliated handful of peripheral courses, coordinated around a minimal number of core courses, some of them taught by individuals who must add it to their already full faculty duties. Courses drawn from various departments to which the program is only peripherally connected means that women's studies offerings often fall victim to the strategies of departments over which the women's studies program has no control (Howe, 1983, p. 105).

None of this is to deny that the presence of large numbers of women students on university campuses has had an impact on how programs are rationalized and organized. Yet, while the educational experiences of most men seem to fulfill the promise of their aspirations, somehow the aspirations of the women sitting next to them, completing the same assignments, listening to the same lectures, reading the same materials, seem to vaporize in the face of women's realities. Despite the apparent opportunities that women's greater participation in formal education would appear to make available, the face of authority and policy making continues to be not only primarily white and economically advantaged but distinctly male.

As Adrienne Rich (1979) suggests, even as we find ourselves inside walls which had previously held us out, we:

> have been made participants in a system that prepares men to take up roles of power in a man-centered society, that asks questions and teaches 'facts' generated by a male intellectual tradition, and that both subtly and openly confirms men as leaders and shapers of human destiny both within and outside academia. (p. 127)

Against this, feminism is posed as a critique in the context of the great unspoken female experience of anger and frustration.

## IMPLICATIONS FOR FEMINIST TEACHING

As a feminist teacher, the core of my work in the academy is the question of how to proceed pedagogically such that I honor the diversity of women's experiences even as I acknowledge our shared violations. I know that simply taking up issues of gender in the context of the course agenda is not enough to guarantee that the analysis used in that context will contribute to building what Thelma McCormack (1987) calls "a cumulative body of knowledge in accord with a feminist agenda" (p. 290). Even individuals explicitly committed to social change cannot always be counted on to interrogate the details of the gender dynamics of their teaching and analysis.

For example, in his article "Pedagogy of the Oppressor?" John Schilb offers fertile ground for a discussion of the tensions that articulate feminist teaching. Expounding on the difficulties he faces in teaching a "feminist course" at an upper-class undergraduate university he identifies himself as both "a teacher of women's studies" and a "feminist teacher." He despairs as he positions himself against the students in his class:

> The ingrained prejudices of the vast majority [of students] cannot vanish upon request and my uneasiness with their world view survives. It intensifies when students take my courses in resentful submission to the requirement instead of genuine sympathy for its concerns. Although I avoid wallowing in my rancor as if it constituted a holy mood, I have grown more willing to reveal it to my colleagues, despite the cherished stereotype of the feminist classroom as a scene of perpetual collaborative bliss. (1985, p. 256)

Despite Schilb's expressions of concern over *his* students apparent disinterest in anything feminist, he states later that "my students feel more comfortable asking me questions about the women's movement than they *probably* would if they had to ask someone from its overwhelming female majority" (p. 263, emphasis added).

If Schilb hoped to be an ally he fell terribly short of the mark. Supporting the myth that women's studies and feminist courses are primarily a social experience of "perpetual collaborative bliss" undermines not only the political aspects of feminist analysis and the women's movement but feeds the fire of those who would wish to use exactly such denigration of women's intellectual work as an excuse to exclude it from the realm of the academy altogether. In opposition to Schilb's claim, feminist work in the academy is constituted by a difficult undertaking aimed at uncovering those lived social realities, the pain of which sometimes makes us "wish we didn't know what we know."

Subjectivities formed in the color of our skin, the varied expressions of our sexual desire, and the differential closeness we live to economic marginality sets us against one another as often as it brings us together in our struggle to learn about ourselves and each other. Without doubt, this learning is sometimes joyful and passionate as we have laughed and cried together, raged and danced together. But at other times, many times, it is difficult and painful as we learn to trust ourselves and each other not by virtue of our similarities but through those aspects of our lived realities that work to divide us.

Similarly, Schilb speculates that he might be a more effective feminist teacher because his *students* "probably" approach him more freely with questions about the women's movement than they would a woman who is a feminist. Here he fails to self-interrogate the reaffirmation of his unproblematized access to the power of meaning making and legitimation. Further, by collapsing the women and men he teaches into the single designation of "student" he fails to make problematic whether his statement can be applied across gender without differentiation. Perhaps, because my experiences, in teaching at a university with a similar socioeconomic profile, do not reflect his, I have to ask whether the political projects of our pedagogical practices might not be the basis of this difference.

Perhaps to his credit, Schilb acknowledges the power of his male voice:

> much as I appreciate the rhetorical leverage granted my sex even in my women's studies classroom, I shudder to think that only a man's voice could legitimize what mine says. (p. 263)

Yet he fails to question the political efficacy of the strategies he employs to "offset" his "authority by having female teaching assistants run several discussions and female guest speakers explain their work" (p. 264).

To be sure, teaching toward a feminist political project is not easy. Nor is it immediately absorbed by all of the students we might teach—female or male. Indeed, there are times when both women and men resist the terms of a feminist analysis. However, it seems to me that the power of a politically informed pedagogy lies in the extent to which it can uncover the ground of such resistance, often located in the hidden privileges of students' dominant social position.

While inviting women speakers to his class in order to legitimate their voices and their work might be seen by Schilb as creating spaces for the public display of the work of women intellectuals, the charitable implications have to be seen as counterproductive to a political agenda directed toward acknowledging feminist analysis on its own terms. Of course visiting speakers are an important aspect of teaching. As Brodribb suggests, sharing the collective knowledge of a discipline is as important in women's studies as it is in any other sphere of intellectual work. However, the potential of men, such as Schilb, teaching from a self-assertively "feminist perspective" must lie not in how they articulate the conditions of legitimacy and validity of women and women's work. On the contrary, the agenda of their practice must arise from their experience of privilege and entitlement as men in a phallocentric culture, not, as Schilb seems to have formulated it, by reaffirming their privilege and power by allowing themselves the prerogative of legitimating women and our work.

Furthermore, for some women, the source of our resistance may indeed arise from a much deeper terror generated precisely by the limits of our autonomy circumscribed by our experience of subordination, a reality requiring analysis not laced with "rancor"—the inveterate bitterness and malignant hate of spiteful cynicism. It never seems to occur to Schilb to question how he might create a context for his pedagogical practice that is not rancorous, but rather committed to the difficult work of lifting up to view our deeply submerged experiences of violation and misogyny, and then finding ways of being there with students, yet without intrusion, when the reality of being a woman in a phallocentric culture explodes into our collective consciousness.

## ANGER AS A SOURCE OF TEACHING AND LEARNING

It has been my experience that, for many women, working through and coming to a feminist perspective on history and biography is not easy. This journey often generates anger and ultimately a politicization of every moment of our personal and public lives until we can come to grips with the positive political potential of our anger—an anger that is freed by the uncovering/ unbinding of centuries of powerlessness and the denial of the conditions for speaking what we know in accordance with our own desires and interests.

Recently a student wrote the following in her critical journal—a weekly writing assignment that forms part of the course requirement for the graduate seminar in feminist theories that I teach:

> Two months ago I would not have believed that a graduate course could change my perspective or change *me* so much! The term transformation is insufficient to explain the effect; I believe metamorphosis is more appropriate because it also implies growth. I have grown up in my understanding and I hope in my self-reflection. It feels like a door has been opened to let in the light, a door that I did not know was closed until the light shone in my eyes. The way I interpret and respond to even trivial events has been altered. . . . Has this transformation been painful? Without hesitation I shout a resounding YES! . . . The feminist perspective for me is a vantage point derived from our shared experiences . . . that has enlightened me not only to gender-related oppression but also race/ethnicity and class. Unfortunately, this enlightenment although positive and "good" has left me angry and frustrated. Now that I am able to see that many social practices were and continue to be formed to support certain interests, I am outraged at these injustices. (Student journal, quoted with permission)

This student is not alone. Many women students arrive in my classes carrying a substantial baggage of dis/ease verging on rage. Mindbindings and body violations articulate the schooling of the dispossessed—women included. This situation has particularly reproductive consequences in a faculty of education where in our relations with our students, the issues we raise with them as important and the perspectives we might encourage in them will ultimately reflect in their relations with their own students. What they carry into their own teaching will either set into motion active, critical processes directed toward the creation of a better world, or, conversely, will create social visions aimed at maintaining cultural inertia and historical amnesia.

In our context in a faculty of education, women students experience the forms of women's exclusion both routinely and vividly. One young woman student teacher described it to me this way:

> When we get out to the school [for practice teaching] you can see it right away. We get assigned to our classrooms and the principal takes us down. He drops me off at the door of my room and then I watch him and the

male student walk down the hall together, chatting, his [the principal's] hand on his [the male student's] shoulder. And you just know, he [the male student] is already on the inside and I am not. (personal conversation, quoted with permission)

These young women teachers know the consequences of such exclusion all too well. Another student describing a similar incident goes on to say:

No one told me how to get from where I was to where I might have wanted to go. I was in science but I dropped out. It's like there was information there about how to prepare for a career and what were the important things I needed to know but no one ever told me. And by the time I figured it out it was too late, I had already chosen the wrong courses and missed other important things I should have done. The boys in the class seemed to know what to do; it's like they already had the information. (personal conversation, quoted with permission)

Whether this vital information is parleyed overtly or whether it is acquired by virtue of the models readily available to young men that provide them with information they could not possibly miss; whether such information is dropped casually in situations from which women are excluded (an economist friend of mine has dubbed this the "washroom theory" of organizational promotion), or is conveyed specifically at crucial moments of decision making, the fact is that women often feel expectantly reticent in educational institutions which are overtly expressive of male interests.

Such exclusionary practices permeate all levels of institutional education. A woman lecturer recently told me that she was potentially up for tenure in a year, but hadn't been aware of the kinds of things she should have been doing all along to make her candidacy acceptable. And, she continued:

Now it's already too late. I wish someone had just said to me at the beginning, here is what you need to do if you want to go on. If someone had been there to show me the ropes and then to encourage me. But now it's too late to pick it up. (personal conversation, quoted with permission)

And finally she articulates the effects of unfulfilled desire: "I don't think I want to go on in the academy anyway."

The experience of women's anger is not unexamined in the feminist concern with pedagogical practices directed toward women's political potential. Indeed, as Audre Lorde suggests, women's anger can be the source of women's energy for action and change (Lorde, 1984, p. 130). There are two faces of this anger in the feminist classroom. Margo Culley (1985) speaks of one and Audre Lorde speaks of the other. Margo Culley articulates the terms of her pedagogy in words that capture my own understandings:

> to permit the acknowledgment and claiming of anger as one's own, and to direct its legitimate energy toward personal and social change. (1985, p. 212)

Culley's analysis proceeds through an important examination of that anger which arises for women from a deep desire to wish well for ourselves and the world in the face of strong evidence against the possibility of such a reality. At such times, Culley suggests, anger may and does explode in every direction. Sometimes, particularly in the case of younger students, such anger is directed at the instructor (me) who is "making us read this stuff and who is old (I am not yet old enough to be their mother!) and who (only twenty years after the feminist movement exploded—yet one more time—onto the political scene) doesn't understand how the world *is now*." It is even suggested that "our talking about it *causes* the problem" and that only when the "old generation" finally "dies" (!) and stops seeing everything through jaundiced eyes will the new (their) generation be able to get on with life as they wish to live it—presumably having eliminated racism, sexism, class differentiation, homophobia, and so on.

Other times anger is directed at other women students who are charged with being "bitter and 'just angry' because they have made the 'wrong' choices and now want to blame men for it." In evaluating the various stages of curriculum transformation, Marilyn Schuster and Susan Van Dyne (1985) suggest that:

> underneath the wide variety of expressions of resistance is a residual fear of loss, a reluctance to give up what had seemed most stable, efficient, authoritative, transcendent of contexts, and free of ideological or personal values. (p. 25)

Culley adds that, while such anger is difficult and often painful to hear and absorb, "they must be allowed or the group will travel no further" (1985, p. 212).

The dynamics of this version of women's anger is important to note and to acknowledge. I have learned from my students that we displace, at our peril, their concerns and anger into the safe ideological category of the falsely conscious. I concur with Schuster and Van Dyne when they suggest that:

> We can readily understand that women students in late adolescence [early adulthood] regard as extremely unwelcome the news that their opportunities may be in any way limited. . . . For women students especially, the temptation is great to disassociate themselves from the disadvantages they perceive as defining women as a group. (1985, p. 21)

Indeed, one of the challenges for feminist teachers in the classroom is the question of how to move students beyond their potentially victim-blaming responses to feminist social analysis without at the same time destroying among these same students the possibilities for intellectual growth and analytical insight.

While this is one version of the anger often displayed in the feminist class-room, I believe, with Audre Lorde, that there is another form of equally transformative anger—the creative anger that comes not from our wish to deny our reality but from facing it head on:

> Every woman has a well-stocked arsenal of anger potentially useful against those oppressions personal and institutional, which brought that anger into being. (1984, p. 127)

Unlike rancor, the destructive hatred fostered by unproblematized structural inequalities that require the subordination of the many to the few, anger, says Audre Lorde is the "grief of distortion between peers, and its object is change" (1984, p. 129). Earlier she identifies the source of this anger in the following way:

> The anger of exclusion, of unquestioned privilege, of racial distortions, of silence, ill-use, stereotyping, defensiveness, misnaming, betrayal, and co-optation. (p. 124)

These angers arise for women of color in a racist society. They also arise for all women in a sexist society which, when "focused with precision . . . can become a powerful source of energy serving progress and change" (p. 127).

Following Virginia Woolf (1929/1977) and Hélène Cixous (1981), Valerie Walkerdine (1985b) also suggests that such anger is the response to that loss out of which hopes are born:

> such losses are indeed the basis of a terrible and important anger and the basis for finding ways of both understanding and working with that loss which will place us once again as historical beings generating "social forms of love and solidarity." (p. 1)

This is not to be confused with a condition of blind rage. Many women experience finding space for the expression of their legitimate anger as a deeply moving personal moment of liberation and relief often expressed verbally and physically in the classroom. At such moments women almost always speak directly to other women through a discourse of recognition.

Our anger is simultaneously marked by our wish to flee from its terrifying possibilities on the one hand and our wish to embrace, as Audre Lorde suggests, its positive potential on the other. About this kind of anger, a young woman student wrote the following on the back of one of her reading assignments:

> Fortunately, I continued to read the articles assigned for our course, and I began a transition from the "anger" stage into one characterized by a feeling of empowerment. . . . I remember that the first time I read Dale Spender's *Man-Made Language* I had to jump up and run around every few pages—empowerment is a very physical, tangible feeling. . . . I "retitled" the section on "Dominance and Tunnel Vision" to "Or Why Women Know More . . . Than Men." I identified with her discussion of consciousness-raising groups because my female roommate and I used to have long talks about how much more aware we were than most of the men we knew. . . . At any rate, after I finished jumping around, I wrote on the back of the last page of Spender's article: Lots of power comes from the ability to be inclusive and multidimensional; to feel that women, collectively, as a 'class' of people don't have to present a unified, uni-dimensional, exclusive, mono-causal viewpoint which is 'logical' and 'objective' in order to be 'right' (my, what difficulty I'm suddenly having with the English language). I can "resolve" the way I feel about pornography, for example, simply by realizing that I don't have to resolve the way I feel about pornography: I can feel that it has terrible social repercussions and that stuff that portrays degradation/ objectification of and violence towards women should be burned and banned, *and* (the *in*clusive conjunction) I can be turned on by some of it. Men take a solipsistic viewpoint (I mean, in the final analysis, we only have one viewpoint each, right?) and call it "objective"—what hogwash!—and then systematically, "objectively" discount the viewpoints of women. So, if all this stuff: science, logic, classics, philosophy, religion stuff isn't necessarily right then I don't have to learn and accept and assimilate it as if it were. I can study it and think critically about it. But how to begin discovering things on different terms? It's as if the entirety of "human" history has just been wiped off the blackboard in front of me; as if the cosmic authority has just said, "Nope, try again" and left us to re-invent -discover -formulate -conceive it all from scratch. How exciting!! I can think of things that don't even have names! Maybe the power comes from knowing that I'm not crazy or over-emotional or etc, etc, etc., and that, since the people saying I am are wrong, I don't have to worry about it. Maybe, instead of being wiped off the cosmic blackboard, the title just got changed from "How It Is" to "How It Is According To The Tunnel-Visioned Dominant Group" and the blackboard has gone from being almost full to being infinitely large. . . . As an independent thinking, feeling being, how can I believe, value, or even tolerate views of the world put forward by men whose views of women were for the most part patriarchal, sexist, and ignorant? How can I accept that views of the world conceived by minds that hold women to be anywhere from soulless to inherently evil could have meaning in the world I perceive? Since I know that many of these "great thinkers" were dead wrong when it came to describing women, I have a

hard time accepting their opinions on other topics as "objective" and representative of those of humanity. (quoted with permission)

Clearly, establishing "the conditions of learning" in a feminist classroom is not only about locating ourselves in history, but as well about the creation of a space for the expressions of anger that are the inevitable consequence of the lacunae left by shifting perceptions, dislodged ideologies, and new ways of seeing and understanding through which we might reclaim both the collective and the individual self.

As Linda Anderson suggests, pedagogy that makes possible the claiming of the self emerges in the spaces that "exist between loss, absence and what might be" (1986, p. 60). Wishing we didn't know what we know, our "grief at the loss of earlier illusions" (Schuster and Van Dyne, 1985, p. 167) turns our desires toward future possibilities. In the feminist classroom, women often articulate such anger first through self-reproach: some version of "how could I have been so stupid" is the beginning point which soon turns to the search for strategies that can fulfill their desire for change.

Women often come away from the experience of the feminist classroom not only with new understandings both of history and of possible futures— the wish for a feminist utopia embedded in practice rather than the death wish for a perfect world—but, as well, prepared to articulate practical strategies for critique which challenge the androcentric biases of their other courses. This does not always gain them favor. Their experiences reflect how difficult this is to do in the face of resistance and the determined power of the status quo to hold firm its privilege to articulate our collective meaning.

Yet, once having glimpsed the vision of a possible future, few women are willing to give it up regardless of personal cost: I have seen them suffer not only ridicule ("you must be taking the feminist course") and goading ("what do you feminists have to say about that?") but as well suffer the effects of intellectual violence, loss of grades, and certainly loss of possibility.

In this context, anger, as an expression of a transformed consciousness is a totally appropriate response to the condition of women worldwide. Rather than challenge it as inappropriate in an academic setting, women's legitimate anger needs to be anticipated and supported, not subverted or diffused. More than this, we need to turn it back on itself and articulate its goals as the transformation of the social relations which generate it in the first place.

The simple dichotomization of the emotional/psychological from the material/concrete undercuts our understanding of the complexity of women's subordination/exploitation as well as makes unproblematic the conditions under which women might appropriate a feminist political agenda. While women's subordination clearly has its brutal psychological/emotional aspects and while phallocentrism manifests itself at all levels of our social encounters (Walkerdine, 1985a), it is their materiality that hammers them into place.

That women cannot exercise the power of "the Father" is not, as Freud would have us so conveniently believe, because we lack the organ of power, a condition that, because it is so singularly unchangeable, would leave us for ever negated against our desires, but because we lack job opportunities, adequate day care and home help, sufficient remuneration, and recognition of our work and talents. Patriarchy exists because it is profitable to be dominant. Men having achieved that status (Stanley, 1992), find it inordinately difficult to give it up. Given the terms of such social conditions it would be a surprise indeed if women did not feel the constraints of contradictory choices and the conflicting articulation of our interests.

These are feminist issues. This is the stuff of feminist pedagogy. This is the substance of our work in the academy. The source of our feminist anger is a response to the all too familiar experiences of exclusion and violation we have learned to recognize. The source of our pain, however, is both more subtle and more powerful, lived through the regret we have all to feel at the realization that the rhetoric of schooling with its promises of equality and possibility lacks the commitment to practices that might make these promises a reality.

If the intent of patriarchy is to reproduce the status quo of masculine knowledge in support of masculine privilege (and I believe this is precisely the political intent of the schooling enterprise), then the role of feminism is to be indiscreet—to speak our experience of alienation, to speak that about which we have been invited to be silent, and to refuse to concede power to the bedrock of that failed yet seductive democracy of individual liberalism. Indeed, as a feminist teacher in the classroom, my most urgent need is to find a pedagogy that:

> can help create a space for mutual engagement of lived difference that is not framed in oppositional terms requiring the silencing of a multiplicity of voices by a single dominant discourse. (Lewis and Simon, 1986, p. 569)

This is a pedagogy that will allow us all to hold up the strands of women's desire to be in the world and to re-examine them through a critical lens that might allow us all to find the roots of our many voices.

# 4 | LEARNING FEMININITY
## SCHOOLING AND THE STRUGGLE FOR SELF

It is a highly radical and subversive act to tell a familiar story in a new way. Once you start to do it you realize that what you call history is another such story and could be told differently and has been. And then the authoritative tradition starts to crack and crumble. It too, it turns out is nothing more than a particular selection of various stories, all of which have at one time or another been believed and told.

—Chernin,
"In the House of the Flame Bearers"

"It's my life, so I'll do what I want. . . . Right?"

—Meagan French

WOMEN'S RELATIONSHIP TO THE ACADEMY—AND WHAT IT IS we are expected to learn there—has not been told very much one way or the other. Yet the development of good and ever more insightful work about our understanding of the dynamics of the challenge brought to phallocentrism by women's education is essential (Rockhill, 1991). Indeed, women's inaccessibility to the word in concrete terms—ie. pen, paper, time, space, and a coding system— has contributed profoundly to our silencing both materially and historically. To be sure, the issue of women's struggle for education is one which always bears more analysis.

First, our absence from and, then, our invisibility in the realm of intellectual work has meant that we have lived our condition as intellectual women mostly as an oxymoron (Spender, personal communication). For women, the contradiction in applying the adjective "intellectual" to the social category "woman" comes from the concrete enact-ments of what it means to be either. Coded through the ideology of reproduction women's capacity for "labor", whether or not we bear children, has historically required us to sustain the work of production not only through the labor of our bodies, but specifically by the labor of our hands: women's place in the family subsumes the ideology of "motherhood" under our expected compliance in embracing "woman's work."

Yet, even as women contribute disproportionately significant labor to the maintenance of the earth, simultaneously we have been, and continue to be, denied the status of meaning makers; we have been excluded from the stories we are told as well as from those we are encouraged to tell to and of ourselves. Lerner states:

> [women] have been kept from knowing their history and from interpreting history, either their own or that of men. Women have been systematically excluded from the enterprise of creating symbol systems, philosophies, sci-ence, and law. Women have not only been educationally deprived throughout historical time in every known society, they have been excluded from theory-formation. (1986, p. 5)

Women's relationship to the socially coded features of maternity is a sig-nificant aspect of our access to schooling and education. In what follows it is my intention to explore the relationship, for women, between education and the ideology of motherhood. This chapter is presented in two parts. I begin with the telling of my understanding of the lived experience of Meagan French, a young female participant in a large-scale research project aimed, in part, at exploring the relationships young adults perceive between education and their future options for work and family life.[1] Following this, in the sec-ond part of this chapter, I draw on my own experience as the source from which to explore the conditions of women's education as a function of our woman/mother work.

## BACKGROUND TO THE STUDY

The data for Meagan's story was collected during a comprehensive large-scale ethnographic study of high school students, all of whom were in the

---

1. Project name: Learning Work. Principal Investigators: Roger Simon and Joel Weiss. Funded by: Social Sciences and Humanities Research Council of Canada. My role: Graduate Research Assistant. For the purposes of this analysis all personal and place names have been changed. Data for this analysis are taken primarily from an interview I conducted with Meagan. Data from the interview with Mr. and Mrs. French were gathered by another Graduate researcher associated with the project.

graduating year of either a general-level or basic-level program in two large suburban high schools and who were participating in a school/work cooperative program at the time of the study. Within the context of the Ontario educational system, in the 1980's and early 1990's the distinction between the general and the basic-level programs was significant. Students enrolled in the general-level program accrued qualifications for entry into community college or apprenticeship programs for the skilled trades. By contrast, those enrolled in the basic-level programs achieved qualifications that suited them, at most, for minimally paid employment in service industries. In order to enter community- college education or an apprenticeship program, students graduating from a basic-level program generally required upgrading. At the time of the study, the Ontario public education system also offered students a third option of study: advanced-level programs preparatory to entry into a university. Even though graduates from the advanced programs could also choose community-college or skilled-trades options for further qualification toward a professional, semi-professional or skilled job, they were the only route by which students could access the higher education options, such as university.

In the school that Meagan attended, students in both the general- and the basic-level programs could choose to participate in the school's cooperative-education program. The co-op-ed. program offered students the opportunity to earn a proportion of their high school credits through job-site experience. The gender specificity of these job-site placements tended to maintain the status quo. Young men were, by and large, placed in such industries as upholstery, garages, auto body shops, woodworking shops and so on. Hairdressing salons and childcare facilities tended to be the placement sites for young women.

In consultation with school staff, students had some say in the nature of their placement. However, teachers played a significant role in encouraging students to choose placements for which they seemed particularly "suited."

The cooperative-education program not only juxtaposed for students the world of school with the world of work but from the students' perspective made immediate the need to consider what they might do after graduation.

For these young adults, as is the case for many of us, "the family" served as a major site where the contradictions and myths of the social, political, and economic conditions of their lives converged as both possibility and constraint. As a researcher, my interest in this study arose because of my concern with the situations of women within the sphere of the family. In particular, my interest was to understand the historical/cultural experiences of women's lives within this context in order to better understand the relationships between gender and power, in particular, the role of the family as a site of social control in creating and maintaining the social and economic imbalance between women and men.

In this analysis I use the case of Meagan because, for her, it was precisely the sphere of the family and domestic life which seemed to present itself as such a massive force. The question of how women might move beyond the specific prescriptions of socially appropriate expressions of femininity without losing the support of their emotional community embedded in the family is the issue of this analysis. With Gerda Lerner, I ask:

> What could explain women's historical "complicity" in upholding the patriarchal system that subordinated them and in transmitting that system generation after generation, to their children of both sexes? (1986, p. 6)

While the story I tell here is related through the situation of Meagan, a young woman who agreed to participate in this large-scale research project in the final year of her high school education, my intention in telling this story is not so that I might present the results of an ethnographic study. Nor is it my interest to tell Meagan's story so that it might serve as an example of how women's lives are socially controlled. Rather, I wish to use what I know about Meagan to reflect on the condition of women—myself included—in a world culture that, through the hegemonic processes of family relations, prioritizes the interests of men over that of women; to make sense of how social contexts work to limit the vision of our own possibilities; to reveal the subtleties of how we come to be complicit in our own subordination; and finally to articulate an understanding of a particular moment of experience that might be used as the basis of a social analysis aimed at politically informed teaching and learning.

In the end, through a process of linking my own biography to the conditions of Meagan's life circumstances as I understand them, I want to make explicit the relationship between power and hegemony: how power creates its own meaning and in turn how meaning reinforces power. I extend this as an invitation to the reader to think about ways in which education may be informed by the personal of everyday ritual.

While my conversation with Meagan is in large part the source of the information I consider in this chapter, it is not my intention to present her case as if she were "speaking for herself." No research instrument—whether quantitative or qualitative, whether minimally or highly interactive—could presume to uncover all of the private ways in which Meagan negotiated her social world. At the very least I know she must have had ideas and thoughts about the research, the interview experience, and me as the interviewer that were never broached, that were not specifically the topic of our joint inquiry, but which nonetheless framed and informed her responses both in what she said and in what she chose not to say.

Whether we understand research as a collaborative engagement between researchers and research subjects (Miller, 1990), or whether as researchers we choose to make our own sense from the information that is shared with us by those we interview, the fact remains that we can never know everything there is to know about the the individuals with whom we share this research space. That this is the case says more about the autonomy of individuals in their capacity to make sense of their own lives than about the limitations of research design or the "instruments" used to gather information (Eisner and Peshkin, 1990).

As researchers, it is imperative that the rights of independent personhood be honored on behalf of our research subjects. We cannot assume that whatever understanding we achieve through the research process gives us the authority to use it to make decisions about people's lives. In this spirit then, I neither wish to lock Meagan's responses into the frames of my analysis nor do I wish to freeze them in time and space. What is presented here is not Meagan's analysis. It is mine. It does not represent Meagan's struggle for understanding of her social world (although I do not rule out the possibility that she might have achieved new understandings as a result of her participation in this research), but for me to understand mine. The questions raised by this investigation and its analysis derived from my interests—a product of my desire to make sense of my world as a feminist teacher and mother within the academy.

Finally, there is no attempt in this text to suggest in any way that the analysis is universalizable to all women or even to all young women in situations similar to that of Meagan. It is not the intent of this analysis to generalize.

More specifically, it is not my intention to reduce the experiences of all women within the situation of white, middle-class, Western experience. The notion of "woman" as a unitary whole, undifferentiated by class, race, ethnicity, age, geographic location, variations in sexual desire, social position, or cultural expression is the reductive legacy of social/theoretical positions that have served the reproduction of the status quo in opposition to the interests of women in all of our complex realities. Indeed, in using the word "women" I do not intend to reduce all women's experiences to a simple monolithic form. I believe that an understanding of the complexity of women's experiences in a phallocentric social cultural setting which is also marked by class differentiation, racism, ethnocentrism, ageism, and homophobia is essential to the understanding of the situation of women. In this regard, the validity of an analysis is measurable not only by its acknowledgment of a two-sexed social system (Hamilton, 1987), but, as well, by how it registers the multiplicity of our differences against the dominant.

As Corrigan (1987b) explains, "the figure in dominance" throughout the world is not only male, but, as well, white, economically advantaged, ablebodied, heterosexual, and intellectually rather than manually inclined (although, this last may only pertain to situations of productive labor: socially, in Euro-Western cultures, the status of non-manually employed men is enhanced by physical prowess usually in the form of some "leisure" sport, requiring both time and money to accomplish—this situation does not generally apply to women).

It is neither possible nor useful to forefront one form of human oppression over another. As is stated by Anne Phillips, "class and race and gender are not parallel oppressions" (1987, p. 10–11), but rather converging/intersecting as well as diverging/contradictory ones. However, language is difficult and often fails to reflect the complexity of how we live our lives. I know that women experience differently from men the social/cultural manifestations of class position, as do women *and* men who are black. Similarly, I know that to be a black woman is to occupy a different social location from that of being a black man. And whether white or black to be lesbian or gay is to experience the world differently from those who carry the normalized assets of heterosexuality. It is also true that economically advantaged women experience their gender differently from women who are economically destitute of whatever race, color, culture or sexual desire.

Yet, regardless of the particular violations experienced by subordinate racial, ethnic, or class groups, the women in those groups have always experienced gender subordination as well. The common feature of our experience as women—defined through gender as a political entity—is that we are all subject to those social forms and power relations that would keep us from naming the world from our own experience; that would deny us the use of the word to organize our collective knowledge; that would deny us the very articulation of our knowledge.

It is my belief that by understanding the terms of a gender analysis we may be helped in understanding the condition of women within patriarchy. We may be helped in understanding how women's subjectivity is both consciously articulated and unconsciously expressed through symbolic practices that mediate, construct, and transform our life experiences not only within our families but as well beyond them in the ways we think about our life possibilities.

While honoring the differences among women across social class, cultural/racial diversity, and the desires of the body, the suggestion that all women are in some way bound to one another beyond these social/cultural definitions is the premise of this chapter.

## MEAGAN'S FAMILY PROFILE

At the time of the study, Meagan was eighteen years old. She was a grade twelve student in a general-level program in a general- and advanced-level high school. Prospects were good that she would graduate at the end of the school year with average grades. In the year of her graduation entry into post-secondary education in Ontario was highly competitive. Even students with high grades in their graduating year had only a small percentage chance of entering a community college program. Given the program in which she was enrolled, Meagan certainly could not contemplate attending university without accomplishing significant upgrading of all of her high school credits from a general to an advanced standing. Such upgrading could be accomplished in only the rarest of cases.

In her final year of school, Meagan's course of study consisted of marketing, business finance, the co-op work-study program and English. English was her only compulsory credit. Over the interval since she began grade nine she had progressively taken and subsequently failed to pursue classes in science, math, history, geography, accounting, and art. Her co-op work placement was at a day care center located ten minutes' walk from her home. As a co-op student, she participated at the day care every other day from 9:30 A.M. until 4:00 P.M. She was one of eight adults in the day care, working with two- and three-year-olds during the early part of the school year and four- and five-year-olds beginning in her second semester in January.

When she graduated in June, Meagan was hired as a part-time assistant at the same day care facility. In addition she was given some full-time work whenever one of the full-time teachers was away. Her full-time day started at 8:00 A.M. and ended at 4:00 P.M. When part-time, she worked two-and-a-half hours a day. As a co-op student she was not remunerated. However, when she was hired as a teachers' aid, she earned the minimum wage of $3.50 an hour. This was exactly half as much as the then current rate of pay for full-time certified early childhood education teachers in the same day care facility.

Meagan had a sister, Libby, who was thirty-four years old, a brother, Dean, who was thirty-two and another sister, Trish, who was twenty-five. Meagan pointed out that "there's seven years between all the girls." As the analysis develops, it will become apparent that Dean is set apart from the other children in the family in ways that are more significant than is indicated by this anomalous relationship in their ages.

Libby graduated with a grade twelve general diploma from the same high school that Meagan also attended. Before marrying and raising her family, she worked for a few years as a secretary with an insurance company. At the time of the interview she had two children with whom she stayed at home. Her husband was a mail carrier. She did not return to work after she married.

Her brother, Dean, also graduated from the same high school. However, he completed what was, in Ontario, then called grade thirteen: the final year of a five-year high school education in the advanced level program. In contrast, both the general level and the basic level programs were four years long in duration. Dean proceeded to a university where he studied computer math—a high employment and lucrative career-oriented program of study. He then worked as a computer analyst in the central office of a large public utility. He also had two young children. Unlike Meagan's older sister, Dean's wife did not stop working outside the home after her children were born. She worked full-time as a secretary at the same public utility where her husband was employed. One of their children attended a day care facility while Meagan's mother baby-sat the younger child in her home.

Meagan's sister, Trish, also graduated with a grade twelve general-level diploma from the same high school as the rest of her siblings. She worked as a secretary at a large oil company. Her husband was a telephone company lineman. At the time of the study they were expecting their first child. Trish planned to quit work when they had saved enough money to buy a house for their new and growing family. Meagan expressed her hope that her mother might be asked to look after her sister's new baby when it was born.

Meagan's father was a sheet metal worker, a trade in which he says he was required to apprentice for five years. The conditions of this apprenticeship were never made clear in the interview. At the time of the interview he was the manager of the small sheet metal company where he had worked for thirty-five years. He started there as an apprentice shortly after quitting school in Atlantic Canada at the age of fifteen. He refers to himself as a "dropout." He did not return to school after grade eight. Even so, Mr. French had a fairly positive attitude toward education and schooling. He said he never really minded it. Talking about his own advancement to his position as manager, he credits his success to his own initiative for continuing education:

> like competition is rough. Even when, going to night school, like, I was competin' against people of grade ten and twelve. But some of the ten's and twelves's went under, and I still came on top. 'Cause I was doing the practical . . . so when I got to theory, I knew sort of a bit of both, you know. But still, like . . . 'cause you had to self-educate yourself and, like I

say, going to night school . . . taking up drafting and taking up all those other courses . . . you had to sort of, well, you gotta upgrade your education. That's what I mean.

Mr. French left the East Coast and came to Ontario when he was seventeen in 1945. About this he has no regrets: "I got the hell out of the place and came to greener pastures." The theme of moving up and doing better and what one has to do to succeed is fairly strong in his understanding about his own life and his prescriptions for those young men (including his own son) whom he encounters on the job. By example, he has always taken the opportunity to upgrade over the years:

> but over the years you have to, like even after you get through your trade, you have to upgrade. Like you have to take courses in order to, well depending on what you want to do. If you want to stay as a workman or go up the ladder and become a manager. So I wanted to get a little higher so I used to take up all of the opportunities that came across, like all the seminars and that, I'd get enrolled in those.

Although he was not quite fifty-five years old at the time of the interview, Mr. French was planning, making provisions for and anticipating his retirement in the near future, perhaps in a year or two. It was his intention that he and his wife move to their cottage just north of the city where they lived. Meagan's plans for the immediate future seemed to play a major part in this decision because Mr. French wanted to see all of his children graduate from high school and holding some employment or "doing something" before they vacated the family home.

Mrs. French also came to Ontario from a severely depressed region of Atlantic Canada in 1945. Like Mr. French, she was seventeen years old at the time. However, unlike Mr. French who came on his own, Mrs. French came with her family not because she, but her father, was looking for work. She did not have good memories of her schooling, possibly with good reason:

> Truthfully, I didn't like school. . . . I didn't like school from the first day I started. I think that the teacher and I didn't get along . . . 'cause the first day we went to school, we lived in the country . . . we had to walk to school. And we were late the first morning and I got the strap [laughs]. So that turned me against school.

Despite her unhappy experience of schooling, Mrs. French once had aspirations of becoming a school teacher. She continued her education to grade ten finally quitting at age seventeen. Meagan's mother worked for a couple of years as a waitress at the snack counter of a large department store. She married Mr. French early and they had their first child when they were both twenty years old. Mrs. French remained at home as mother and housewife immediately after the birth of her first child. It is interesting to keep in mind that Mr. and Mrs. French adjusted to three fairly major changes in their lives within a period of three years: they immigrated to an urban center from a part of the continent that was, in 1945, a rural, resource-based, marginal economy and not a province of Canada but a colony of Britain; they quit formal education and married; and they became parents. Their second child was born when they were twenty-two, and their third child when they were twenty-seven. At this point, Mr. French had been working at the sheet metal firm for ten years. Around 1955, in the midst of the 1950 postwar boom period, they bought a house and moved to a then newly developed suburban residential area consisting of moderately sized and affordably priced brick bungalows. Seven years later, when they were thirty-four years old, Meagan was born. Eventually, starting when Meagan was eighteen months old, Mrs. French worked as a foster mother and had young children in her care until about six years prior to the interview when she took her first part-time job outside her home since the birth of her own children. She worked as a cleaner in a hotel. She subsequently quit this job and stayed home to look after first the older and then the younger of her son's two children.

Like her sisters, Meagan had never held a formal part-time or summer wage-earning job during her high school career, although she helped her mother look after the various children in her care and did baby-sitting for mothers in her neighborhood. One presumes her sisters did so as well. Dean, in contrast, held a variety of wage-earning part-time and summer jobs throughout his high school and university career. The best-paying and longest-lasting of these were at the sheet metal company where his father was manager.

This quick family profile should be sufficient to introduce the research site and subjects. By drawing out connections among seemingly disconnected features, by tracing the gendered patterns of this family's life, by locating points of contradiction, contestation, and struggle, by paying attention to concrete and symbolic practices, I hope to make some observations about the socially organized everyday life of this family to contribute to our understanding of the role of the family as a site of social control. It was by reading and rereading the transcripts and listening to the taped interviews, that I began to understand more and more the conditions of Meagan's life within those social contexts in which she moved: her home, her school, her co-op work placement (which became her part-time job), and her peer group. Out of this data began to emerge for me an understanding of the subtleties of how women's lives are organized not only within those idiosyncratic peculiarities which make each of us an individual and therefore different from any other individual, but also as individuals who participate in, conform to, and accept, while also contesting, challenging, questioning, refusing, and subverting those social, political, and economic structures that would contain and confine us.

## THE ANALYSIS

It is a simple statement to say that it matters where, how, and with whom we live. The question I ask myself in this analysis is the following: How do the conditions of lived experience shape our subjectivity and understanding simultaneously as these become the hegemonic forms that in turn shape ideology and culture?

There are several key places in the interviews where we can see how, for Meagan, there are subtle and sometimes not so subtle pressures to take her "proper" place in the gender structures seen to be appropriate by her family. Looking at what she is encouraged to see as a desirable future for herself focuses attention on the sexual division of labor and social practices embraced by her family. Her father, in particular, is instrumental in constructing a clearly patriarchic home environment that is successful in its intent and has obvious prescriptive overtones. When talking with Mr. French about a possible future for Meagan in relation to his imminent retirement to the cottage, the following conversation took place:

> Int.:     And are you planning to live (at the cottage)?
> Mr. F.:   Yeah, well we spend every weekend up there now . . . in summer.
> Int.:     Are you waiting for that?
> Mr. F.:   Retire or get out, in other words.
> Int.:     What about the children?
> Mr. F.:   Well, there's only one left, you know. Meagan. So . . . she gets married, I guess or doing something.

Beyond the specificity of marriage Mr. French makes no concrete suggestions about what Meagan might do after leaving formal education. As will be seen again later, conformity to heterosexual aspirations for gender relations and the implications of this for women seems not to be questioned by Mr. French in his general hopes for his children. In a later interview, Meagan elaborates on the pressures brought on the female members of the family to conform to the traditional division of labor and, therefore, economic relations of dependency. The discussion here starts with Meagan talking about her father's displeasure because his wife is baby-sitting their granddaughter, the younger child of his son Dean and his daughter-in-law who holds a full-time job. She says he would prefer that his son and daughter-in-law put the child in a nursery. On the surface Mr. French's position is rationalized in terms of his belief that the work is too taxing for Mrs. French. With a little probing, however, it becomes clear that the more fundamental issue has to do with his daughter-in-law's determination to keep her job despite her growing family and with his son's willingness to support his wife in her decision by helping out with household chores. The following conversation arose in the midst of a larger discussion concerning Meagan's understanding of her father's opinions on the role of women and men in the family:

Int.: Does your brother help out at home?

Meagan: Oh yeah. . . . He does a lot, like he takes the kids out and, and that. And he'll do the laundry and he'll do the dishes. He'll do whatever he has . . . that has to be done. And his wife sits back and watches.

Int.: Does his wife work outside the home?

Meagan: Uh, yeah. They both work at [the public utility]. . . . They've just got to go do this and Barbara will go shopping and Dean will have the two kids.

Int.: What does your father think of that?

Meagan: He thinks Dean's crazy to do it.

Int.: Does he say so?

Meagan: Yeah. He doesn't come out and tell Dean, but he tells Mom and I that he doesn't think it should be that way. Dean shouldn't always have the kids, and Barbara should be doing the . . . well . . . the . . . um . . . laundry or whatever. And Mom goes, well she's got him trained (laughs). Don't let it bother you, like you know.

Int.: Yeah. . . . What does your father say to that?

Meagan: Not much (laughs).

Int.: No?

Meagan: He just shuts up. Because he never did it you know. So he can't understand why his son's doing it, which I can see why . . . I can see why he doesn't understand why Dean does the things that he does. But a lot of people can't figure it.

Int.: What does he say, like, when he says that Dean shouldn't be doing that, why does he say he shouldn't be doing that?

Meagan: Because he figures the wife should be doing it. Barbara should be home with the kids. Barbara should be doing the laundry and . . . and the dishes and that sort of thing and you know, shopping and just things like that. . . .

Int.: What do you suppose he'd say if you, uh, if you called him on it? If, you know, if you said well . . .

Meagan: Well, he'd probably say, like a woman's place is in the home.
They should be doing all the stuff. A man should be working
downstairs with the furnace or something like this.

The fact that Mr. French does not tell Dean of his objections to his son's
participation in the housekeeping and child-rearing functions in his own
home should not come as a surprise in this interview. The objects of Mr.
French's control, after all, are not Dean, but Mrs. French and those of his
daughters still under his influence, namely Meagan. His discourse regarding
the appropriateness of Dean's behavior and, by strong implication, that of his
daughter-in-law are frames Mr. French wishes to impose on the women in *his*
household within his sphere of influence, not necessarily that of his son.

Despite his efforts, Meagan and her mother have their philosophical
moments about this:

Int.:    What does your mother think about this?
Meagan:  Well, she just ignores him too now. She doesn't listen to him. She
knows he's wrong, and he won't admit that he's wrong, like he's
so . . . old-fashioned. He hasn't, um, grown up yet from the
times. Whereas Mum is in the what's going on now. She just says
. . . oh Fred, you're old. Shut up. And it works.
Int.:    Do you and your Mum ever discuss it?
Meagan:  We just let it ride. If that's what he wants to do, you know, let
him. . . . We have nothing, no control over him.

With this keen bit of insight Meagan penetrates the guts of patriarchic
hegemony and possibly points our way to understanding the analytical relationship between all socially and politically unequal groups. In the North
American version of democratic capitalism, social, political, and economic
relations are such that they systematically, ideologically, and institutionally
support the interests of some individuals against the interests of others
through the unequal distribution of and access to resources and power. The
dichotomies which articulate broadly defined social categories such as gender,
race, ethnicity, age, desires of the body, and social class manifest themselves
in such power dualities as male/female, white/non-white, Anglo Saxon/all
others, middle aged/young and old, heterosexual/gay and lesbian; and those
who control social, political, and economic decisions/those who do not have
direct access to the influencing of these decisions. Dialectically, the fact that
power is vested in the hands of some and not in the hands of others affords
the former the possibility to construct, reconstruct, and manipulate these
social, political, and economic structures in such a way so as to give

the appearance that this particular distribution of power is rational, natural, and immutable.

In other words, the power that certain vested interests have to legitimate the hierarchical ordering of relations which are not in and of themselves hierarchical, by making them appear either non-hierarchical, or in the best interest of both the dominator and the dominated, serves to mystify these relations. Mystified also is the social processes which create these divisions. By turning to notions of "common sense," questions regarding the politically motivated ideologies of social inequality are discursively repositioned as "senseless." This is no less the case for issues of gender than it is for issues of social class, ethnicity, race, or sexual orientation. In this respect Chris Weedon makes the following point:

> Common sense has an important constitutive role to play in maintaining the centrality of gender difference as a focus of power in society. The degree to which particular theories of gender can be assimilated into common sense discourse varies since common sense itself tends to privilege conscious knowledge and experience, more often than not reproducing the liberal-humanist version of subjectivity. It is common sense knowledge that gender difference is of primary importance, though the reasons used to justify this are varied. (1987, p. 76)

What counts as common sense is not an arbitrary matter but a matter of power. In the case of gender, while one does not negotiate one's biology, for certain one negotiates its meaning. For the purposes of this analysis, this distinction is particularly relevant in the lives of women in a phallocentric society.

In the larger social, political, and economic structures, struggles arise out of the fact that the very survival of social/institutional forms is premised on the power of some to extract labor from those who have labor to sell in return for their own survival. In the workplace, these struggles manifest themselves as they arise out of negotiations around issues of labor power, wage, surplus production, capital accumulation, and profit.

Similarly, as is the case with relations of commodity production, gender relations in the home are defined through a particular set of practices, discourses, and ways of engaging the world such that women's labor is unproblematically appropriated by those in power for the purposes of maintaining the family unit in the interest of only some of its members. This relationship is such that, in general, men are invested with the prerogative to determine for women not only how the maintenance of the family will be accomplished, but, as well, what the dynamics of the family relationships will be. In contrast to sites of commodity production, in homes constituted through heterosexual relations, the negotiated currency takes on forms which are articulated through the socially constructed aspects of gender and inscribed in the complex interweaving of emotional investment, conjugal relations, social taboos, and access to outside resources. When women's inequalities in the public realm and in the work available to them beyond the home are added to this, it becomes clear how women's situation in this relationship is one of disadvantage. To the extent that the power to influence the outcome of these struggles is not equally distributed between the dominator and the dominated—whether this be in the context of class or gender—insight or no, the consequences are severe.

As in the larger society, for the women in the French household, the naturalized "common sense" notions of gender hierarchy have equally severe implications. Meagan draws on the life situations of those people who are closest to her—her family. Her lived experience, in the context of her home and social environment, is significantly circumscribed by, while also reconstructing notions of traditional female and male roles. This is not to say that there do not exist some contradictions and some challenges to these relationships. However, both the traditional pattern exemplified by her parental home and the challenges brought to this, primarily by the example of her brother's home life, have the effect of enforcing the "rule" by juxtaposing the "exception." The power of Meagan's father to challenge the possibilities in Dean's home contribute to how Meagan makes sense of her notions of family life as well as, it will be seen later, how she understands her day care work, and her future prospects with regard to job and family.

Despite what he sees as his son's failure to sustain traditional patriarchic structures in his own home, Mr. French has been quite successful at organizing his family in such a way that those power relations supported by the attendant economic consequences have militated against the women in his family.

For example, as we shall see in the interview passage below, according to Meagan, Mr. French has been fairly unreflective of the differing economic possibilities afforded his daughters in comparison to his son in relation to their hopes for advanced education. Whether or not he acknowledges it, the fact that Mr. French does not problematize the meaning of "equal treatment," under conditions where "unequal opportunity" has been socially inscribed, means that he wields considerable power through his apparently equal distribution of family finances. The effect of this economic control is such that gender expectations of work and family life are accomplished without making obvious the patterns of coercion which require the compliance of family members even when such compliance does not serve their interests. This has significant consequences in the lives of the other members of his family.

At one point in her graduating year, Meagan gave some thought to enrolling in a community college in order to earn a two-year diploma in early childhood education. Given her present employment at the day care/nursery, having this qualification would certainly have been in her best interest not least because this would gain her an immediate increase in wages. However, she did not pursue this route. When questioned as to why, we had the following conversation:

Int.: Is that, uh, would it [the prospects of better pay] be an incentive for you to go back to school and get . . .

Meagan: No.

Int.: No? What made you decide not to go to community college?

Meagan: I didn't have the money at the time. That was one reason I didn't—decided not to go. And right now I'm not fussy about going back. I don't think I could handle the pressure of subjects and after being out almost a year, it'd be too much on my system. So I said "no." I'm not going back.

Int.: You say you didn't have the money at the time. How could you have got the money?

Meagan: Well, my Dad would have gave it to me. But I didn't . . . but I didn't want to . . . him to bother, right? And that.

Int.: Why is that?

Meagan: Because he, when he gets like that, he always says, I did this and I did that, right? Even though we have done it. Like he put all four of us through school. He's taking the credit for us getting through school. He's taking the credit for us getting through school when we did it ourselves. Things like that. And I just didn't want that. I'd never hear the end of it.

Int.: Who paid for your brother's university, for example?

Meagan: My Dad helped, but my brother paid Dad back.

Int.: Once he started to work? (Meagan nods). I see.

Meagan: Yeah. Because he was working and going to university at the same time. So Dad gave him his first tuition, and Dean paid the rest and then paid Dad back what he gave him.

While taking care not to ascribe a unitary cause to decisions people make, it cannot help but come to attention that, of the French's four children, each of whom, we can only speculate, were provided with the same restricted option of financial support to continue their education beyond high school, only their son took it up. Meagan's concern about her father using his children's successful educational career to raise his image of himself as benefactor did not seem to have the same effect on her brother. Further, we might wonder whether

Meagan's decision not to borrow money from her father is the consequence of a distinctly articulate awareness of women's general financial situation.

Given the social realities of work, employment, and remuneration, young women know that their ability to "work their way" through university is economically a more difficult project for them than it is for men. Nor must it be forgotten that women's and men's education does not ultimately accrue them equal job opportunities and equal financial remuneration. Hence the prospects of repaying financial debts accumulated during the process of credentialing for a job can only be perceived as a more daunting task by women than by men. For the children in the French family, the financial support for further education that may have been quite acceptable for the son to request appears to have been impossible to negotiate for his daughters—in particular Meagan. For at least these reasons, and perhaps more that were not raised in the interview, Meagan did not avail herself of financial assistance from her father.

In order to understand the effects of this financial arrangement, we need to look at how it is supported at another level by the patriarchic ideology embedded in the social, emotional, and psychological relations in the family.

The division of labor in Meagan's home is clear. The ideological effects of this division makes a difference in how she formulates her understanding of what it means for women to commit themselves to the work of home and family, on the one hand, and, on the other hand, of forming notions about what it might mean for women to work outside the home. The basis for this tension is seen in the following interview segment:

> Int.: What if your mother decided to get a job? Would [your father] go for that?
>
> Meagan: Well, she had a job a long time ago.
>
> Int.: Yeah? Before . . . ?
>
> Meagan: Before Alexi was born or Lisa [her brother's children] was born. And he didn't like that idea either because he . . .
>
> Int.: You mean after you were, what in high school or what? (This question was asked in a tone of noticeable excitement because the information not only came as a surprise but, as well, suggested the possibility of disconfirming my growing unease about the extent to which Meagan's family forms seemed to reproduce the status quo in seamless and uncontradictory ways. Forever hopeful that "things are better now," throughout this interview, I actively searched for information that might have offered counter hegemonic possibilities. The fact that the data seemed not to offer challenges to the status quo was, and continues to be, for me, a source of dismay rather than pleasure at having found informa-

tion that might be seen to confirm what my experience tells me about gender and possibility.)

Meagan: When I was in junior high in grade seven and eight.

Int.: Oh. I see. What did she do?

Meagan: She made ... worked in a hotel making beds and that. And tidying up. So she didn't really like it. Like, she didn't mind. It was money coming in. But he didn't like the idea because he came home and his dinner wasn't ready and things weren't done around the house and things. ...

Int.: Like what?

Meagan: Well the dishes might have been left there from breakfast. They weren't done or the vacuuming hadn't been done. Mom would come home and have to cook dinner and then have to clean the house, and it'd be too much on Mom, right? And he got fed up with that after a while too. Even though it was his idea for her to go out and work.

Int.: Was it his idea?

Meagan: Yeah.

Int.: Why?

Meagan: To give her a break. ... Because she was getting bored at home from doing nothing. ...

Int.: Does your father help out? Like when your mother was working, did he help out with the housework?

Meagan: Not very often. No. (Laughs).

Int.: No? He didn't like it or what?

Meagan: He doesn't do very much around the house. Like ... he'll do his work but he won't ... he doesn't like doing dishes or ... or vacuuming. He says it's ladies' work, you know. That's the way he is.

Meagan's brother and sister-in-law offered to Meagan an example of possibilities for oppositional notions of family life. Despite this, however, the source of the constructs that seemed to define for her the relationship between home and job and between female work and male work arose from those practices in which her father and mother engaged. For Meagan, as is the case for many children, encouragement to embrace the ideologies fostered in the home is overtly supported and nurtured by emotional and familial valuation and affirmation. In nuclear family settings, livable familial relations often carry the weight of compliance to family norms. As Chris Weedon suggests:

> the reality of the family as a social institution materially supported by the law, the tax system, the welfare system, education, the media, the churches and a range of other social institutions, together with the lack of a real alternative to the patriarchal nuclear family, means that it is very difficult for women to opt out of family life. (1987, p. 40)

Jane Jenson (1986) offers a similar discussion of the relationship between capitalist modes of production and state support of particular familial forms and of the ways these contribute to ideologies of "proper" family life and attendant notions of "appropriate" femininity and masculinity. "Common sense" discourse does not often articulate what concrete practices are required to support alternate family forms. Nor does it often raise issues concerning the difficulty of negotiating the sharing of work and household responsibilities among all members of the family. Consequently, young women, even if they are able to imagine idealized notions of transformed family life, do not easily have the strategic knowledge required to accomplish it.

Because Meagan's brother and sister-in-law were not interviewed for this study, we know even less than does perhaps Meagan of the terms under which their apparently more egalitarian family forms were negotiated. For many women such terms often imply difficult choices and compromises regarding children, conjugal relations, financial independence, and emotional well-being. The decisions women and men make in this regard often take place not during open discussions with members of the extended family, but, rather, in private, away from the publicly observable outcomes of these negotiations. In other words, the social complexity of these decisions cannot be made sense of by a simplistic interpretation of observable outcomes. Nor can we refer to an unproblematized notion of choice, as is often suggested by apologists of a patriarchic system of power and privilege. Examples are not hard to come by. In response to an interview question a young man offered the following comment:

> every individual has a choice. It is up to the person to wear make-up, the latest fashion, to stay home and have children or to pursue a career. Ultimately it is her decision. (Lee, 1992, p. 2)

The refusal to factor in social context as a ground of individual practices continues to hide the fact that inequalities mediate human relations; that "choice" is never simple and personal; and that consequences for non-compliance with the status quo are not always livable. Meagan's understanding of her brother's family life, of how household work is actually accomplished, and of how these divisions of labor, production, and reproduction are struggled over in their own private moments by her brother and sister-in-law are details available to her only as an outside observer. Moreover these understandings are filtered through the influences of her own parental family which must clearly superimpose on her observations.

As is shown by studies such as that of Jane Gaskell (1987, 1992), for young women (and for women more generally), reality confirms the relentless message that the choices they face about what to do after graduation are massively different for girls/women than they are for their male peers. Connell expresses this as the dilemma of the "marriage *or* career" duality for women. In contrast, the operative phrase for men is "marriage *and* career" (Connell et al, 1981, p. 109). For women, the resolution of the conflict requires, as Connell suggests, "constant compromises."

Meagan has seen this played out most graphically in her own home. Mr. French, despite his initial educational handicap, has managed, over his lifetime, to increase both his job status as well as, one presumes, his income without compromising the social/emotional benefits accrued from family life. His wife, in that she seems to have carried the weight of the responsibilities for home and family care, could not, despite her two years of high school education, participate in labor activity which would have given her a commensurate rise in status or income. This was in fact put to the test and confirmed for her by her hotel job experience a few years previous. Whether the motivation to return to work was economic or social, when Mrs. French sought wage-earning employment after her family was grown she could find only a low-paying, oppressive, depressing, and dehumanizing job. Since she still carried primary responsibility for care and maintenance of the family home on top of this, she willingly retreated away from the double burden of work outside as well as inside the home. In that her home life was marked by the hegemony of patriarchy—however benevolent—she was caught between the dubious choices of continued financial dependency and the plight of the double ghetto (Armstrong and Armstrong, 1982). To understand this is to know what it feels like to live in the double bind of a Catch 22. In a world culture that unproblematically supports male interests through the specific organization of work and family life, many women know this scenario well:

> The unrealistic expectations placed upon "successful" women to emulate "superwomen" generally leads to great strains, affecting both physical and psychological health. That the domestic sphere remains women's primary responsibility has meant that the full weight of the "double burden" has rested on women's shoulders. . . . [As a consequence] many women appear very willing to give up low-paid, low-skilled work in favor of a "family wage" for their spouses. (Corrin, 1992, pp. 33–34)

Based on the example of her parents, Meagan could choose work, she could choose marriage and family, or she could choose, as her mother did for a short time, to do both. The consequences and contradictory outcomes of these choices are made clear to her by the example of her own family situation.

When I began my interview with Meagan I wondered why she did not choose to go on to community college and increase her wage-earning possibilities by completing her diploma in early childhood education. My conversation with her led me to believe that a major reason why Meagan did not consider the option of further education in this field had to do with the considerable value her family placed on the activity of child-rearing and homemaking within the context of the nuclear family. Issues of where and how this activity is best done and how, through the work of mothering, women's self-worth is articulated in her family are significant sources for the development of Meagan's understandings of the work of childcare.

What the women in the French family did have—despite Meagan's earlier statement that they have "nothing"—is "a way with children." This is a description Meagan appropriated for herself continually throughout our discussion. The valorization of this activity and Mrs. French's proficiency in it can be seen not only from the fact that there were, over a period of several years, foster children in the home to whom Mrs. French and Meagan in particular became quite emotionally attached, but also in Mr. French's efforts to force his daughter-in-law to take up her "proper" child-rearing function in his son's home. The impact of this ideological construction of the family is not lost on Meagan. As will be shown later, this became a constant and recurring theme for Meagan as she talked about prospects for her future.

Mr. French's articulated aspirations for his children confirms the point that his relationship with his children is structured through the taken-for-granted assumptions implied by the specificity of gender identity.

Int.:     What was your, what were your aspirations for Meagan when she was at the elementary level, for example?

Mr. F.:   Well, this is, well I guess we are from the old school, you know. Let me put it this way and after raisin' three others ahead of that. Like all we can do, you can't sort of push a kid into anything they don't want to do. . . . You sort of, all you do, as a father and mother, you coach 'em if you're not . . . you're not their superiors. You can't say, I want you to be this or I want you to be that. Whatever you wanna do . . . all you do . . . you either go along with it or you discuss it, but you . . . you can't just say you know. . . . Now Meagan never indicated . . . like she wanted to be a doctor or a nurse or anything else. She just wanted to go to school. And you know, she sort of picked her own profession. And she asked us what we thought about it. She did come back and say, well, Dad, what do you think of . . . well if this is what you want in life, be my guest. Have a go at it. You know. So she decided to tackle on that condition. Now all the kids the same way, you know. Like my boy. I said to him, if you ever be a sheet metal

> man, I said, I'll break your arm, you know . . . 'cause I've had
> enough of this. It was a good trade . . . still is . . . but I said, I
> never want you to be a sheet metal guy. And he'd o' made a bet-
> ter sheet metal man than I ever made.

While on the surface Mr. French appears to overlook the gross inconsis-
tency with regard to how he talks about his aspirations for Meagan in contrast
to how he articulates his aspirations for his son, there is, in fact a deep-seated
and sedimented consistency in his thinking. Meagan did not after all choose
to be an auto mechanic, or a riveter in a car-manufacturing plant, or even a
nurse or a secretary. When she told me on one occasion that her class had
gone to tour a car-assembly plant, I asked her if she thought she could work
in a place like that. She responded with: "Too farfetched for me." We can only
speculate about what else might be "too farfetched" for her.

There is good reason to believe that it is mostly through the activity of
childrearing that both Mrs. French and Meagan gain approval and some
measure of status in their home. While for father and son consistency is
clearly maintained in that they participate in a dual-generational upward
swing in status, such that the upward social mobility of Mr. French (from
that of sheet metal apprentice to that of plant manager) taken up and continued by his son, Meagan and her mother also share in constructing and
maintaining a particular kind of status in their home—this structured
through the act of mothering—that of the important distinction made
between "rearing" children on the one hand and of "looking after children"
on the other. The significance of this distinction will become clear when we
note the sense Meagan makes of her childcare work at the day care/nursery
and her aspirations for her future.

At this point, however, I think it is crucial to say that it would be a mistake
to see Mr. French as a mean-spirited cynical man uninterested in fostering his
daughter's future. Parents are not, by and large, determined to create impossible futures for their children. Rather, as Chris Weedon says:

> the overriding concern of most parents in bringing up their children is with
> 'normality', the normality necessary for future success in two privileged sites
> of adult life, the family and work. This concern with socially defined nor-
> mality will lead most parents to accept dominant definitions of the necessity
> and meaning of gender difference. (1987, p. 76)

Instead of attributing to them cynical intentions, it is more appropriate to
see these familial relations and practices as precisely promoting those attrib-
utes which parents think will prepare their children to "make the best of it" in

the society in which they live. If this society is also phallocentric, then women's and men's identities must be marked in difference and their social relations in hierarchy. Chris Weedon goes on to explain:

> Common sense has an important constitutive role to play in maintaining the centrality of gender difference as a focus of power in society. [This is] why it is necessary to put so much time and energy into establishing [gender] difference. (1987, p. 76)

Unfortunately it is this very striving for "normality" that also handicaps our daughters and vests power with our sons. In a culture where the norm is inequality, injustice, and exploitation of the many by the few, the discourse of "normality" means that proposals for equality, justice, and freedom often appear at best as socially inappropriate, sometimes abnormal and often "hysterical." As a result the possibilities for contestation are limited. As Minnie Bruce Pratt (1991) suggests, women know that:

> if we ally ourselves with the "other" group, in a direct, personal or public way, even if it is an issue of justice, if we threaten our folks' or self-interest, or definition of self, then there is the risk of being thrown out. It is a real fear: we know the stories. . . . This is a fear that can cause us to be hesitant in making fundamental changes or taking drastic actions that differ from how we were raised. We don't want to lose the love of the first people who knew us; we don't want to be standing outside the circle of home with nowhere to go. (p. 65–66)

While considerations concerning family life were never far from Meagan's thoughts about her future, the immediate prospects of marriage were not obvious in our conversation. Therefore, she, like many of her peers, was faced with finding something to do after graduation. Added to this was the pressure Meagan felt to move out of the house and become financially independent of her parents. This was intensified by the fact that her father in particular was anxious to retire and move north, where he planned to open a small, private sheet metal shop in his garage. For Meagan the choice of becoming a childcare worker seemed to be the obvious route to economic independence in that it provided a continuity to her life which appeared sensible to her for two reasons. It allowed her to earn a marginal income. At the same time and perhaps more importantly, it allowed her to capitalize on her accumulated skill in an area that was valued in her home and which accrued her some measure of status in that environment. It also provided a ready answer to that incessant query often posed to young graduates to make clear what it is they are going to *do* after high school (Simon, 1987). That this question has as much to do with the need to confirm normality, and therefore parental success (Caplan, 1989), as it does with the wish to see children become financially viable adults, requires that young adults have a ready and acceptable answer available such that it can satisfy these concerns.

In our conversation Meagan repeatedly articulated her interest in childcare work in a variety of ways:

> I've always been around kids. . . . I baby-sit now. . . . I help my mother baby-sit. . . . I like playing with kids. . . . I like playing kids' games. . . . I will be prepared to be a mother. . . . I will help raise other people's kids or I will raise my own.

For Meagan, the work of caring for children made it possible to draw on her experience and in this regard she spoke about her competence with certainty: "that's the only background that I have and because I've grown up with kids I have the knowledge of it. That's the only thing I've had." Later in the same interview she goes on:

> Meagan: I love children.
> Int.: Is that a consideration in choosing a job?
> Meagan: It was, yeah.
> Int.: Yeah?
> Meagan: Right now . . . and I work better with children than I do with adults (laughs).
> Int.: Yeah?
> Meagan: Yeah. I get along better with them.
> Int.: How do you mean?
> Meagan: I relate more to them, I think, than I do with adults.
> Int.: Why?
> Meagan: I don't know, I just do. It's . . . I guess it's natural instincts or somethin'.
> Int.: Does your mother?
> Meagan: Yeah.
> Int.: How about your Dad?
> Meagan: He's more for adults, I think (laughs). 'Cause he's always with adults.

When questioned early on about her experience at the co-op work placement, this sense of competency and relationship with kids seemed to be maintained as she clearly articulated it:

> I still like it, yeah. I think with the disappointments they help you later on because if you get a disappointment you say, well, why isn't this right? What did I do? And you think back, well, I should have done this and it would have helped me. And by making a mistake and being disappointed, it helps

you later on. And that's why I think the kids understand me. Like you think, they don't understand me, I'm older than them, I've got authority. But they know how to manipulate you, like, get around this person like this, and they do, some of them, too. Or they just have to go, "ah, come on please" and that does it sometimes. I can't take that. But, um, when they feel like, um, aware, like they do something good, you say, well, that's good or else, um . . . and that way you feel a sense of accomplishment, 'cause you accomplished something with them and sometimes just before I leave a little kid will come up and give you a hug, and it makes you feel like you're number one in the world. Nobody can stop you. And that's what I like.

As is apparent in the following interview segment, Meagan's interest in child-care work is very much reaffirmed for her by her parents in ways which draw significantly on their emotional relationship to her. The dialectical relations which mediate the gender struggles in her home are difficult to unpack precisely because often they are so thickly frosted over with the emotional relations that attend this social formation. When questioned about her parents' reaction to her choice of co-op placement in the day care/nursery she says the following:

> Dad thought that I was like my Mom. And Mom looked happy for me. She says, um, she says, good idea, because I get along with kids and because, um, I've always grown up with kids since I was a year-and-a-half old, and I've gotten used to having them around, teaching them different things as I got older. I just fell in love with the field.

Several factors, however, militated against Meagan's ability to sustain this positive attitude toward her relationship with children and toward the activity of child-rearing in the context of institutionalized childcare settings. For Meagan and her mother, the patriarchic relations in their home environment are given substance through the valorized activities which constitute mothering and care of the family home. Set against this is her experience in the day care/nursery:

> It's boring. . . . They have the same routine every day. . . . They don't do anything different. . . . They don't do anything exciting or, you know, just the same routine every day. . . . All day long . . . and I got bored of it . . . and I'm still bored of it.

To some extent, this boredom is constructed for Meagan precisely out of the realities of her not being a certified early childhood education teacher. When we talk about the fact that only the teachers are allowed to establish the day care/nursery program Meagan says:

> Meagan: I let the teachers program. I just sit back and watch. Nothing else to do.

Int.:     The teachers do most of that, you're saying?
Meagan:   Yeah. They, they program because they're qualified to program.

Later, she speaks about the day care children being equally as bored. When I ask her if there is anything she could do to alleviate this boredom, she answers:

> No, not that I know of because if you mention anything, they kind of well, you're not a qualified teacher, so to speak, you know. Why should you have anything to do with what the kids are doing?

Meagan's day care/nursery experience grossly devalues that which she and her family have come to value very highly, and that from which the women in her family gain a special status. Meagan draws a great deal on what she believes to be her "natural abilities" for child-rearing, a talent which her family believes she shares with her mother and which she seems to speak of as a skill/talent she acquired through "osmosis" because they've always had children around. Hence it makes little sense to her to study something that one acquires by "instinct"—you either have it or you don't. Furthermore, the belief that this activity is best done in the home is clearly articulated in the following conversation when I asked her if she thinks she would go back to work once she has her own children.

Meagan never doubted that she would have children and her quick answer to my question was that she would indeed return to work. However, as her thinking about it elaborated, her commitment to this position weakened. She says:

> I don't know. I *think* I would go back to work. It depends how, what I was doing and if I liked what I was doing. If I didn't, I'd stay home with the kids and *teach them everything I know*. . . . It's easier to stay home and teach them what you know than, um, put them in a day care. Because I know how they're run now, so I wouldn't want to put my kids in one. (emphasis in voice)

This tension between her own sense of competence with children as this is constructed in her home and the extent to which this is disorganized for her by the idea of institutionalized childcare work and certification is clearly a problem for her. Meagan's words are interesting in this regard:

Int.:     What kind of setting would you like [to work with children]?
Meagan:   Mm . . . like a day care center is nice. There are so many kids, and so many different things happening, you can't really sit a kid down, talk to him, find out why they're doing certain things. . . . I think a home setting would be better.

In our conversation I heard Meagan trying to legitimate her day care/nursery work experience without having the discursive resources with which to do it. Despite her wish to legitimate a possible career future for herself, we can see how Meagan's experience of the institutionalized childcare setting and the home based child-rearing practice stand in a dialectical relation, mutually constructing and deconstructing each other. As Roger Simon (1987) suggests, this discursive difficulty is informed by the socially produced and contradictorily articulated notions of women's relationship to our "freely compelled" choices surrounding childcare/child-rearing practices. Discussing how young women are positioned in relation to this social reality in the context of day care/nursery work, he offers the following:

> To do childcare work in a day care center would require her to submit to the commodification necessary for her to participate in the wage-labor exchange that is basic to the institutional organization of such work. . . . To "choose" child-rearing in the home would have been to refuse such commodification—a "choice" not without its own limiting features: economic dependency and the submission of a private social "contract." (pp. 175–176)

For many young women these tensions are often instrumental in dissuading them from pursuing further education—in this case a certificate in early childhood education—and bring them full circle back into the home confined to social/familial terms not of their own making. And the patriarchal agenda, to use Connell's word, is "achieved."

Meagan's situation reveals how both the internal forces (those tangible and ideological possibilities which are provided for her in her home) and the external forces (those social, political, and economic conditions which permeate her own understanding of her life situation and the possibilities which these conditions expose or conceal) come together to create a complex problematic having to do with issues of gender and the social construction of women's femininity as a function of the converging and diverging needs of democracy, capitalism, and patriarchy.

While, for young women, these are difficult issues to work through, this is not to say that Meagan does not problematize either patriarchy or the attendant web of social/political/economic structures. But she is stuck. This is most clearly articulated by her (and most important for her) when she contemplates other possibilities for work. The following interview segment is instructive:

Int.:    So if you don't like day care work, what would you do instead? Have you looked into doing other things?

Meagan: I've looked into marketing. I want to get into marketing sales or market research. But it's harder because you need your maths and things like that, and I don't have my math. I need two years of math, which I don't have. . . .

Int.: So that means you can't do marketing?

Meagan: No, but I can get in, like if I can get into a store I can get into the sales department and that because of the two years marketing that I have [this is her grade eleven and grade twelve general-level courses in marketing] and work my way up from there into a business.

Int.: What do you mean by sales department? You mean as a sales person?

Meagan: Well . . . like . . . yeah. . . .

Int.: Like behind the counter? And then work your way up from there? [Meagan nods yes.] So if you went to work at Eaton's you'd start out as a sales clerk? And then work up to what?

Meagan: Well, you could work up to, um, floor manager of that section. Then from there you can go up to the offices and then up to management. Which I guess I would like. It'd be, um, hard work but it takes determination.

Int.: To what?

Meagan: To do it.

Int.: To work up?

(Much of this conversation was marked by my astonishment at the level of naivete Meagan seemed to show about how one moves into the executive levels of large corporations. I believe she may have been influenced by her father's notion of "getting in" and "moving up" and how "anything is possible" if you have the "determination to DO it." The other side is, of course, that should she fail to accomplish such an outcome—which, given the state of current economic and corporate practices, is a good possibility—she is given no discursive position that might allow her to think about it in any way other than that she has only herself to blame.)

Meagan: Yeah . . . into . . .

Int.: What about getting a job? Have you looked?

Meagan: Yeah, I've looked but there's . . . there's not much out there. You have to be . . . everything is, you have to have experience. And I don't have very much experience (laughs) now. I only have experience with kids and that's it. So that's kind of a bummer.

Int.: So what's down the road for Meagan?

Meagan: Not much.

## REFLECTIONS ON THE STUDY

Caught between her aspirations and her reality, Meagan's words trace the web of her own contradictions marked by her hope, energy, and determination, on the one hand, and doubt, impotence, and helplessness, on the other. My interview with Meagan began with her assertion of self: "It's my life so I'll do what I want. . . . Right?"

What happened in that long pause before her wavering plea for confirmation? As for many women, for Meagan those three dots represent a chasm across which her words are barely heard. For me, as teacher and researcher, they also represent that space across which I strain to hear what she cannot say.

Meagan is aware that the "consent of women to definitions of femininity which locate their primary role as keepers of the home with only secondary involvement in waged work" (MacDonald, 1981, p. 31) means that her lived reality, as this is articulated through her home and refracted back to her through the possibilities she sees for herself in the world of work, is constructed within those familial relations within which its members must survive not only economically and socially but, as well, emotionally.

Meagan's family articulates specific forms of "man's work," "woman's work," division of labor in the home, division of capital in the home, and the legitimacy of claims made by members of the family for the use of the collective labor and capital resources. Meagan's experience of this web of material/emotional resources suggests that they have all played a part in configuring the future possibilities she sees for herself. While Meagan's situation may have found its expression within those cultural forms and social discourses specific to Canadian working-class culture, the reality of her subordination finds expression, although differently, in the lives of all women. The ideology of motherhood, the specific outcomes of schooling/educational experiences and the struggles to accommodate contradictory social demands is a major feature of this reality. It is to a discussion of this that I now wish to turn.

## UNBINDING THE MINDBINDINGS OF GENDER

> If you care for a son, you don't go easy on his studies; if you care for a daughter, you don't go easy on her footbinding. (Chinese saying, Ts'ai-fei lu, quoted in Daly, 1978, p. 134)

While the specifics that mark foot/mindbinding as a feature of social control may vary between cultures, geographic locations, and historical times, the outcome is often more coherent than diverse. Like most of us, Meagan enters the social world by way of her family. Anyone who has ever lived in a family—whatever form that family may have taken, however conforming or nonconforming it may have been to the currently persistent ideology of the "proper" family—will know that the social world in which the family is embedded, and of which it is a component part, constantly and simultaneously constructs and disrupts the personal and collective relations within that structure. Forms of political, economic, and social relations outside the home often dictate the possibilities for people inside it. We may be good or poor parents, we may be attentive or disloyal children, we may be committed or estranged mates, but, in our culture, all of these ways (and more) of being in or outside of the family are measured against a socially constructed and idealized version of family life—one that is explicitly directed toward socializing its members to accomplish the work of our culture through particular forms of production, reproduction, consumption, and emotional/sexual relations. How young women construct viable notions of self and possibility is confounded by the contradictory dialectic between productive/economic possibilities and reproductive/psycho-sexual desires.

Encoded in language, as in, for example, the Euro-American marriage ritual, it is women's hands and the labor they promise which are "given" by the father to the groom. It is precisely in this exchange of "taking" a woman's hands that a man becomes publicly proclaimed and celebrated as the "head of the household" regardless of his actual relationship to the mode of production in the public realm; regardless of the conditions under which he toils; and regardless of whether or not he benefits from the toil of others.

While in the public realm, race and class may equally delimit the participation in mental labor of particular men, the fault lines that mark power relations within the private realm of the heterosexual nuclear family are socially institutionalized in deeply gendered ways. Hence, mental work—the work of the "head"—is masculinized and defines intellectual labor as man's work against which women's intrusion is seen, at best, to be benignly irrelevant. More commonly, the masculinized social forms of intellectual exchange overtly, sometimes violently, exclude and marginalize women from, as well as in, sites of intellectual exchange [See: De/Siring the Text, this volume]. For women committed to the work of the intellect the possibilities for achieving coherence in their social lives are deeply contradictory: if we embrace the practices required by the mandates of intellectual work we are marked as "aggressive," "pushy," and, in the final analysis, "inadequate" women, but if we agree to display socially prescribed practices of femininity, we earn the label of "incompetent" thinkers.

Regardless of how—or even whether or not—women take up the practices of mother/wife, the contradictory social coding maintains. The power of patriarchy to universalize the principles of heterosexuality, femininity, and the nuclear family, whether or not one participates in these social forms, means that engagement in intellectual work, by *any* woman, is, by social-historical contingency, named questionable.

Women are "allowed" access to the work of the intellect only to the extent
that we agree to the terms suggested by the material realities of men's lives—
terms that take account of neither women's realities nor of the social forces
that prescribe these realities. Conversely, the very raising of questions regarding the processes of intellectual production leave us named inadequate or
indiscreet or both.

The popular discourse delineating this dialectic is generally available to
young women. For example, the January 1988 issue of the *Report on Business*
featured four women graduates from the class of '78 of the School of Business
at the University of Western Ontario—one of the more prestigious institutions of higher learning in Canada. Entry into the program is competitive and
the course of studies is rigorous. Ten years later, in 1988, only one of the four
women had a job at which she considered herself to be successful as well as a
growing family within an emotionally supportive home life. There are two
interesting points to be made here: first, the description of her work/family
life is one that is a common profile for the vast majority of men successful in
business for whom the intersection of work and family life is not a liability but
a career asset; and, second, this particular woman's job was anomalous by
comparison to jobs generally available to business graduates in that, rather
than work for an already established business interest, she had started a farm
implements firm in partnership with her husband.

Of the rest, one had a successful career but had "chosen" to forgo marriage
and children; another was a single working mother, supporting her two
children from a failed marriage, who had had to pass up lucrative job opportunities in order to spend the required time with her growing daughters; and
the fourth, married to a successful professional (for whom there were, apparently, no collisions between career and family), struggled to find adequate
childcare for her two children and eventually gave up working outside the
home to take up full-time mothering. This just about sums up the possible
options for women in the work force intent on establishing their own economic independence and gives a new meaning to the accusation that "women
want it all." For young women, such scenarios reaffirm what they already
know. That:

> women's familial location and responsibility signify a completely different
> material position in the structure of society to that of men. (Brittan and
> Maynard, 1984, p. 57)

In a society where a high premium is placed on economic independence
and where the measure of adulthood is the ability to provide basic economic

survival for one's self and one's children, women's identity and sense of self-worth is as much a function of our economic viability as it is for men. Nor is it only a question of self-worth, but profoundly the material conditions of survival. Yet how women might achieve such economic viability and emotional well-being is continually organized, disorganized, and reorganized within the frames of phallocentric interests: the psychological, social, and sexual parameters drawn by the discursive power of patriarchy and the nuclear family.

That women bear children is not insignificant either to how the work of the household and parent-child relations are organized or to how intellectual work is accomplished. As Roberta Hamilton has argued so effectively:

> children are a primary cause both of domestic labor and the sexual division of labor. It is not an ahistorical accident that women are the domestic labor-ers; indeed it would have been a miracle if they were not. And it will require a major and sustained struggle accompanied by a collective and planned effort to go about changing it. (1987, p. 149)

Simultaneously, we continue to expect women who choose to work in non-traditional areas to fit into routines which do not take into account women's responsibilities for home and family life. Or else we ask them to pay for their participation by forgoing the potentially emotionally and psycholog-ically supportive environment of family life. When women finally collapse from the exhaustion of the double shift or are numbed by the impossibility of having to make diametrically opposed choices, it is used not only as confir-mation of our political and economic marginality, but, as well, proof of our psychological, social, and sexual inadequacy. For women this reality has par-ticular consequences most clearly articulated by Joan Kelly when she says:

> [Women] are living in the sphere of the family and of social production, and as we do so, we become increasingly aware of how the social relations arising from each sphere structure experience in the other. To be a mother in one domain deeply affects one's position, tasks, and rewards in the other domain. Mothering determines where and at what hours women work, and thus the jobs for which they are available. Conversely the inferior pay and benefits of women's work in a sex-segregated labour market perpetuate women's eco-nomic dependence upon men. They pressure women to form sexual and/or familial attachments to men; and in the family ensure that the man's position will determine the place of residence and the unbalanced allotment of responsibility for domestic work and childcare to women. (1984, p. 5)

Both the strictures as well as the possibilities offered by the larger social, economic, and political constructs in which are embedded our personal lives are tied in with the details of the everyday. The minutiae of the everyday comprise a practice, language, and discourse so subtle and piercing that they can barely be articulated even as they are cutting us to the core. The conditions under which most of this chapter were written are significant to the understandings which it is my aim to develop.

## "THE PERSONAL IS POLITICAL" IS LIVED IN THE BODY

I understand that the transformative power and social significance of feminism lies in the coherence of a process that articulates a politic out of the personal. The importance of the feminist focus on experience is not to prompt a vacuous, gratuitous telling of our intimate stories as a cathartic moment, but indeed to emphasize the political meaning of our personal reality: that subordinate groups live subordination and marginality through our subjectivity. We live it precisely in the context of the details of our individual experiences which to the extent that they can be made to seem private cannot then offer the ground for a collective political practice. Carrying deep within me my commitment to the politics of feminism confirms for me that understanding can begin only from where we are.

This political position has a profoundly concrete and historically significant meaning for me. As is the case for many women, for me the creative processes of intellectual work are articulated through the specifics of my personal but politically charged realities that have a history and that bind me still to the materiality of "woman/mother work." For many years, our house, full and noisy with young children, was, for someone who requires quiet and solitude when she writes, not conducive to the task. Were it just the incessant chatter of young children learning language, themselves, and the world, I might have found there some quiet moments late into the night during which to read and write. However, my desk, the only possible writing surface that might have been consistently and privately available to me was, three subsequent times, converted to a baby's changing table, and my study into a nursery. As a result, I still read Tillie Olsen's question with particular poignancy:

> How is it that women have not made a fraction of the intellectual, scientific, or artistic-cultural contribution that men have made? (1978, p. 27)

While I don't believe that we have not, it being more true that our contribution has gone unnoticed, unrecorded, and unvalued (Smith, 1978), were it the case, it is at least in part because our desks—metaphorically or in reality—have had to hold both books and diapers, each threatening to overpower and consume the other while our minds have worked to mediate the struggle.

Traditionally women have not had and continue to be restricted in our access to the public forum of intellectual exchange (Luke and Gore, 1992; Bannerji et al, 1991; Lewis, 1990). Hence, to write about the blocks to the exercising of women's artistic/creative talent is itself a privileged practice, even as it is contradictory. For am I not a woman writing, and am I at least, therefore, not silenced in my creative work?

I was a graduate student during those years, and it became a "habit" for me to return often in the evenings to the institution where I studied. I was grateful for the small office space to which I had been assigned: a space that was, for the most part, uninterruptable and where I routinely worked late into the night. After our shared moments of family dinners, riotous baths, story telling, and tucking in, I would return daily to this private space arriving usually around eight thirty or nine o'clock to work often till one or two in the morning. The memories of that time still bring back deeply powerful feelings of the pain of the contradictions of my double life.

Sustaining the exhaustion of mothering three small children during the day was the knowledge that with the evening I could return to my books and writing; and sustaining the exhaustion of being a graduate student, were my children who would, with our mutual pleasure, draw me away from those very same books and writing into the world of playgrounds, "mucking" in the kitchen, and our weekly visit to the museum dinosaur display.

I intend no romanticization of this period of my life. Despite my relative "success" at mixing the intellectual with the mundane—and I have yet been unable to decide which was which—my feeling was always that potentially I could be judged inadequate in both spheres. In a culture that defines mothering through the binary opposition good/bad, women have had no option but to choose between our children and ourselves. The following news item in my local paper is telling. The headline reads: "Woman Claims Sex Bias as Department Vetoes Her Bid to Be Firefighter." The source of the controversy was based on the following incident: a woman had responded to an advertised position as a part-time firefighter on the force of a small south-eastern Ontario town. When she was turned down without apparent cause, she charged sex discrimination at which point a debate ensued at city council. In part, the text of the news report read:

> (the Counsellor) says that with two preschool children, (the woman) would have difficulty responding to a daytime call. "With the kids, she's tied up, as far as I can see—if she's a concerned mother. From my point of view I'd consider her not available." (*Whig Standard*, 1988)

Male firefighters, it seems, are not asked to account for their children while on the job.

For women, the option of choosing both a job and motherhood, labels us inadequate in both. Adrienne Rich is helpful in making this contradiction visible and livable:

> My children cause me the most exquisite suffering of which I have any experience. It is the suffering of ambivalence: the murderous alternation between bitter resentment and raw-edged nerves, and blissful gratification and tenderness. Sometimes I seem to myself, in my feelings toward those tiny guiltless beings, a monster of selfishness and intolerance. . . . There are times when I feel only death will free us from one another, when I envy the (childless) woman who has the luxury of her regrets but lives a life of privacy and freedom.

> And yet at other times I am melted with the sense of their helpless, charming and quite irresistible beauty—their ability to go on living and trusting—their staunchness and decency and unselfconsciousness. *I love them.* But it's in the enormity and inevitability of this love that the sufferings lie. (1986a, p. 21–22)

Over the intervening years I have come to reconcile the necessary compromises that were required of me to get my work done. Yet while intellectually I am able to persuade myself that no harm was in fact done, my body has not yet forgotten the pain that my repeated leaving imprinted on my cells. I continue to relive my memory of "leaving home" in the image of my then young son, his body silhouetted dark against the pane of his upstairs bedroom window imploring me, night after night as I backed my car out of the driveway, to please not go.

I still don't know what compelled him to demand my physical presence at home even when he slept. Nor do I know how the neighbors understood my evening ritual of pushing the car out of the driveway and part way up the street before I turned on the ignition in hopes that my child might not hear me leaving and, therefore, not suffer the apparent trauma of my absence—or was it I, his mother, who was suffering the trauma of the projections of his unfulfilled desire? While my work as "mother" seemed invisible in its presence it became indispensable in its absence. By the same turns, was my intellectual/academic work made both unnecessary in its presence and unmissed in its absence? Roberta Hamilton states that "mothering our children is about leaving them." Yet I also understand and live through my body, as does she, the knowledge that:

> we are expected to be, and indeed are, for all practical purposes, given the social organization of this society, indispensable to our children. (1990, p. 24)

The little boy in the darkened window demanded that I understand this.

The category "mother," a social position that identifies me as unmistakably "woman," both gives and denies access to social process in particular ways (Kristeva, 1986, pp. 186–213). Thinking beyond these strong social forms is difficult and painful work. I find myself the mother of three children, whose growing up I sometimes catch myself actively resisting, like many women, because my social category as "mother" has been one I have engaged with unqualified rigor and joy for over nineteen years. At the same time, I wait impatiently to be needed less in fulfilling the exhausting physical and emotional demands of such a relationship. I continue still to vacillate between these contradictory desires for my children and myself.

My commitment to working as an intellectual woman has been, and in big ways continues to be, marked by the contradictory reality of public and private worlds even as their fusion offers the rich tapestry out of which I struggle to carve out legitimate spaces for the solitary work of thinking and writing. I now have a study that does not have to double as a nursery, and I have three growing children who no longer need one. It is a small room at the back of the house overlooking the lake on which my home is located. It is three fifty-four in the morning. Although I can hear the waves crashing on the rocks I cannot see the lake because it is very dark. Indeed I cannot see beyond the circle of light cast by the single desk lamp that lights up this small space I call my own. I sit inside this pool of light surrounded by the deep darkness of a world that, for the moments of my being at my desk, disappears as a concrete reality. The social prescriptions of motherhood fade into abstractions: if there are dishes in the sink I do not see them; if there is laundry piled in their baskets, I will neither wash nor fold it; I am comforted by the security of knowing that in their bedrooms no one stirs; the matter of whether children's homework is or is not done is at the moment irrelevant; no one has to be picked up or delivered to any other place; no one is being anxiously waited on for having missed their bus; forgotten lunches and lost mittens are realities saved for the moment when the rising sun streams once again across the bay signalling that this period of uninterrupted time is no longer my own.

This room, this pool of light, this place where I sit alone, is a space with which I am deeply familiar—it is a space where for a brief moment I am not defined, nor do I define myself, as "mother." Yet, I still struggle against the contradictions in my life, between the mental and the manual lived through the realities of the social category implied by the terms "intellectual woman." I still negotiate the oppositional desires that continue to mark my double life. And I still struggle with the possibilities of "telling" as a political/pedagogical agenda, aware that academic discourse precludes the putting to public scrutiny the moments of our private life, an act which not only judges us indiscreet but as well is seen to confirm our inadequacy. How I might do this work in the midst of raising three children is as problematic for me as my struggles to transform through my work our collective social understanding of the situation of women.

As I reflect on the familiarity of the moment and on my "habit" of finding most comfort when I write at night, I realize that the legacy of those early times, both as constraint and as privilege lived simultaneously as pain and possibility, has stayed with me for these many years. I contemplate the words of Jane Gaskell:

> there is . . . a tradition of feminist scholarship that has emphasized that women's consciousness is not simply an internalization of male forms but contains its own alternate interpretations, commitments, and connections. . . . The relations between women's consciousness and man's world is complex and involves accommodation, resistance, and self-imposed and externally imposed silences. (1987, p. 167)

Women do not leave unquestioned our assumption of the given social relations. Yet, what we might do about it is not always obvious nor easy. The political economy of creative work means that for women writing is an intrusion into dangerous territory as much as it is a concrete and unambiguous claiming of the word to effect social change. I am aware that, for women, choosing to write is to participate in a passionately political project knowing all the while that "the economy of this system requires that women be excluded from the single true legislating principle, namely the Word, as well as from the (always paternal) element that gave procreation a social value" (Moi, 1986, p. 143). The discourse of silence is one salient feature of our engagement of the social world. Caught in the vacuum between the myths and the realities of what is possible for us, I wonder what private spaces might be found by those women for whom a desk caught in a pool of light is not a possibility.

## CONCLUSION

Were this all of the telling of this story it might have stopped here with some self-reconciliation, a conclusion that as difficult as I might have found it, I at least could negotiate those necessary moments during which to work, think, and write. The story might have ended here with an acknowledgment of the privilege of my economic/social status which continues to allow me access to the academy and to provide for the physical sustenance of myself and my children. To be sure, economic marginality/possibility *matters*, as do inequalities that define social/cultural/sexual difference in a society that is deeply racist, ethnocentric, and homophobic. However, it is important to question as well the embeddedness of the idea that women's creative/economic engagement is something to be squeezed into the routines of our daily life and to be tolerated only so long as it does not effect our responsibilities for woman/ mother work. In the act of taking up this text, I am struck not only by the enormity of the contradiction which its production requires me to overcome, but by the memory of a young woman in her blue uniform with whom I shared, over the course of a year or so, long and frequent conversations late at night: I sitting at my desk with papers and books strewn, pen in hand; she pushing a cleaning cart and wearing a uniform while she cleaned the offices where my desk was located.

That this young woman and I met at all was a function of the social/familial contexts we both lived. Hidden in the folds of the ideology of the patriarchic nuclear family are the contradictory realities for women marked by the promise of the comfort and closeness of family life, on the one hand, and, on the other, the materiality of the unequal distribution of work organization, the marginality of our economic self-sufficiency, the lack of social support for our autonomy, and our emotional/affective investment in the nurturing aspects of "woman's work". Women's relationship to the seat of phallocentric power is scored by the substance of the economic and social inequalities left unquestioned within modern family forms. These inequalities limit women's possibilities through our unequal responsibility for home and child care. Had I not been required to seek the necessary private spaces and had I not felt the contradictory moments that were thereby highlighted, the questions that haunt me in this writing might never have occurred to me.

As it is, the conversations between the young woman and myself became the pivotal point for my own growing understanding of the material realities hidden in the ideology of "home." Simultaneously, her private world became the mirror in which I caught the ever more articulate reflections of the contradictions that create the nuclear family as the site of socially acceptable expressions of gender/sexuality set against the possibilities for women's intellectual, cultural, and personal expression.

This young woman and I talked often, mostly about her: her aspirations, her future, her boyfriend, her home, her family, her job, her school. Having recently graduated from a basic-level high school program she had subsequently enrolled in a community-college, part-time, high school upgrading program in order to improve her secretarial skills and to take accounting. She wanted to be a secretary, because, as she said pointing to the trash can, "I wasn't meant for this job." Her boyfriend and, as plans were at the time, her future husband, did not mind her wanting to be a secretary, at least as she told me, until they have children. But he did not want her to go back to school. So her return to school was a secret she, with the support and help of her parents, was able to keep from him. Her parents frequently lied to him about her whereabouts, she told me, so that she might attend classes without his finding out and imposing limitations on her activities.

To be sure her parents might have perceived themselves to be acting in her best interest. They supported her in her desire for further education. Simultaneously they were able to conform to the mandates of male privilege by affirming her boyfriend's prerogatives to dictate possibilities for her future. While the specifics might have been played out in particular idiosyncratic ways in this instance, the general scenario is not an unusual one in the lives of many young women. Parents' complicity in supporting the gendered violations of heterosexual social/marital relations has a long and worldwide history (Daly, 1978). Historically, geographically, and socially, the cultural imperative requiring that parents, particularly mothers, undertake to make young women marriageable on terms not of their own making differ only in content not in intent. "If he knew I was going to school," she said to me on several occasions, "he'd get very angry. But I don't care, I have to do this. I just hope he doesn't find out."

In one of our conversations this young woman and I talked about her grandmother. Her grandmother, she told me, "is a very wise woman. I listen to my grandmother," she said, "because she knows how things are. She told me women have to learn not to talk. They have to know how to keep quiet. A woman must never tell a man what she knows or what she thinks. Women must listen a lot, hear everything and keep quiet. Then we can do more because the man will never know":

> Let no one tell me that silence gives consent, because whoever is silent dissents. (Barreno, Horta, daCosta, 1975, p. 86–87)

I had images of this "grandmother" in my mind—what she might have looked like, what the sound and intonation of her voice might have been when she was telling this young woman these things. My young acquaintance related her grandmother's words to me almost in a whisper, moving closer into my room, telling me a secret, as if she were sharing the profound wisdom of Mary Daly's hags and crones (1978). I thought at the time and think even more so now that this young woman must have considered me in need of such wisdom, surrounded as I was by my papers and books, telling her as I did that she should not allow herself to be bullied by this young man, that he had no right to assume control of her life in the presumptuous ways he did.

The irony of my relationship with this young woman still strikes me profoundly: each of us, while sharing the secrets of our different worlds, were simultaneously engaged in the genuine caring for one another signalled by our wish to impart the knowledge we thought the *other* needed in order to survive.

And yet the disquiet with which I have carried this story over many years has continually forced me to reflect not on our difference, but on what we had in common made graphically concrete in that shared space and time. The same social forces that give patriarchy its power to silence, on that occasion brought us together in conversation when others slept. I don't intend this as support of some romanticized notion of women's developing consciousness. We both knew what we wanted: I wished I could have done my work differently as much as she wished she could have done different work.

I continue to wonder: how typical was this young woman; of what particular social group was she a representative; to what extent did her realities and insights transcend class boundaries, social boundaries, race boundaries, age boundaries? I still don't know the answer to these questions. It would be comforting to believe that I and those women who form the circle of my social and political life don't keep quiet, don't just listen but are listened to, don't have a social and political existence shrouded in silence. Yet, . . . I also continue to wonder: how much of my daily life is rationalized as political strategy; how much is material, ideological, psychological, and emotional constraint; how much is marked by the limited choices offered by compliance to socially acceptable forms of femininity; how many of my "choices" are a function of my culturally contained reality as "woman"?

Simultaneously, how much of what we do goes unnoticed, unaccounted for, forgotten, not seen to be "doing anything," considered unimportant and inadequate? And at what point might our "telling" overstep the boundaries of discretion because for women to speak about these things is like peeling back layer by layer the gauze that covers our wounds, gagging those who have violated us even as it exposes us to the healing powers of the wind and the sun.

Sitting at my desk, I think about Meagan, I think about the young woman in her uniform pushing the cleaning cart, and I think about myself. The images merge and intermingle as they dance back and forth supporting as well as contradicting each other. What do we share? What about our situations are different? My questions push their way through to the fingertips that hold my pen.

Not only the young women in Gaskell's study, but Meagan and the young woman in the powder blue cleaner's uniform:

> knew, for their own good reasons, what the world was like, and their experience acted as a filter through which any new message was tested, confirmed, rejected, challenged and interpreted. Changing their minds would have meant changing the world they experienced, not simply convincing them of a new set of ideals around equality and opportunity and the desirability of a different world. (1987, p. 168)

Women's physical, social, and emotional relationship to bearing children and to the organizing features of home and family are lived most often in such a way that we occupy a non-arbitrary position within these social forms. Women's relations to home and family is matched by social, political, and economic relations which make the realization of women's aspirations beyond the home easy or difficult depending on the extent to which the individual woman conforms to or contests the structural configurations present in our lives.

Young women often have a much simpler explanation of this process. As one of my students said in class recently: "Guys can't handle it if they think you're smart, so if you want a boyfriend you have to pretend to be dumb." The expressions of this reality may be coded differently in the home, in the workplace, in school, and on the street. The terms of the code may have their particular and specific manifestations across racial, ethnic, and class lines; and indeed for those who choose not to invest themselves in heterosexual relations. Nonetheless, for all women, the hegemonically coded forms of family is a reality within which they have to make meaning even as they acknowledge the struggle.

Because "the governing of our kind of society is done in concepts and symbols" (Smith, 1987, p. 87) the delineation of what is possible for women has not only a material basis, but a symbolic one as well. Gender struggles begin in the inequalities expressed within patriarchy and the competing interests of women and men forged in our condition of unequal access to the terms of our social relations. Just as "the measure of power" within a capitalist economy is "the control and disposition of property of all kinds" (Morton, 1988, p. 257), so the measure of power within a patriarchic discursive economy is the control and attribution of meaning. Finding the transformative practice that both confirms the existence of these realities *and* breaks the symbolic/ discursive code through which women's subordination and men's entitlement is articulated is the ground of a feminist politics.

The pedagogical implications of this reality are many and complex. It is not sufficient to wish to dream a new reality into existence. Oppressions and subordinations are embodied in concrete practices enacted in our social relations. To be sure, the project of transformative pedagogy is to change these relations and practices. Yet:

> for women, who are so often excluded from the public sphere, the question of whether resistance can lead to change if it is only expressed in individual critique or private opposition is a very real one. And this leads back to the schools. Can schools become a possible "public sphere" for the encouragement of resistance and the building of a critical counter-hegemony for girls? (Weiler, 1988, p. 52)

For feminist teachers this is a question that throws its shadow across all of our relations with our students and all of the possibilities of what we might do in the classroom.

# 5 | DE/SIRING
THE TEXT
### FEMINIST STUDENT
### IN THE CLASSROOM

Feminism exists because women are, and have been, everywhere oppressed at every level of exchange from the simplest social intercourse to the most elaborate discourse. Whatever the origins of this oppression—biological, economic, psychological, linguistic, ontological, political, or some combination of these—a polarity of opposites based on sexual analogy organizes our language and through it directs our manner of perceiving the world. Whether or not we can in fact escape from the structuring imposed by language is one of the major questions facing feminist and non-feminist thinkers today.

—Marks and de Courtivron,
*New French Feminisms: An Anthology*

I believe increasingly that only the willingness to share private and sometimes painful experience can enable women to create a collective description of the world which will be truly ours. On the other hand, I am keenly aware that any writer has a certain false and arbitrary power. It is *her* version, after all, that the reader is reading at this moment, while the accounts of others—including the dead—may go untold.

—Rich,
*Of Woman Born: Motherhood as Experience and Institution*, 1986a

I BEGIN THIS CHAPTER WITH THE DETAILS OF A CONVERSATION, IN the spring term of 1985, among seven women graduate students enrolled in a graduate seminar at the Ontario Institute for Studies in Education, the graduate school of education associated with the University of Toronto. One of the comments is my own:

> I don't understand what [the men] are talking about. I feel like I'm not as well educated as them. I haven't done too much reading in this area. They know so much more than I. I just feel

that if I said anything they'd say, what is she doing in this class, she doesn't know anything, so I keep my mouth shut.

I haven't got the right language so I always feel like such a dummy. I don't really want to talk because if I do [the men] will realize how stupid I am.

I feel very angry and uncomfortable in that room. They have no right to talk about us like that. I feel so embarrassed. It's like men passing around pornographic pictures. I don't think it's appropriate.

I've talked a few times, but nothing I say seems to make a difference. What I say never gets taken up. It's like I hadn't said anything. So I've given up. Why bother?

They talk about those women [in Radway's study] as if they were me. I don't sit at home reading junk like that. I've worked all over the world and have done many interesting things. In this class it's like none of that counts. You're a woman so you must sit at home reading cheap romance novels. That life isn't my life, and I resent being compared to them. But then I get angry at myself for saying that. Why do I want to distance myself from those women? We are no different, they and I.

I always have the feeling you get when people are talking about you as if you don't exist but in fact you're sitting right there. It's the way people talk about children or people they think are mental incompetents.

You know, they are just like little boys, always demanding attention and monopolizing all the time. I just sit back and think, let them have their say. Sometimes I think it's quite funny.

These are the words of women, mature students, most of them professionally established prior to their enrollment in one of the most rigorously academic and research-oriented graduate schools of education on the North American continent. It is an institution into which entry is highly competitive, and which brings together students and faculty from around the world in an atmosphere, in large part, of intellectually challenging and politically progressive perspectives on education and schooling. The question of the social circumstances that brought these women to speak words so clearly in contradiction to their intellectual abilities and sense of professional competence is the point of this chapter.

## THEORETICAL FRAMEWORK

In 1964, Herbert Marcuse pointed out that one feature of the liberal organization of the modern technological state—which Western liberal democracies are—is the way in which they embrace discursive forms as modes of governance in the context of freedom from overt physical constraint:

> by virtue of the way it has organized its technological base, industrial society tends to be totalitarian. For "totalitarian" is not only a terroristic political coordination of society but also a non-terroristic economic coordination which operates through the manipulation of needs and vested interests. It thus precludes the emergence of an effective opposition against the whole. Not only a specific form of government or party rule makes for totalitarianism, but also a specific system of production and distribution which may well be compatible with a "pluralism" of parties, newspapers, countervailing power, etc. (p. 3)

In social systems marked by the ideology of liberal democracy, the power of the word to create the world takes on a significance that is at once subtle, pervasive, and contradictory. The political effect of the contradiction between our experience and the rhetoric of liberal democracy which embraces notions of freedom, equality, and possibility is the way in which it invites us to internalize our limitations as if they were of our own making. In such a social system, critique and dialogue is closed out at the very moment it is offered up as a possibility.

For the dispossessed—those for whom autonomy and self determination are not uncontested assumptions—social experience is overlaid by difficult and ambiguous questions: how does one identify that moment when a seemingly insignificant individual event becomes a moment of possibility, a moment of transformation, a revolutionary moment, or conversely a moment of closure and loss; what is the measure of significance of these everyday relationships and events; what are the possibilities for discourse—the communicative and meaning-making stance of social interaction?

By discourse I mean a set of social practices that signify positions in subjectivity which are always multiple and which are always negotiated within the broader political and economic relations that mark our day-to-day lives. What access we have to the decision-making apparatuses, and what claim we can lay to the economic resources that determine in fundamental ways our very survival, are given meaning and are constructed and regulated through discursive practices. In short, discursive practices are the stories we believe we can tell to and of ourselves and also the practical engagements these stories imply. Thus, discursive practices do not simply overlay the particular political and economic power relations that are a feature of our private and social lives. Rather, they are a way of negotiating our subject position within these relations of power. Coincidently, how we are positioned subjectively organizes our perspective and the discursive practices that are the vehicle through which we articulate our experience.

As is suggested by Marcuse (1964), what makes discourse political and hence a form of governance more powerful than brute force could ever be is that it is arbitrated by a set of social relations among groups of differentially empowered individuals in such a way that it necessitates the discursively disadvantaged to participate in the construction and legitimation of their own disadvantage. It is an attempt to minimize the critical moments and maximize the reproductive moments in the service of the dominant interest.

Volosinov (1973, pp. 216–217) states that discourse is not merely socially constructed in dialogue; it is *accomplished* in the exchange of meaning and signification within those frames and power relations out of which it arises.

Roger Simon (1987) elaborates on the regulative relationship between discourse and power:

> Power works through discursive and material practices that in their moment of concretization already delimit and condition action. (p. 175)

The relationship between discourse and power is mediated through meaning and meaning making: power is having access to those processes which legitimate *and* enforce meaning as this is inscribed in language and supported by concrete practices. The discourse/power relationship is not just a handy theoretical construct; one never just makes up discourse in the abstract or in a solitary moment outside of the social locations we occupy. Rather it is attended by concrete acts with concrete outcomes: it is a way of seeing our everyday living, loving, eating, sleeping, and waking, in the myriad of social contexts in which we find ourselves, as at every moment political and negotiated. Concretely, then, discourse is an action taken upon the world. These actions may be transformative or they may be tenaciously preservative of the status quo; whichever the case, discourse is socially negotiated through power.

Under conditions of social inequality, individuals have differential access to both ideological and material resources. Power develops from such social relations where for some the possibility exists to control other individuals by naming these relations on their own terms derived from their own experiences. That language, discourse, speaking, and writing are not neutral but political acts becomes clear when we realize that who "speaks" and by what authority their "speaking" is governed cannot be disassociated from those relations of power that mark the social, political, and economic structures within which individuals live their daily lives. Put more simply: it matters who tells the story and what social power they hold to enforce their meaning. In a phallocentric social structure this has particular consequences for the specificities of women's lives.

For women, the particularities of the relationships between personal experiences and the larger social context within which they occur are significant. Whether at the level of common, daily social interaction or at the level of intellectual, political engagement, women have been, and continue to be, either excluded from the dominant discourse or have found ourselves to be marked as deviant in relation to it—a deviation marked in difference rather than in experience.

In an uneven society marked by the constraints of discourse and power, women's social situation is lived in oppositional terms. As Gerda Lerner (1986) elaborates:

> The contradiction between women's centrality and active role in creating society and their marginality in the meaning-giving process of interpretation and explanation has been a dynamic force, causing women to struggle against their condition. When in that process of struggle, at certain historic moments, the contradictions in their relationship to society and to historical process are brought into the consciousness of women, they are then correctly perceived and named as deprivations that women share as a group. This coming into consciousness of women becomes the dialectical force moving them into action to change their condition and to enter a new relationship to male dominated society. (p. 5)

"Feminist consciousness," says Sandra Lee Bartky (1985), "can be understood as the negating and transcending awareness of one's own relationship to a society heavy with the weight of its own contradictions" (p. 32), contradictions born in the ideology of the primacy of the phallus.

Yet, despite the possibilities of "feminist consciousness," the ideology of liberal patriarchy enforces that, as social experience, we live our life closely. We make daily investments in survival such that the political nature of our everyday lives are not easily revealed. We suffer concrete physical constraints all the way from not being able to walk the streets in freedom and without risk whenever we choose to do so to not being hired for jobs because we happen to be women, or being hired for jobs but paid less than men are for the same jobs. In addition, significant psychological constraints work actively to discourage us from pursuing our dreams. The situation of women in the academy runs parallel to these larger social situations.

It is in this context in which I reflect on the incident with which I began this chapter. The details of the incident out of which the women's comments came took place in the public space of a graduate seminar. To this extent, the story I relate here might be construed as a public story. However, while this story clearly has its public face, for me, both the incident and my retelling it here are also moments of reflection on the relationship between the public and the private. Inasmuch as women are invited to believe that our experience of marginalization and diminished opportunity is a function of our own *private* inadequacy rather than the intent of *public* social organization marked by the subordination of the many for the benefit of the few, a feminist analysis of the culturally supported distinction between the public and the private is aimed at showing the inadequacy of the arbitrary ideological separation between them. As is suggested by Jana Sawicki (1991):

> if we are to free ourselves from rigid adherence to the standards and practices of our disciplines that constrain and neutralize feminism, personal reflection on the conditions out of which our discourses are produced is crucial (p. 3).

In telling this story, through a dialogue with my own experience, I make distinct the inseparable relationship between the private and the public of personal experience.

What is of interest to me in the stories I weave together in this chapter is how they reveal a lived reality of contradiction and disjuncture: among other things, I want to show that while our private ways of being are deeply felt, their social display is often quite unremarkable.

## POLITICS OF THE ORDINARY

In the spring of 1985 I was nearing the end of my doctoral studies at the Ontario Institute for Studies in Education. Despite the embracing environment I experienced there in the form of colleague and faculty support, the trepidations with which I had returned to complete my PhD in the fall of 1982 were still with me.

Initially I had returned to school under rather unplanned circumstances. Having been at this same institution in the early seventies as a graduate student in the Master of Arts program, my life took an unsurprising turn. I was married at the time to another graduate student whom I had known since my mid-adolescent years, and with the completion of each of our Master's degrees, we moved out of the world of "schooling" and economic marginality and into the world of work and economic independence. The gendered reality of this moment had not yet made itself apparent to either of us.

For each of us, schooling had been the most significant preoccupation throughout all of our early adulthood. Entering the world of work meant that much of our future seemed unclear. The only thing we knew for sure as we embarked on our new life in a small community in northern New Brunswick was that my partner was going to have a job and I was going to have a baby. He was, as it turned out, to provide the material wherewithal in exchange for my work of keeping intact the physical and the emotional environment of family life. I don't recall this turn of events having been the outcome of any extended debate or even a benign discussion. That at the time I asked no questions about this situation should not be a particular surprise. As Roberta Hamilton suggests, the questions we ask are both limited by and in turn limit the situations we live out:

> Along with most "girls" of my time and station I did not question my economic dependence on a man or that this man had an obligation to support me and our children. Nor did he. (1990, p. 26)

I want to resist the inclination to indulge in revisionist history and say that at the time it truly did not occur to me (nor, it seems, to him) to risk other discursive forms through which I could have engaged possibilities for my life—discursive forms other than the one I was encouraged to embrace: the unquestioned economic, social, and sexual relations lived out in the heterosexual, North American, nuclear family. While I recall being sick to my stomach during most of the "trek" east and for several weeks after our arrival, I did not associate this with a body in severe disconnection with the mind and calling out for attention. I was determined that it was possible for me to make the best of it. Indeed I remember how much pride I took in being a "self-starter." I convinced myself that regardless of how disadvantageous the situation seemed to be for me I could always "create something out of nothing."

While for both of us in this nuclear partnership, parenting was a new and exciting adventure, for me mothering became a calling. Indeed, it seems to me now that at the time I had no options but to create in my head mothering as a fully engaging activity. While I had not given much thought to whether or not I was "cut out" to be a mother at all, let alone a mother full-time, the community in which I lived seemed to leave no options. I still recall the naivete with which I applied for a job as a community youth worker, a line of work in which I had had at the time several years experience while working through my graduate program. The minute details of the moment of my failed attempt to secure a "real" job after so many years of schooling are still vivid in my memory.

At the time of my application it was equally obvious that, in this small lumbering and mining community, I was quite likely the most well experienced and well educated person available for the job *and* that I was nine months pregnant. Interviews were held in the provincial capital, a two-hour drive from where I lived. The letter inviting me for the interview indicated that in every aspect, experience, and education, I seemed the perfect person for the job and that the interview was a formality.

I arrived for the interview in good time wearing my deep moss-green corduroy pant suit—cut to fit the proportions of a woman about to give birth. Images flood the memory of that incident. I recall vividly the moment of walking confidently through the door for the all but redundant interview. In my eager anticipation I registered the eyes and face of the man behind the desk as he looked up at me only to realize, in that millisecond of recognition, that the redundancy was not the interview but me. I remember the interviewer's soft-spoken voice as he explained his "concerns" about my impending motherhood. I recall his incomprehensible explanations as to why he could not offer me the job. It was a voice attendant to the social graces of an apology yet carrying the implied indictment that held me responsible for "wasting his time." Couched in words that expressed *his* concern for *my* not yet born child, his gentle, paternalistic demeanour hid the sharp edges of his accusing words that held me responsible for my failure at "motherhood" even before I became one. The interview ended before it began. I did not get the job.

In retrospect I stun myself still with the realization of how willing I was to accept that I had made a deeply culpable social error in presuming to apply for the job in my condition of almost motherhood. Instead, I returned home, curiously amused, but astonishingly not angry.

I proceeded to commit myself to the birthing and raising of my child telling myself, and others, that, despite my "non-work" status, my commitment was to mothering and not to housework. I even told myself (and other people), in those ways we have of convincing ourselves, that I refused to do housework. Only occasionally did the human capacity for self-deception catch up with me and in these moments I often found myself holding a toilet bowl brush or crawling on my hands and knees pushing a wet rag across the kitchen floor. To this day I engage the activity of "keeping house" with ambivalence and feelings of self-betrayal.

Except for an acceptable level of intrusion of socially conscious community work politicized by a short stint on the board of trustees of the local school district (ended abruptly by our return to the city—and my partner's new and better job) my life proceeded in this way for a number of years of child-bearing/raising.

It was not until a few years later, having returned to the city that felt most like "home," that I ran into an old colleague with whom I had previously attended graduate school. We had begun and completed our Master's program in the same year. Unlike myself, he had continued to teach during those years after my departure from the city. He was, as he told me, now contemplating his future as a result of having been granted a one-year sabbatical from his teaching position. I remember our meeting and conversation well. Moving past old reminiscences and the "how's" and "who's" of our shared past, he wondered what I would do if I were in his situation: would I spend a year travelling around the world working in areas that might be of interest to a social activist of the seventies remade in the image of the eighties, or would I go back to school and complete a PhD?

One more time in my life that feeling of being stunned washed over me. His request that I contemplate his dilemma seeped through to my body so much so that I can still feel—in ways that bodies don't forget—the weight of his question as it mingled with my life reality. Concrete images continue to serve as the metaphor for the abstractions of our socially constructed gender difference. His light and eager steps highlighted mine weighted by and feeling the resistance of the three smaller bodies that surrounded me: one sitting in a stroller which I pushed with difficulty through the urban slush of early spring; the second engaging the world from a pack on my back; and the third, tucked against my chest in a "snugly," clinging to the familiar heartbeat he and I had shared over the nine months of his wombed existence.

My head spun with my own questions: Why had I not thought of these possibilities for myself? Why had the contemplation of such choices not occurred to me? Why, even as I knew these were things I too really wanted to do, did the possibilities seem so remote? So remote, indeed, that it had not even come to me to think about them.

I reminded myself of a cousin living in the then cold war conditions of the European East Block whom I had visited several years previous. I had asked him, with as much simplicity as my friend asked me on this occasion, if he would like to come and visit in the West. I recall his sardonic chuckle as he replied with some compassion in his voice for my naivete: "the possibilities do not exist that might make that question sensible for me." How we attend to and formulate ideas about the possibilities that exist for us come directly out of the lived realities of our daily lives. It is out of these realities that we draw the meanings we allow ourselves to make. And these meanings can confine as much as they can create possibilities.

As Roberta Hamilton suggests:

> the usefulness of my own biography is not that it is particularly interesting
> or unusual, but that, for its type, it is so ordinary. (1990, p. 24)

Yet, it is out of these ordinary and deeply idiosyncratic moments that the politics of the personal emerges. As I reflect on the historical/biographical conditions that construct for me the moments of my daily life, it is clear that the roots of my feminism did not materialize as a sudden response to an incident of brutal violation. Rather my developing consciousness and understanding has been a slow coming-into-being through a steadily shifting perspective. Like a lens which we work until the image is clear this feminist perspective has enabled me to notice details I might never have noticed, to make connections I might never have made, to ask questions I might never have asked, to offer understandings that might never have been available to me.

Yet I also know that as social analysis our "telling" is transformed into an act of indiscretion. "Telling" betrays our social contract. It is in return for protection and security that we are required not to tell. And "our fear of the losses can keep us from changing. [Yet] what is it, exactly that we are afraid to lose" (Pratt, 1991, p. 57).

In *Reflections on Gender and Science*, Evelyn Fox-Keller tells the story of Barbara McClintock and her struggles to gain recognition among her almost exclusively male colleagues:

> Her expectation that she would be rewarded on the basis of merit, on the same
> footing as her male colleagues, was itself read as a mark of her ingratitude—of
> what he [her male colleague] called her "personality difficulties." (1985, p. 159)

To speak of such things is in itself judged to be indiscreet. The very act of putting to public scrutiny our private experiences is seen to confirm our inadequacy. There is literally no legitimate way to politicize women's experience within the terms of phallocentric discourse without making ourselves into the authors of our own violation and subordination. The exploration and delineation of the terms of our marginalization are the same terms that create us as beings capable of being marginalized.

The parallels with victims of rape are not accidental. Although I would never want to diminish the immediacy of the terror and genuine fear for life that often accompanies that act of violence, the forms of the violations have some parallels. Victims of rape are often made responsible for their own experience of violation by pointing to some social indiscretion or inadequacy in the lives of the women concerned—a social indiscretion that somehow is used to justify the violence perpetrated against them.

And yet it is the stories we tell of and to ourselves that provide the conditions for transformation. Deborah Britzman elaborates:

> To understand the process whereby experience becomes meaningful requires that we situate ourselves in history and recognize as critical the relationships and intersections—both given and possible—of biography and social structure. Theorizing about such connections allows individuals a double insight into the meanings of their relationships to individuals, institutions, cultural values, and political events, and into how these relationships interpellate the individual's identity, values, and ideological orientations. This kind of insight can help individuals participate in shaping and responding to the social forces that affect, impinge on, and construct how experience becomes lived. (1991, p. 232–233)

There was for me in the moment of that crisp spring afternoon, faced with the request that I contemplate the dilemma of one whose privilege to assume possibilities went for the most part socially unexamined and unquestioned, a desire to claim for myself possibilities I had not assumed even though at the time I did not understand the social relations and historical/biographical moments that had made the assumption of such privileges impossible. Nor, having made the decision for myself to return to graduate school as a PhD student, had I anticipated how difficult it would be to transcend the boundaries posed for women by the academy as a masculinized social/intellectual site. The story that follows is the telling of how those boundaries were crossed in a graduate seminar entitled "Discourse, Text, and Subjectivity."

## METHODOLOGY OR SETTING THE STAGE

A noticeably different version of what follows appeared in the *Harvard Educational Review* as an article co-authored with Roger Simon (Lewis and Simon, 1986). The specifics of the production of that text are relevant to the inclusion of my parts of it here. In the article, Roger Simon and I share in the telling of the story through a two-voiced narrative. In that publication, each part of the text is, by turn, assigned with our names so that we each take responsibility for our own words. This happened, in part, because our two separate texts were not originally written jointly.

Following the events of the graduate seminar each of us had written our own stories separately. Simon wrote for the 1985 AERA Annual Conference. My original paper was an attempt to sort out for myself my experience of the events of the seminar in which I was, at the time, a student. Admittedly, the motivation for my writing was partially influenced by my need to inscribe my own understandings knowing that the seminar instructor had done the same. Subsequently, I presented my paper at the 1985 JCT Conference on Curriculum Theory and Practice.

While the experiences that were described in the joint Lewis/Simon text and retold again here were encountered at the same time in the same place—our weekly three-hour meetings in the context of a graduate seminar—neither of us contrived the events of this class so that we might write about it. We anticipated neither the events that took place as a result of the assigned readings and personalities of those in the course, nor did either of us direct the events to a particular outcome except in as much as each of us (and all of us in that class) desired certain outcomes to resolve the contradictions and violations of a lived situation.

Initially, in submitting a paper to the *Harvard Educational Review* in the spring of 1986, we had intended to create a single text that might carry for the reader some concrete sense of how we experienced the class sessions. For this purpose we tried to meld each of our texts into a single-voiced version with joint authorship. It soon became obvious that this task was impossible. For each of us, our words held our own meanings and descriptions of the events as we understood them. In our attempt to integrate our separate texts each of our "I's" refused their subordination to the collective "we." To talk about how "we" experienced the events of this weekly encounter inevitably violated one or the other of our experiences.

Had it been textually possible to present the words of two people speaking at the same time we might have presented the story in that fashion. The metaphor that comes to mind is captured in the technology of modern music making described as "mixing," the superimposition of multiple "voices" in order to create the collective effect of a simultaneous speaking of many voices. Since then an almost possible (were it not for common restrictions on publishing format) textual presentation has presented itself.

Recently one of the graduate students with whom I worked as thesis supervisor used transparent plastic pages to accomplish the effect of multiple voice. Laying one page on top of another—one of which was a transparency—enabled her words to be superimposed and "mixed" in such a way that each of her texts sat juxtaposed as mutual informants for the other. These multiple texts were not speaking in dialogue but rather as independent texts reflecting differently on a multiplicity of possible meanings. In this way the two texts were able to stand independently of each other and yet share a common political project (McDonald, 1990). Similarly, for Simon and I, in the original text of the *Harvard Educational Review*, it was not our intention to present a dialogue in the usual sense of that term. Nor was there a contrived attempt for either of us to "respond" to or "take up" points made by the other. Rather the viability and strength of the presentation, while using a more conventional form than had been used by McDonald, was located precisely in how we negotiated our difference in the context of the shared agenda.

For this reason it is possible to read the text as it appears in the *Harvard Educational Review* in the linear fashion in which it is presented. But it is also possible to read each of the texts, identified as authored by Lewis or Simon, independently of the other in a consecutive rather than integrated fashion. For the purposes of this text I have used only my own portions of the journal text except where I quote Simon from Lewis and Simon (1986).

And finally the undifferentiated texts in the introduction and the conclusion of the article in *Harvard Educational Review* were written in the same manner. However, even though specific parts of those sections were written by each of us we chose not to identify our individual contributions by name because we concurred on the final analysis.

Reflecting on the nature and process of the presentation of the joint text and of its reincarnation as a single-voiced text in this book calls into question the nature of academic work. There is strong ideological myth surrounding the work of intellectual production: that as intellectuals we do our work apart from how, where, and with whom we live our personal and intellectual lives; that in order to do this work in its most pure and therefore desirable form we need to disassociate ourselves from the lived "trivialities" of our everyday lives; that the best text is one that silences what Roland Barthes calls "the most delicate mechanisms of social exchange: not only in the State, in classes, in groups, but even in fashion, public opinion, entertainment, sports, news, family and private relations, and even in the liberating impulses which attempt to counteract it" (Sontag, 1987, p. 459).

Yet, it seems to me, valorized academic practices steeped in notions of "objectivity" and "independent" work guarantee that what ought to be considered most important is trivialized into insignificance and what is elevated to truth is generated mostly out of irrelevance. "The academy," says Linda Brodkey (1987), "has traditionally demonstrated a limited tolerance for lived experience, which it easily dismisses as 'anecdotal' or 'stories' and in some quarters that intolerance is so great that any ethnographic narrative would be an affront to scholarly sensibilities" (p. 40). Fortunately such conditions of knowledge production are only a pretense which while put forward in the interest of power and mystification has nothing to do with how knowledge is actually produced. Knowledge production is always the result of our intellectual efforts to make sense of our most mundane and most profound social experiences, motivated by our moral/political agenda and laced with conversation, casual remarks, the circulating of books and articles that have interested us and which we think might interest others, and the mutual critique of texts that may alternately find themselves thrown on the flames or be the focus of our next work. Despite claims to the contrary, were this not the case not only I but no one would ever write again. Our claim for authorship/authority over any text must be understood in this context.

## TEACHING AND LEARNING WITHIN PATRIARCHY

Even as I prepare to tell the story of this experience, I realize and acknowledge that my whiteness, my economic viability supported at the time by the social/economic forms of liberal patriarchy embedded in the nuclear family, my able-bodiedness, my relative youth, and the outcome of the well learned lessons of Euro-American cultural forms provided me with privileged entry and, as well, having been allowed access, a less alienating environment than would have been available had I not carried any or all of these forms of social acceptability.

Term after term, I worked under the strenuous conditions that superimposed full-time mothering with full-time student work until the spring of 1985 when I was coming close to completing the course requirements of my program. What brought me to this particular course was my specific interest in exploring the questions concerning the relation between text and discourse seen in the light of a consideration of the relation between language and power. What fueled this interest, particularly as my academic work moved closer and closer to an articulation of the specifics of the political nature of curriculum, defined broadly as "life text," was my growing uneasiness with the fact that much of what I saw pass for social theory—explanations that attempt to account for why the world is as it is, how particular social forms come to be created, how economic and political relations come to be experienced, and how these experiences come to be understood—simply did not seem to me to conform to what happens to women as we go about living our daily lives. It seemed to me that there exists a language/discourse that systematically describes the social world and, simultaneously and consistently excludes women.

That the overwhelming experience of women in a society dominated by men is that of being silenced was an impression I had carried with me for a long time. Nor, it seemed to me, was I alone in this idea. Like fireworks, the explosion of feminist scholarship over the past twenty years has documented the complexities of the marginalization and exclusion of women from the social/intellectual traditions that claim to know and speak the word/world on behalf of us all. But while collective historical accounts are crucial for the purposes of identifying the systemic forms of our exclusion, every woman carries a bag full of personal experiences drawn from our daily lives. The search for examples does not have to be long or intensive.

Some years ago, returning by train from an academic conference, I sat next to a woman who summed up exquisitely the situation of women. After the conductor, the steward, and the railroad's public relations representative overlooked her in their various dealings with the passengers, she turned to me and said, "Sometimes I think I must be invisible. People don't see me. They don't hear me. Sometimes I wonder if I am really here."

This was a woman, a grandmother, a secretary, who had never read Dale Spender's *Invisible Women* (1982). I passed on that reference along with a couple of others and she promised to read at least one of them. But she admitted feeling reluctant to buy and bring into her home titles such as *Sex, Gender and Society* (Oakley, 1972), or *Women's Oppression Today* (Barrett, 1980). She thought *Invisible Women* sounded sufficiently like the title of a science fiction novel that she could smuggle it into the house without arousing her husband's suspicion. She indicated that if her husband were aware of its subject, the book would surely be banned from the house and her reading even more closely monitored.

Is this an extreme example? I don't think so. The situation of my seat-mate on that trip home is instructive in what it says about how we might understand the socially supported power relations between women and men. That there is an assumed privilege accorded the interests of men's lives even as these circumscribe those of the lives of women is the experience women have of patriarchy. I equivocate deliberately on the word "interest" for I do indeed intend both meanings of the word—what interests men as well as what is in their interest.

Conforming to the ideologies of colonialism, the monitoring of women's words is simply a particular manifestation of a general social condition that is played out among women and men on a daily basis in a variety of forms and places. As Sarah Hoagland states:

> One of the first acts of colonizers after conquest is to control the language. . . . Further, values are embedded which disavow the colonized's ancestral ways and economic independence. As the colonized are forced to use the colonizers' language and conceptual schema, they can begin to internalize these values. This is "salvation," and colonizers pursue what they have called mani-

fest destiny or "the white man's burden."

The theory of manifest destiny implies that colonizers are bringing civilization (the secular version of salvation) to "barbarians" ("heathens"). Colonizers depict the colonized as passive, as wanting and needing protection (domination), as being taken care of "for their own good." Anyone who resists domination will be sorted out as abnormal and attacked as a danger to society ("civilization") or called insane and put away in the name of protection (their own or society's). (1988, p. 32)

Taking apart the parts that form the whole of "manifest"—man/I/fest—reveals interesting possibilities for understanding. "Fest" means "to have a feast," "to celebrate"; hence to manifest is to "celebrate" the "feast" of the Man/I who, as The Father, holds the Power Of The Word to name the world; he holds the power to describe and therefore to prescribe how the world can be understood and lived. The significance of this becomes obvious when we understand, as Hoagland does, that:

The purpose of colonization is to appropriate foreign resources. It functions by de-skilling a people and rendering them economically dependent. . . . This de-skilling of conquered peoples is crucial to domination because it means that the colonized become dependent on the colonizers for survival. Actually, however, it is the colonizers who cannot survive—as colonizers— without the colonized. (1988, p. 33)

Phallocentric discourse not only colonizes women but renders us irrelevant in the context of the struggle for power among *men*. In her now classic article, Hartmann (1984) defines patriarchy as a social system characterized by "the systematic dominance of men over women" (p. 194). While later in the same text she goes on to say that "patriarchy is not simply hierarchical organization but hierarchy in which particular people fill particular places" (p. 199), she also makes a finer point not often noted in our discussion of the social construction of masculine power. As Hartmann suggests, what is significant about the social workings of patriarchy is that it emerges as a:

set of social relations *between men*, which have a material base, and which, though hierarchical, establish or create interdependence and solidarity among men that enable them to dominate women. Though patriarchy is hierarchical, and men of different classes, races, or ethnic groups have different places in the patriarchy, they also are united in their shared relationship of dominance over their women: they are dependent on each other to maintain that domination. (p. 197)

Patriarchy is often seen only as a set of social relations and enactments between women and men (resulting in a negative outcome for women), but the significant point of Hartmann's analysis lies in how it establishes patriarchy as a system of relations among men. As she suggests, men as a social group do act in concert to establish collective power over women, but I also take from Hartmann's analysis a more complex understanding of the internal workings of patriarchy. Patriarchic practices and social relations are not a simple binary opposition between dominant and subordinate social groups such as women and men. Rather, there are those social moments when, in order to establish power relations among men themselves, the focus of men's attention is not specifically on the violation of women (although this is surely the outcome—at the very least the violation of considering women to be irrelevant), but the struggle for dominance of one man over another whether this be in the area of physical or intellectual superiority. (Understanding this sheds more light on the social meanings of contact sports restricted exclusively to men). In those aspects of patriarchy defined through this struggle for power among men, women are not only irrelevant, but often seen as getting in the way of the otherwise unimpeded struggle for power.

When a woman speaks, it means that a man cannot speak, and when a man cannot speak it means that the social relations among the *men* are disrupted. It occurs to me that, in as much as women's colonization within patriarchy has a long, if contested, history, it may be that men are not so much concerned with losing power to women. Rather women's engagement of social/cultural interactions disrupts masculine duels and joustings and interferes with the contest for power among men. Women, therefore, have no place in the contests of this playing field except to support them by their absent presence; simultaneously enacting the practices of the spectator and those who toil; indeed, women are peripheral to the organization yet central to the labor of society.

Women's reading of the words of women is a challenge to this process. Contestation is that act when the powerless refuse to live by the definitions of the powerful. It is the acknowledgment of the experience of the Other demanding equality. The relation between power and contestation results in struggle. As Teresa de Lauretis says, women know that:

> the edge is there: the sense of struggle, the weight of oppression and contradiction. The stakes, for women, are rooted in the body—which is not to say that the body escapes representation, but quite the opposite. (1986, p. 12)

As we parted company, my seat-mate said, "You younger women have it made. You know what you want and you are so outspoken, people listen to you. Women my age never had a chance." Had there been time I could have explained; I could have told her what I am about to say here: that she and I inhabit the same world, that we are both engaged in the collective struggle to claim our voice, to be heard, to become visible.

While not free of overt, sometimes physical violence against women (McDonald, 1990, 1991, 1992), schools and educational institutions are a significant site where the struggle for intellectual power among men perpetrates the violation of labeling women irrelevant. The department I was in, not the most extreme example of sexism in academic institutions, consisted in the vast majority of male faculty members. I make this point simply to highlight the fact that as women graduate students we were not unfamiliar with the negotiations and accommodations that were required of us to survive in the world of male academe (Spender, 1981; 1982; Miles and Finn, 1989; Rockhill, 1987a; Aisenberg and Harrington, 1988). My daily experiences in this context fed my growing interest in feminist issues, particularly the relationship between language and other more subtle discursive practices and the moral regulation of subjects.

While all of us—students and teacher, women and men—came to this new course, "Discourse, Text, and Subjectivity," for a variety of personal and professional reasons, we also came with an intact social repertoire. We came carrying the baggage of our governed selves. For the women this meant that we already knew that what we said and how we said it was not quite as problematic to our male colleagues as the fact that we spoke at all. As Dale Spender (1980) has suggested, in a set of social relations where women's ideal discursive state within phallocentric discourse has been defined as silence, a woman speaking is seen to be in and of itself a political act. Under these conditions the very act or intention of speaking becomes an intrusion and a potential basis for a violent reaction on the part of those who have decreed our silence. Ultimately, for individuals who transgress the discursive limits of phallocentrism, the forces of regulation are without doubt swift, sure, and relentless.

As we began to take up the first of the assigned readings, an interesting and significant work by Ariel Dorfman (1983), *The Empire's Old Clothes*, the social dynamics in the class were annoying but not unusual: the men monopolized not only the speaking time but the theoretical and social agenda as well. They sparred, dueled, and charged at each other like gladiators in a Roman arena. Yet their camaraderie intensified with each encounter.

The instructor's social positioning was interesting in this respect. While he tried to mediate the encounters among the men, and at the same time registered (although not until later in the term, verbally with the class) the women's growing discomfort and frustration, he was continually positioned by the men in the class as the arbiter of the verbal/intellectual skirmishes they enacted on one another. The metaphor of scoring points for the approval of the instructor was an image that continually sat with me as I observed the exchanges. Whether or not the male students also registered the women's growing dis/ease was not obvious to me. If they did, they did not act on this insight.

Throughout these exchanges, the women were relegated to the position of spectators. The discursive dynamics of this exclusion are complex. As Bakhtin claims:

> utterance is not speech conceived as a holiday from system, representing the individual ability to will language elements into freely chosen combinations. Besides forms of language, there exist as well forms of combinations of these forms. The determining role of the other in actual speech communication shows not only that there is a system in language outside of any particular articulation of language but also that there is a system governing any actual utterance. (Volosinov, 1973, p. 222)

As women, we experienced this seminar and lived this system as phallo-centric. Feminist critique has shown how the phallocentric universal "I am a man, nothing human is foreign to me" (Volosinov, 1973, p. 212), represent-ing the power of discourse, is transformed into practices based on the particular "I am a man, nothing foreign is human to me," representing the discourse of power—and then made to seem equal. For women who must survive and negotiate our way within this system, this reality has profound implications. Catherine MacKinnon says:

> Women, have been deprived not only of terms of our own in which to express our lives, but of lives of our own to live. The damage of sexism would be trivial if this were not the case. A feminism that seeks to under-stand women's situation in order to change it must therefore identify, criticize, and move those forms and forces that have circumscribed women in the world and in the mind." (1987, p. 15)

The feeling of being in a space that is not one's own is familiar to women in a society marked fundamentally by patriarchy (Imray and Middleton, 1983). In our seminar, ideological differences existed among the men in how they took up the agenda of the class or in how they envisioned its pedagogical implications. Indeed, in many instances, whether defined through a radical or a liberal stance to educational content and practice, there was often more in common both pedagogically and ideologically between groups of men and women than between people of the same gender. But since the overriding issue which constructed the class dynamics was not the politics of curriculum but rather the politics of gender, ideological differences among the men were obliterated by the desire to structure gender solidarity. Independently, we women felt our exclusion more and more intensely the more we struggled to find room for our voices and to locate ourselves in the discourse.

Because patriarchy organizes the political and economic forms within which we must survive, regardless of our gender, social class, sexual desire, or racial and ethnic identification, all men can benefit in some way from belonging to the dominant group. At the most mundane level, this means that, for men, the boundaries of social relations are so extended that a whole range of social behaviors, that is seen to be acceptable for them, is deemed to be inappropriate for women, irrespective of our social class or ethnic and racial origin.

In the context of our course this meant that the men were allowed to speak at length—and did. Their speaking was seldom if ever interrupted. When a woman and a man began speaking at the same time, the woman was expected to defer to the man and most often did so. Women's speaking was often reinterpreted by a man through phrases such as "what she really means is . . . ". More than just a few times the actual talk of women was attributed in a later comment by a man to a man. Women's ideas—sometimes reworded, sometimes not—were appropriated by men and then passed off as their own, sometimes only seconds after the words were spoken by a woman. Whenever a woman was able to cut through the oppressive discourse, the final attempt at silencing took the form of aggressive yelling.

It became clear to the women that, socially, the reversal of this dynamic would have been totally unacceptable to those who held the power of legitimation. Designations such as "hysterical" or the less political descriptor, "rude," are often attributed to women when we attempt to use forms of discourse deemed to be "vigorous" and, in the academy, "intellectually dynamic" when used by men. That "assertiveness training" for women has not enhanced the success of many affirmative action programs attests to the liability for women of engaging in social and discursive practices seen to be appropriate for men. "Assertiveness training" does not work precisely because it fails to acknowledge that women's social position is a function of the differential social meanings assigned to practices enacted similarly by women and men. In this social context, for women, assertive responses become a liability whereas for men they are an asset exchanged for power and defined as a commodity.

Gender solidarity is not rooted first and foremost in vague notions about sociality but rather in the politics and economics of patriarchy. This is not to say, however, that "homosociality" is not an important strategic position from which to maintain and reinforce male dominance, or that such homosociality does not have extremely effective and deeply felt results (Morgan, 1981).

Rather, men's political and economic advantage continues to be confirmed, supported, and legitimized through a social discourse that arises from their particular relations to one another. In the course, to the extent that we women drew our discourse from a different perspective—one that did not/could not conform to the forms of male homosociality—our discursive intrusion seemed irrelevant and disruptive. Conversely, because it was only the women who could both genuinely interrupt the male discourse and question the singularity of the male interest, it was our very presence as women that disrupted the logic of the phallocentric project.

Feminist social analysis has taught us that within the terms of patriarchy the legitimacy of men's dominant discourse is no less circular than women's powerlessness. Men set the boundaries and then act as gate keepers and arbiters over both men's and women's discourse. Within this closed system men need to be legitimated and to legitimate each other. Women, because we occupy a deprived political and economic space, are denied the power to set the social agenda. Hence our powerlessness continues to be reinforced and supported. Moreover, because of our relative powerlessness, women cannot assume the position of legitimators of men's *or* women's discourse nor as supporters of our own interests. It is this reality precisely that often persuades women to vest their interests with patriarchy hopeful that they might be *the* exception to the gender-selective symbolic power of the phallus.

The phallus as the symbol of entitlement is central to this. It is a term which allows for the possibility of extending the enactment of patriarchic power into the realm of symbolic discourse. Drawing together the concrete and the symbolic power of masculine embodiment, the notion of phallocentrism refers not only to the concrete ways patriarchic forms enact control through political power and economic viability, but as well makes it possible to consider those forms of social control whose power is affirmed through the symbolic: concepts of desire, sexuality, language, representation, self, and so on. As such the use of the term "phallocentrism" also allows the possibility of new namings, meanings, and referents. It allows the possibility that women, to the extent that we are not "either totally powerless or totally deprived of rights, influence and resources" (Lerner, 1986, p. 239), might participate in transforming the symbolic phallocentric system. It also allows the possibility that those (mostly men) who benefit from the symbolic power of the phallus may begin to shift their perspective and join in transformative practices that take them and us outside the frames of current symbolic discursive forms. Understanding the power of the phallus as symbolic makes all the difference in the world. The "scepter" is just a wooden staff, after all, and the "Conch" an empty sea shell serendipitously washed to shore (Golding, 1962). This means that how social meanings are assigned is always political. Hence as a social/political act where we assign meaning we can also reassign meaning.

Despite conversations and discussions that took place between small groups of women as the course proceeded, by the time we came to Janice Radway's book *Reading the Romance*, the women in the class had been all but muted. As course instructor Simon's own words describe the centrality of this text to the agenda of the course:

> In this book Radway examines extensively both the production and con-
> sumption of mass-marketed popular romance novels. Radway's work is
> unique in that she not only develops an ideological critique of the novels she
> examines, but she also analyzes empirically and theoretically the reading of
> these books as part of the discursive practices of a particular group of
> women. She not only identifies the way they use and read romance novels,
> but also gives us an understanding of how packaged forms of romance are
> integrated into daily lives that are historically and structurally constituted
> within patriarchic social practices of courtship, sexuality, and marriage.
> Radway questions how, why, by whom, and with what purposes and mean-
> ings such books are read. In examining the readings produced by the women
> she studies, Radway reveals contradictory constructions of resistance and
> regulation. Hence, she shows how we can investigate the reading of a text as
> a form of social practice that can be examined for the work it does in orga-
> nizing subjectivity. (Lewis and Simon, 1986, p. 463)

Either because we had been marginalized into silence or because we had made a conscious decision to refrain from the discussion as a form of resistance to being silenced—how ironic that the result in both cases should be the same—we had become prisoners or exiles within a wall of silence. In part the reasons the text of Radway's book enraged us was the context within which we read it and our realization that what was going on with the women in Radway's study was precisely what was going on with us in the classroom.

Radway's study demanded a response. How were we to do this? We knew from experience that to insert ourselves into the social text required that we speak/write without words of our own (Assiter, 1985). Our history had taught us that our tongue or pen, like the tongues and pens of our mothers "have needed no turn of an iron key, no leather tong" (Mairs, 1986, p. 103) to know where they belong. Historically, women have found legitimation only to the extent that we have been able or willing to appropriate the male agenda, a particularly self-violating form of escape from domination which in the end turns out to be no escape at all. The words of Jana Sawicki (1991) make this clear:

> Recent French psychoanalytic theorists such as Luce Irigaray and Julia Kristeva both have suggested that Western cultural discourses are univocally masculinist. They claim that these so-called "phallocentric" discourses offer no place for women to speak except in so far as they speak in ways that men have preordained. Thus women's only alternatives are to speak in a masculinist voice, construct a new language, or be silent. (p. 1)

The price we pay for this appropriation is the disclaiming of our collective experience of oppression, an act that forfeits our voice and gives overt support to dominant social, political, and economic forms.

As women, to a large extent we have appropriated the terms of our own subjection. This is not a case of false consciousness. Rather, we have accepted the powerlessness of these terms to define a discourse within which to speak, partly because we are powerless to do otherwise. While many feminists are clear about the need for women to legitimate each other and thereby begin to break away from the patriarchic stranglehold, it is also clear that intellectual assault is just one of many forms of violation that act in concert to disempower women and moderate revolt. Given the complexity of the relationships between physical, emotional, psychological, and intellectual abuse, it is clearly not easy for women to subvert this assault.

As a social text the simple act of women speaking comes to defy allowable discourse within patriarchy. This reality often leaves our words struggling to find their political significance even as it makes possible those discourses intended to marginalize to be transformed instead into embodiments of belonging and power.

As the male-defined resistance to the formulation of our response intensified, it became clearer to us (the women) that what we were engaged in in this class was a struggle not just for ourselves but for all women—including those women who are reading romance novels.

Had we not been required to read Radway's study in the context of this seminar, we might never have been pushed to the outer limits of our marginality. While we could doubt ourselves, our capabilities, our understanding, and even our experiences within the context of most male-defined academic discourse, in this instance the disjunction between content and process became obvious, as did the disjunction between what we knew about who we were and what the men in the class insisted in telling us about who we were. We knew we had not only an experiential base from which to take up Radway's agenda, but, as well, a lived theoretical framework from which to understand it.

In contrast, framed by the focus of Radway's study, in this class the men could only speak about Radway's text in distanced, abstracted theoretical ways free of the grounding in experience that might have given a different meaning to their discourse (Lewis and Simon, 1986, p. 465). However, given the social precondition of male prerogative it did not occur to the men in the class that the women might have had something salient to say about the study that might have helped them and us to better understand the nature of the relationship between language and power. Nor did it seem to occur to them that the women's increasing silence might have had meanings other than consent, compliance, agreement, or ignorance.

Taking the risk to speak our social experience is often difficult. This was certainly the case in our seminar class. While experiences are socially produced, they are individually felt. Social practices coded and regulated through specific cultural forms articulate "acceptable" discourse and social/linguistic exchange.

Taboos delineating appropriate topics for conversation work to mystify the intrinsic connection between the social and the personal. Given the condition of women's discursive subordination, feminist critique has shown us that women's first-order transgression is not a function of how we participate in the utterance of the word, but rather the fact that we speak at all. Politics— those relations of power and appropriations of discourse that inscribe us—arise out of how we are positioned within/against the word/world. While our desire is to transcend the alienations that such power relations prescribe, the great hoax of woman speaking is that she is allowed to speak only so long as she is not saying what is really on her mind:

> so long as she is not a "subject," so long as she cannot disrupt through her speech, her desire, her pleasure, the operation of the language that lays down the law, the prevailing organization of power. (Irigaray, 1985, p. 95)

Our speech is measured in silence. Consequently, it becomes difficult to express our experiences of personal brutalizations in terms that can link such experiences to regulative social forms and practices.

As an example, not long ago a student where I teach asked my help in sorting through the incredibly brutalizing experience of having been raped in her coed residence. Since such occurrences are a routine and all too regular feature of women's educational experience, the anonymity of the particular incident is guaranteed. The conundrum she faced—and that for which she came to get help—was the issue of telling. Having been threatened with retaliation (either by the assailant himself or his friends), she was reluctant to press charges. Yet she wondered, if she didn't tell, what would prevent him from doing it again with repeated impunity? Her own safety and as well her feelings of obligation to other women who were potential victims were significant factors in her concern.

The question was serious and our solution only ambiguously effective. What I want to highlight, however, is that the experience left both of us feeling the constraints of finding a way of speaking a truth for which there were no words or social frames within which their meaning—at the level of practice—could be articulated. All that the police wanted to know was did she or did she not want to press charges. Their embeddedness in the very phallocentric frames which allowed the crime in the first place made it impossible for the police to see/understand that not only was there no easy answer to their question but that the question itself was the wrong one: a blindness made possible by what Audre Lorde calls "the power of unaddressed privilege" (1984, p. 132). What is often forgotten by both women and men but is important to remember, is that this process of blinding is man-made—although not without a struggle—and therefore neither natural nor neutral.

To speak about rape, violence against women, and our struggle for transformative politics should not be seen as a retreat into the safe moral indignation of a victim. Our pain and tears are not a wall of safety from behind which we can point the finger of blame and guilt. To see it that way is in fact to reinforce existing power relations and to continue to limit the horizons of our vision for how things might be otherwise. However, when only silence can speak our refusal to participate in the myth making that has for so long enhanced women's subordination we need to examine both the political edges of such silence as well as political possibilities for breaking it. In this instance, I am using Corrigan's sense of the term "myth making" (1988, p. 9) and in so doing I want to juxtapose "myth" as a debilitating concept against the possibility of speaking our *dreams* and *desires* as a revisioning of a longed-for, better future:

> Repetition by a different-sex speaker is a creative act of reading involving a new locus of desire and a non-oedipal act of identification. Identification in this case does not render the identifier identical to the text, it changes the desires. (Modleski, 1986, p. 126; see also Brodkey, 1987)

That words are inscribed by/in the masculine means that the very same words mean different things when spoken by a woman or a man.

To be sure, women are not the only social/political group who has been subordinated by the myths of the oppressor. Historically blacks, Jews, the working classes, lesbians and gays have all borne the consequences of tales fabricated by those who would wish not to take responsibility for their complicity in practices violent against the Other. Indeed the access we have to myth making is directly proportional to the power we derive from our social, political, and economic positions. All subordinate groups have less need for myth making since their interests lie more in uncovering the realities that are the consequence of the myth makers' practices.

> That most such myth makers are men is entirely to the point. (Corrigan, 1988, p. 9)

This seems to capture the entire essence of an issue in language so plain and simple that every syllable reverberates with meaning. The words, like stones dropped into a still pond, create crests and troughs which move out in ever widening circles. They intermingle with one another creating higher crests and deeper troughs, disrupting the quiet still of the pond, which until that moment had reflected an image that could satisfy nothing beyond the narcissistic desire to mirror a surface reality back to us.

## "THAT MOST SUCH MYTH MAKERS ARE MEN IS ENTIRELY TO THE POINT."

Hence we need not simply point out how we might be in peril from the embodied forms of men's myth making; we need as well to focus our attention on how we might think about change.

In this seminar class we understood that what we were experiencing was indeed a collective experience, and we knew what this collective experience was about. Our reading of Radway's *Reading the Romance* was the catalyst that enabled us to understand how, for the women, the divisive and individualizing process was embedded in the taken-for-granted prerogative of male discourse. As a collective we could more easily challenge the oppressive boundaries and limited interpretations imposed through such discourse.

In the context of socially produced and collectively, yet privately, lived gender inequalities, it is important to understand that the disjunction between male and female discourse does not arise out of the distinction between the objective knowledge associated with masculinity and the subjective knowledge associated with femininity—a discursively constructed disjunction that forms the basis of Western philosophical thought. Rather, objectivity is male experience elevated to the level of theory.

Reflective of the disparity of relations of power between women and men, this gendering of objectivity as male implies that women's experience and discursive forms are defined by men as illegitimate within the terms of men's experience and men's discursive forms. The assertion that women's knowledge is based on personal experience while men's knowledge is based on objective grounds obliterates, above all, the relationship between education, personal experience, and politics. Yet, the only education that can have meaning is education that is personal and therefore political. The ingenuousness of an educational process that attempts to obliterate the relationship between the personal and political is profoundly silencing of all subordinate groups and guarantees the priority of the dominant interpretation of social, political, and economic relations.

While the experience of being consciously, deliberately, and overtly dismissed is painful, the experience of being invisible is brutalizing. To have had our ideas, work, and talent considered and contested might have challenged our critical sense; to have them not even noted denied our existence in the most profound way. The fact that for women such denial may not be an unusual experience does not make the living of it each and every time less brutalizing.

"Silence can turn into rage" (Lewis and Simon, 1986, p. 465) when we realize that who "speaks" and whose authority governs that speaking cannot be disassociated from those relations of power that mark the structures within which individuals live their daily lives. Eagleton's elaboration is helpful:

> The critique of ideology . . . presumes that nobody is ever *wholly* mystified—that those subject to oppression experience *even now* hopes and desires which could only be realistically fulfilled by a transformation of their material conditions. . . . Someone who was entirely the victim of ideological delusion would not even be able to recognize an emancipatory claim upon them. (1991, p. xiv)

For the women in the seminar class suddenly and forcefully the revolutionary moment became concrete. While we were waiting for the elevator during one of our breaks, a moment of solidarity was precipitated by what may have begun as an off-hand comment made to me by one of the other women in the class. She said in a quiet whisper: "I can't go back into that room." I shared her feeling and responded with an invitation to talk.

I don't know how we knew that this was the occasion to cast aside our silence. I don't know how we were able, in that moment, to identify our mutual safety and solidarity. It is not always easy or possible to identify all of the details (the soft data) that come together to articulate a moment of possibility. While a shared sensibility to body language and to nonverbal discourse becomes, at times, the only means of communication between and among members of oppressed groups, such coming together is neither predictable nor guaranteed.

> The underground language of a people who have no power to define and determine themselves in the world develops its own density and precision.

> It enables them to sniff the wind, sense the atmosphere defend themselves in a hostile terrain. But it restricts them by affirming their own dependence upon the words of the powerful. It reflects their inability to break out of their imposed selves. It keeps them locked against themselves. (Rowbotham, 1973, p. 32)

Despite the contradiction, as women in the class, we knew we had to confront our silencing concretely and we took the risk of doing so.

It is important to signal that what happened to the women in this class was consciousness-raising. Catherine MacKinnon's recovery of the naming and practice of women's political activity as consciousness raising is central:

> Feminist method is consciousness raising: the collective critical reconstitution of the meaning of women's social experience, as women live through it. Marxism and feminism on this level posit a different relation between thought and thing, both in terms of the relationship of the analysis itself to the social life it captures and in terms of the participation of thought in the social life it analyzes. To the extent that materialism is scientific it posits and refers to a reality outside thought which it considers to have an objective—that is, truly nonsocial perspectival—content. Consciousness raising, by contrast, inquires into an intrinsically social situation, into that mixture of thought and materiality which is women's sexuality in the most generic sense. It approaches its world through a process that shares its determination: women's collective social being. . . . The process is transformative as well as perceptive, since thought and thing are inextricable and reciprocally constituting of women's oppression, just as the state as coercion and the state as legitimizing ideology are indistinguishable, and for the same reason. The pursuit of consciousness becomes a form of political practice. (MacKinnon, 1983, p. 255).

Catherine MacKinnon has convinced me that the politics of consciousness-raising has earned a bad name precisely because it is a profoundly effective practice. This always implies collective action and, to the extent that it challenges the status quo, such action is always revolutionary and difficult. That this event took place in the privileged setting of a university does not diminish the social meanings and political implications of our experience. Perhaps "in the world of wrongs done" our experience may not have seemed a "big thing. . . . But small moments or decisions often reflect and/or presage larger dynamics which are important. This [was] one such moment." (Pickard, 1992, p. 1)

The usual practice during breaks had been for the men and women students to sit together which, while it created a time of informal discussion, did not obstruct the prevalence of the same dominant discourse. Despite the fact that the instructor chose not to join the class during these times, the men, regardless of the women, continued to work at impressing each other with their own self-regard. The two of us took our coffee and tea and moved to a private space. Other women noticed and joined us. Some went to get the rest of the women until all but one of us (she had gone to the library directly from the class and so was unaware of what was happening) were gathered.

Our gathering was noticed by the male students whose body language and joking demands to know "what's going on" punctuated our construction as Other. Again, the soft data of sexism is something we don't often hear or read about because its subtlety defies the starkness of words. How do we describe the look of vagueness or hostility in someone's eyes, the position of their body, the shoulder turned just barely perceptibly, that gaze that just misses its mark, that attention just barely out of focus, that laugh that isn't quite, that "joke" lived and felt as violation. How do we draw the line between the trivial and the profound:

> There is nothing ambiguous about racial segregation or economic discrimination: it is far less difficult to point to these abuses than it is to show how, for example, the "tone" of a news story can transform it from a piece of reportage into a refusal to take women's political struggles seriously or even into a species of punishment. . . . It is difficult to characterize the tone of an article, the patronizing implications of a remark, the ramifications of some aspect of practice, and it is even more difficult to describe what it is like to be bombarded ten or a hundred times daily with these only half-submerged weapons of a sexist system. This, no doubt, is one reason why, when trying to make a case for feminism, we find ourselves referring almost exclusively to the "hard data" of discrimination, like unequal pay, rather than to those pervasive intimations of inferiority which rankle at least as much. (Bartky, 1985, p. 29)

Only one of the men asked if he could join us in a show of solidarity. While his gesture was appreciated, his presence, however unintrusive, would have been silencing. We said no. It was at this point when the conversation reported at the beginning of this chapter occurred. Our meeting was seen to be and was an overtly political act. As we talked, the anger came in floods.

It was now not as individuals but as a group that we uncovered the perspective from which the men in the class discussed Radway's work, drawing as they did on their own version of what women were supposed to be like. Thus we were able to discern the subtleties of how they twisted the analysis until the subjects of Radway's study fit the image that was required to sustain the notion of male superiority (Haug, 1987). We came to understand the oppressive relations within which women become the subjects of male discourse. And it became clear that the only difference between us and the women in Radway's study was that as graduate students we lived out and contested the patriarchic social relations under different circumstances. The oppression was no less felt, and the struggle was no less difficult.

We were the women in Radway's study. The women in Radway's study were us. In a moment of collective insight we understood that we are our history, and our history is laid within patriarchy. To deny that we are a collective body is to deny not only our history, but the possibilities for healing and recovery. Realizing our identity with the women in Radway's study was the first step in releasing us and them from the bonds of patriarchy.

When we connected with, talked, and listened to each other we became a viable political force in this context. We reappropriated our voice, found support in each other, and were able (for a short time and certainly not completely) to lift the oppression. Our act of refusing silence produced a moment of speaking. It produced as well the possibility for political action.

We considered a number of strategies for subverting our marginalization, exclusion, and violation. Among them, importantly, were suggestions for politically motivated enactments of silence. We thought we might not return to class at all—a proposal that would have highlighted our absence from the discussion in concrete ways. It was proposed that we might return to class but, by sitting together at one end of the seminar table rather than intermingling with our male colleagues, choose not to speak with the intention of reappropriating our voice through silence. Thereby we would publicly embrace the politics of absenting (Woolf, [1938]1966). And finally it was suggested that on our return to class we request from the instructor time to speak when we would each make a statement concerning our experience of exclusion. It was clear to us that any one of these propositions might have accomplished the same end. Nevertheless, in part out of respect for the instructor, after our extended break we returned to the class, each of us prepared to make a statement. What we could never have accomplished individually became possible for us as a group. We disrupted the male agenda and appropriated our space.

## CONCLUSION

As is often the case, this is not altogether a happy story. It was clear that, as the term continued, a true attempt at equality and understanding was achieved on occasion between some of the women and some of the men. Yet this was not a miraculous transformation of the phallocentric agenda. While the men became conscious of their own speaking—sometimes catching themselves speaking too much—and began to monitor themselves and each other, by and large most of them seemed unable to move beyond defining women within male terms; employing that power which confirmed their privilege to validate us and which, thereby, simultaneously confirmed their power to withhold validation.

This "validation" took a number of forms. By some, our "speaking up" was seen as the manifestation of the presumably desirable characteristics of those who "carry the public persona of the strong woman" (O'Brien, 1987, p. 59). We became, in Adrienne Munich's words "the exception that proves the rule" (Munich, 1985, p. 250). In response to our statements, one man even assumed the prerogative to explain to us how wrong we were to think so poorly of him and that we would surely see it differently if we knew how well he had spoken of us to his wife! In elaborating he explained that on repeated occasions he had shared with her how much he enjoyed talking with us precisely because we were strong, powerful women who had ideas. If he intended to flatter, he succeeded in violating. That his statements exemplified the problem did not occur to him. The silence that followed his words only left him wondering at our rudeness in refusing to acknowledge his benevolence. What he did not understand is that by standing us apart from other women he, in effect, denied that we were "women"; he denied the possibility that to be a woman is to be strong, to be intellectually rigorous, and to be autonomous. Rather, our "strength" became that against which other women's presumed "weakness" made them (and by the terms of the dialectic, us) the cause of their/our own misfortune.

Moreover, the patriarchic foundations of racism and class privilege (Lerner, 1986) were confirmed in his statement. As women we might wonder with Adrienne Rich (1979) what it was exactly that determined us as "strong." By ignoring the conditions of our access to the academy—access to a seminar class shared with him—we might wonder at the implications of his dismissal, by omission, of our own good luck at being born white, at a historical moment when however difficult our existence inside the academy by virtue of our being women, its doors at least were not overtly barred to us, having achieved relative economic advantage, and not being required to look after "his" children. Under such conditions, being designated "strong" is feeble praise when women can say with Audre Lorde:

> like Virginia Woolf, I am aware of the women who are not with us here because they are washing the dishes and looking after the children. Nearly fifty years after she spoke that fact remains largely unchanged. And I am thinking also of women whom she left out of the picture altogether—women who are washing other people's dishes and caring for other people's

children, not to mention women who went on the street last night in order to feed their children. (1979, p. 38)

The invitation to accept our designation as strong "according to *their* ideas of what a special woman ought to be" (Rich, 1979, p. 38) was directed toward denying all of our personal and collective histories and struggles as women.

Other times, catching themselves reenacting practices the women had critiqued, the men would turn to one or the other of us and utter some version of "Do you want to say something?" or "Maybe x has something she wants to say about that." Yet, being "given" time and space had its own oppressive moments in that the power of control over such time and space had not changed. Our inclusion, by virtue of the terms of our special status, had the effect of "confirming through [our] deviation from the female norm the larger rule of exclusion" (Silverman, 1984, p. 327). In that the terms of our allowable discourse had not changed, the granting of such "speaking time," as an act of charity, had the effect of bringing us into silence amplified even beyond our original muted state.

> Being muted is not just a matter of being unable to claim a space and time within which to enter a conversation. Being muted also occurs when one cannot discover forms of speech within conversation to express meanings and to find validation from others." (Lewis and Simon, 1986, p. 464)

Despite the fact that the power dynamics were now made explicit, the violation continued mostly without understanding.

I suspect all women, like those of us in this class, have lived this struggle, have felt anguish in response to the strength-sapping power of the oppressor pushing us to the edge and demanding of us to conform, and have felt terror and rage welling up from the depths of our being when sometimes in hopelessness we think that conforming would be so much easier. I think often of the despairing words of that young woman in an undergraduate sociology seminar who said: "Sometimes I wish I didn't know what I know." Most of the time the strength is there to keep up the struggle. But when it seeps away, it is these golden touchstones, the reference points signifying a collective struggle, that enables us to say we are not alone.

We have to ask: What might have facilitated the terms of our speaking? We must go beyond the meaning, consequences, and import of the effect of including women in the social landscape and beyond prescriptions about how this project might best be accomplished. We need rather to uncover/propose an explicit feminist version of community life framed by a specific moral discourse of utopian political/social vision grounded in practice and directed toward livable alternatives.

Yet:

> to live for a particular definition of human being without a guarantee of its historical possibility is not an easy task. (Welch, 1985, p. 91)

Clearly to dream a utopia is not enough unless such dreaming projects a future grounded in suggestions for practice. Dreaming with no possibility for action (doing) is self-consuming. The dream becomes impoverished. To dream about:

> unity that rubs out divisions as if they were chalk marks only . . . to over-flow the boundaries and make unity out of multiplicity . . . would be . . . to dream the recurring dream that has haunted the human mind since the beginning of time; the dream of peace, the dream of freedom. (Woolf, [1938]1966, p. 143)

But this dream is a dream of naive optimism, not the dream of possibility. Given human history, the growth of unprecedented military weaponry world-wide, and increased political tensions even among friendly nations, to be an optimist today is truly to succumb to the seduction of power, injustice, and dishonesty. It is to dismiss the possibility of an alternative altogether.

But on what basis do we establish a utopian discourse that has any legit-imacy? The answer is in the feminist call for a transformed practice—a practice whose aim is not to humanize our phallocentric culture but to transform the very ground of its existence. Feminist utopian practices imply not closure, but steady, relentless acts that defy oppression—like the Mothers of the Plaza de Mayo, or the Women of the Greenham Common—our vision is our practice. It is not "clean," tidy and complete. It is always in the process of becoming, such that our dreams are projected out of our his-tory, out of our memories of: those who died or were maimed; those whose lives have been contorted by acts of oppression by those who we know could have done otherwise; those whose lives have been violated by those whose assumed power to do so went unchallenged by those who shrank from the risk of challenging.

These are not dreams that envision magnificent tapestries, but rather dreams that seek to reweave the tattered threads of our history. These are not dreams that desire to avenge the deaths and oppressions of a violent past, but dreams that capture the shimmer of joy that celebrates life—the prism that reintegrates the scattered colors of a shattered past into a steady piercing white light—dreams that transform the past into a future marked by an alternative practice.

Utopian visions are never neutral. They always and only arise out of the particular needs and desires framed by the social, political, and economic positions—the history—of those who propose them. History is the story of the collusion between governance—the overt and covert regulatory practices embedded in our social, political, and economic relations (Corrigan and Sayer, 1985)—and the gendered/sexualized/eroticized conditions of our human be/ing.

This means that men, too, as well as women need to examine their social practices. In the context of our seminar, what could the men have done differently that would have rejected the assumption of male privilege? First, it would have been necessary for them not to see the women's developing political protest as individual moments of hysteria, for which the cure was the calming word of the Father. Second, it would have been necessary for them to take equal responsibility for naming the discourse of phallocentric power as an immorally oppressive social form that denies freedom and human possibility.

There is no question that these are not easy mandates. However, if men are to participate in the emancipatory project, they can neither assume the burden of providing women's freedom and legitimacy nor enjoy the luxury of remaining silent in the face of oppression. To declare solidarity with women under either of these conditions can be rightly challenged as insincere. Men needed to risk more than a comfortable indignation that declares solidarity with women without requiring action based on that conviction. One cannot simply donate freedom from a position that does not challenge privilege. As is the case for any oppressor group, for men to ally themselves with the oppressed, they must understand the power of their privilege and the privilege of their power, and self-consciously divest themselves of both. This requires the envisioning of a pedagogy that simultaneously articulates the possibilities for accomplishing freedom from power over us as well as freedom from our power over others.

# 6 | INTERRUPTING PATRIARCHY
## FEMINIST TEACHER IN THE CLASSROOM

Consciousness of self . . . is a particular configuration of subjectivity, or subjective limits, produced at the intersection of meaning with experience.

—de Lauretis,
"Feminist Studies/Critical Studies: Issues, Terms and Contexts"

If feminism is to survive as a galvanizing force, then it must—at the very least—give us access to the hard truths of how we live in the world. The ideals of how we *would* live are simply not enough. Measured only by our ideal we are all found wanting. But if we can allow one another to probe the harder realities, then we might forge bonds of mutual trust and acceptance that make the ideals finally possible.

—Kolodny,
"A Determined Life"

The truth . . . is always easy and simple. And in its simplicity lies a savage power.

—Rockhill,
"The Chaos of Subjectivity"

WHETHER WE TYPIFY THEM AS "EASY" OR "HARD" THE CONDITIONS of women's situation in the academy are contradictory. Universities are both the site where reactionary and repressive ideologies and practices are entrenched *and*, at the same time, the site where progressive, transformative possibilities are born. Historically, while many revolutionary movements have begun in the minds and hearts of socially and economically subordinate groups engaged, for the most part, in physically draining and emotionally brutalizing work not of their own design, the support and energy of individuals in the intellectual community have contributed substantially to the realization of emancipatory social goals. Poverty and physical exhaustion are not conducive to the realization of one's creativity not because the poor and the constrained (the vast majority of whom worldwide are women) are not capable of it, but because such conditions consume the physical energy required to concretely enact social, political, and economic change (Olsen, 1978). In contrast, the academy provides a potentially privileged space from which women might speak. What we do with this privilege is the challenge of any revolutionary project including that of feminism.

Yet, with Jana Sawicki (1991), I note the particular implications for women of the fact that the academy is "an instrument of domination as well as liberation" (p. 9). Institutionalized educational settings are a major site where women's subordination is reaffirmed and the ideology of women's social place is reproduced, ultimately by the techniques of meritocracy, credentialization, and a particular definition of standards that lock us "into the *terms* of ongoing social arrangements" (Elshtain, 1981/82, p. 140). The neutral language with which notions of ability, interest, and motivation are articulated in educational discourse makes unproblematic the question of what constitutes the acceptable. Simultaneously, the internalized practices that support the reproduction of the status quo hide the terms of how the acceptable is designated.

Women's struggles to gain a place inside the academy are framed by our desire to disrupt/interrupt phallocentric voices so that they might no longer speak in singular gendered chords. Yet we know that because we have been, by and large, excluded from this academic community, our interests have not often been served by the transformations for which we have struggled.

If we are to stay true to the politics of feminism we need to begin with where we are. Academic institutions *are* profoundly patriarchic in how they reproduce knowledge in masculine bodies. Likewise, they are profoundly phallocentric in their reproduction of a particular version of theoretical discourses supportive of ideologies that discriminate against women and other subordinate social, cultural, and economic groups. And they are also enormously powerful.

What are the possibilities for feminist practices within the academy that will not send our words to hide behind a wall of silence washed by pain? To be effective, the focus of a pedagogical project that can address the discursive meaning of women's silence must explore the political struggle over meaning.

To this end, my interest in this chapter is to reflect briefly on my own teaching practice. My reason for doing this is to make sense of what, for me, constitutes feminist teaching. In the university where I hold my position as "one of the feminist professors," the terms and nature of my practice are continually debated and questioned. In the academy, those of us who teach from a feminist perspective know that the intense scrutiny of our teaching stands in stark contrast to the review of the teaching of those who instruct from social/political positions that do not challenge the status quo. Similarly, only those who embrace the ideology of "objective" knowledge can claim "disinterested" practices, not because objectivity can be made sense of in teaching/learning contexts, but because ideas that do not question "the given" of dominant ideology—Barthes' "that which goes without saying"—do not carry with them the requirement for self-reflection (Ellsworth, 1989; Britzman, 1991; Freire, 1972; Simon, 1992).

As a feminist in the academy, I know no one who undertakes to propose and engage feminist alternatives lightly. Recently, cynics have suggested that proposals for feminist alternatives to traditional intellectual work are not to be seen as a commitment to social change. Rather, it is suggested that feminism is a fashionable display of political correctness. Yet as feminist women we know that intimidation often accompanied by the threat of the denial of tenure or promotion, often articulated through limits on our intellectual freedom, is the consequence of our choice to embrace a politics of possibility aimed at broadening access to political and economic viability for all marginal and socially disenfranchised groups. It is difficult to transmit in writing the amount of frustration that attends the work of feminists in the classroom, whether we are teachers or students. I despair for the loss of energy expended by this struggle as I despair for the more or less cavalier attitude that marks the responses of many of our colleagues.

However, neither the anger nor the frustration are totalizing or the most important experiences. The liberating potential of community, vision, hope, and laughter (of which there is a great deal) are the positive moments of our collective struggle. At the practical level, we look for strategies and techniques that make our work as feminist teachers within the academy more effective. We look to share materials and teaching methodologies that bring women's experiences out of the shadows and make them legitimate curriculum content. We seek to share strategies on classroom practices that make the daily rigor of classroom teaching less draining and more supportive between students and teacher. We attempt to share in finding effective ways of making clear our political position not as an ideological construct, but as a perspective or vantage point derived from our experience. We seek also to find ways of addressing in our classrooms the skepticism of students who have been well-schooled in the ideological notion of the possibility of neutral social science research and educational practices. And finally, we reach out for support from one another in those moments of despair and disillusion when we are faced with that student who has come for the easy *mark* (for what else could a course in feminist theory, feminist research or women's studies, taught by a woman, be); or when we are faced with the anger of this same student for not having delivered on their hopes for the "easy" course. I use the word "mark" deliberately because "grade" does not have the double connotation embedded in our relation as student and teacher under these conditions. The word "easy" also carries a double social meaning which would be, by and large, irrelevant were we men, but has deeply violating implications in the lives of women.

Such discussions and articulations are one side of feminist politics and pedagogical practices within the academy. To be sure they are important. But they are insufficient for understanding the import of feminist politics and, therefore, the possibilities for feminist pedagogical practices. The potential of women's studies taught from a specifically feminist perspective lies in the uncovering of those human relations which are scored by deep and brutal inequalities, and as well the proposing of ways of healing these social wounds by challenging those bases on which social relations rest. Conceptions of power, equality, justice, freedom, and so on need to be rethought and practiced differently.

It is in this context that I take up the examination of my own practice as a feminist teacher in the academy. In her now classic article, "How Does Girl Number 20 Understand Ideology," Judith Williamson (1981/82) provides a useful map for this examination. Like myself, Williamson is concerned with the political and ethical parameters of teaching and learning from a feminist standpoint, and provides a clear statement about the difficulty of negotiating social relations within the feminist classroom. Many students enter our classes acknowledging the social existence of sexism or racism or homophobia or class privilege. Yet they often stop short of the necessary self reflection that might reveal how we ourselves might be complicit in practices that perpetuate exactly these same social inequalities even as they make invisible and deny the social, cultural, and economic benefits we might derive from our privileged social positions. Practices complicit with creating social inequality are made invisible by students' comfortable indignation and outrage at social injustices that, nonetheless, allows them to displace such practices outside of themselves, even outside of our classroom, to an abstracted OTHER they call "society". In this context, both the agenda of the curriculum and the political project of feminist teaching practice are potentially seriously disruptive of students' world views.

That students—all of us—carry our privilege, or lack of it, in our bodies, that our access to or denial of privilege exists inside as well as outside of us, is often not something those who embody the social privilege of gender or race/ethnicity or social class wish to hear and see. Nor indeed, as Williamson's analysis would suggest, is it necessarily something that they *can* hear and see:

> students learn best to "see" the "invisible," ideology, when it becomes in their own interest to—when they are actually caught in a contradiction, believing things which are directly hindering their own well-being or wishes, or which conflict with a change in experience. (1981/82, p. 85).

The questions that arise for me out of Williamson's analysis are the following: how do we make "of interest" and "contradictory" to our male students the experiences of subordination and violation of the women in their classes; how might we construct a contradictory reality for male students whose privileges and entitlements are not contradictory but rather consistent with and coherent within phallocentric social structures; how do we reformulate notions of self-interest for the women students who know all too well that often their immediate self-interest (often within the confines of the classroom) lies precisely in acknowledging, negotiating, and even supporting the inequalities of phallocentric privilege; and finally how do we offer the possibilities for the deeply self-reflexive critique of the social and political forms that are required for wholesale social change?

Because students often find it difficult to engage the self-reflection required for the questioning of unequal and violent social relations in which we ourselves are social actors, there is often the tendency to conflate the notion of collective responsibility with guilt. Attendant to this is the strong desire to deny one's own social identity, to "depersonalize" the social actors and to disembody and displace them into a "black box"—a theoretical construct—that does not require that we ask difficult and often painful questions of ourselves concerning our own everyday practices. However, to the extent that sexism, racism, homophobia, and social-class inequalities represent social systems within which we appropriate or struggle against particular personal relations, men can no more escape the embodiment of their entitlement than those of us who are white can escape the embodied entitlement of our race. In this context, commitment to social change requires a moral/ethical attitude toward equality and possibility.

Scrutinizing the pedagogical practices necessary to bring students to an understanding and embracing of this attitude is the point of this chapter.

## SOCIAL/POLITICAL CONTEXT

In Canada, the fall of 1989 marked a particularly hostile environment for women on university campuses. On my own campus the events surrounding our "NO MEANS NO" campaign drew national attention. "NO MEANS NO" was an educational campaign organized by the Gender Issues Committee of the undergraduate student government (Alma Mater Society), aimed at alerting young women, particularly first-year students, to the forms and expressions of date rape. The reaction of a faction of the male students was to respond with a counter "sign campaign" that made explicit their belief that women's refusal of male sexual demands could appropriately be countered with violence ("No means tie me up") or with their own definitions of women's sexual deviance ("No means dyke"). To the extent that the signs were accompanied by active verbal threats and physical intimidation, many women experienced the atmosphere as misogynist.

My campus was not the only one experiencing what appeared to be an increasing backlash to a feminist presence inside the academy. As women academics across and between campuses shared stories of violation, more and more examples of misogyny surfaced. Our isolation and small numbers (women still comprise only a very small fraction of academic faculty) precluded any possibility of collective action (Brodribb, 1987; McCormack, 1987). In the face of an academic community complicit in its complacency, and unwilling to acknowledge its own oppressive practices born of the sexual subordination of women, we were atomized and held inside the private spaces of our own violations. And yet, despite the isolation of our struggles, we worked with our students to create an intellectually and emotionally supportive environment for them.

It was within this context that we witnessed with horror the spiraling momentum of woman-hating explode, in the early evening of December sixth, with the massacre of fourteen women at the Université de Montréal by a gun-wielding young man. He had convinced himself that women, transposed in his own sad head into the phrase "you bunch of feminists," were the cause of his own personal misery.

This incident focused, on several levels, my concerns about teaching and learning as a feminist in the academy. The historical context of our individual and collective experiences as intellectual women enabled me to see that what the media identified as the "idiosyncratic" madness of this young man actually reflected infinitely multiplying images of male power transformed into violence—a polished surface facing the mirror of masculine privilege. The selective nature of his violence, and his identification of intellectually active and successful women as both feminist and the cause of his misery and anger, made it clear that this was not the single act of a deranged mind, nor the outcome of peculiar conditions on that specific campus. That the events at the Université de Montréal could have happened on any campus in this country—indeed, any campus on this continent—became a tangible reality (Malette and Chalouh, 1990). Our identification with a politics that makes explicit our critique of women's subordination as a function of masculine privilege put my students' and my own safety into question.

Now, years later, I am still haunted by the image of young women—not unlike the women I teach—lined up against the wall, while their perplexed, perhaps helpless, male colleagues and male instructor vacated the classroom. I am haunted, too, by the words (reported in the media) of that young woman whose vain efforts to save herself and her women classmates were captured when she screamed at the gunman: "You have the wrong women; we are not feminists!"

The words, "you have the wrong women; we are not feminists!" provides a backdrop for the questions I raise: How might we bring about the social changes we desire without negating women's perspective on our reality, or turning it, yet one more time, into a self-perpetuated liability? More specifically, how might I create a feminist pedagogy that supports women's desire to wish well for ourselves, when for many women the "good news" of the transformative powers of feminist consciousness turns into the "bad news" of social inequality and, therefore, a perspective and politics they want to resist? More than resistance, which, drawing on Willis (1977), I characterize as the struggle against social forms that are experienced as oppressive, transformation is the fusion of political perspective and practice. Transformation is the development of a critical perspective through which individuals can begin to see how social practices are organized to support certain interests. It is also the process whereby this understanding is used as the basis for active political intervention directed toward social change, with the intent to disempower relations of inequality.

Given this context of backlash (Faludi, 1992) and implied or actual violation, how might we understand the basis from which a viable feminist pedagogy of transformation might be fashioned out of student resistance, *not to patriarchic meaning making, but to feminist politics*.

Using my experiences in Foundations 490, in this chapter I continue to raise the dilemmas I face as a feminist teacher in the university classroom.

I explore the possibilities and limits of feminist teaching and learning in the academy under conditions that directly contradict its intent.

Foundations 490 is a sociology of education course I teach in the faculty of education at Queen's University. While it is not one of the core women's studies courses, it is cross-listed in the women's studies program calendar. For this reason, the course often draws students from a wide range of disciplines. The specific title of the course, "Seminar in Social Class, Gender, and Race in Education," is explicitly descriptive of the course focus. In the course outline, I tell students that the theoretical framework we are using draws on critical and feminist theory and method. More specifically, the course proposes to "examine and develop a critical understanding of the implications for children's educational experiences of the effects of social class background, sex/gender differences, and racial background." It also proposes to "locate school practices as part of the larger social context within which schools exist."

The course format is a seminar which incorporates class discussion around assigned readings and student presentations. The class presentation component requires students to articulate the social meaning of a cultural artifact or practice of their choice. Students examine how the artifact or practice reflects the social/cultural context out of which it has arisen. The purpose of the assignment is to help students develop their skills in raising questions about our culture regarding practices that they had previously taken as given. My intention is also that, through this exercise, they might see differently how sexism, racism, class differentiation, homophobia, and so on, are embedded in concrete cultural products and social practices.

I begin the course with an introductory lecture that outlines to the students what I intend we take up during the coming term and the perspective from which my analysis proceeds. By doing this, I attempt to incorporate many aspects of women's lives articulated within feminist politics.

The course is attended by both female and male students, although women tend to outnumber the men four to one. This, in part, is accounted for by the fact that student enrollment in faculties of education is still largely skewed in favor of women, who comprise approximately seventy to seventy-five percent of the undergraduate teacher education complement.

Because the majority of students in Foundations 490 are women, in this text I use the general designation "student" to refer to women or to the students in general. When I refer to the men in the classroom I shall use the qualifier "male."

While in this chapter I explore the context of my teaching practice and the politics of the classroom, it is not my intention to offer prescriptive and generic feminist teaching strategies abstracted from the particular situations of feminist classrooms. Although it might be possible to employ suggestive approaches, we cannot artificially construct pedagogical moments in the classroom to serve as moments of transformation toward a critical political perspective. Nor can we predict how such moments will be responded to when they arise in particular situations given the personal histories of the students and instructors involved.

Rather, I believe questions about the politics of feminist teaching have most specifically to do with how we identify those pedagogical moments whose transformative power lies precisely in the understandings we bring to the gendered context of the classroom. Ruth Pierson (1987) provides a clear and comprehensive definition of feminism, which frames the intent of my own teaching from a feminist perspective:

> One identifiable characteristic of feminism across an entire spectrum of varieties has been the pursuit of autonomy for women. Integral to this feminist pursuit of independent personhood is the critical awareness of a sex/gender system that relegates power and autonomy to men and dependence and subordination to women. Feminists start from an insistence on the importance of women and women's experience, but a woman-centered perspective alone does not constitute feminism. Before a woman-centered perspective becomes a feminist perspective, it has to have been politicized by the experience of women in pursuit of self-determination coming into conflict with a sex-gender system of male dominance. From a feminist perspective the sex/gender system appears to be a fundamental organizing principle of society and for that reason it becomes a primary object of analysis. (p. 203)

From this perspective I raise the psychological, social, and sexual dynamics of the feminist classroom as a site where, I believe, the political struggle over meaning must be seen as the focus of our pedagogical project. It is a context in which a serious intrusion of feminist pedagogy must concern itself, as Rachel Blau DuPlessis (1985) suggests, not with urging our women students to "resent the treatment of [their] sex and plead for its rights" (p. 33)—a project that acts to reaffirm women's subordination and encourage our exploitation—but to self-consciously examine and question the conditions of our own meaning making and to use it as the place from which to begin to work toward change.

In taking up the psychological, social, and sexual dynamics of the feminist classroom, in this chapter I propose to examine the violence/negotiation dichotomy environment as a feature of women's educational experience. In this context, I share the strategies I employ in specific instances as a feminist teacher to subvert the status quo of classroom interaction between women and men. Finally, in the conclusion I suggest a specific framework that articulates the terms of feminist teaching.

## THEORETICAL FRAMEWORK

In the largely unchallenged practices of the school setting marked by patriarchic privilege (Corrigan, 1987a, 1987b), for women, the dynamics of contestation born of knowledge are more complex than is often implied in the resistance literature. By paying close attention to practices in the classroom, forms of discourse, directions taken in discussion, the subtleties of body language, and so on, it is clear that, for women, a dichotomy between desire and threat is reproduced and experienced inside the classroom itself.

The salience of this dichotomy for women is suggested by Kathleen Rockhill (1991) in her powerful and moving article, "Literacy as Threat/Desire: Longing to be SOMEBODY," in which she articulates women's contradictory reality as an educational dilemma. For the women in Rockhill's study, the knowledge and power made potentially available through becoming literate contradictorily also repositioned them in such a way that it threatened familial, conjugal, and ultimately economic relations. Rockhill explains:

> It is common today for education to be ideologically dressed as the pathway to a new kind of romance for women, the romance of a "career," a profession, a middle-class way of life; the image is one of a well-dressed woman doing "clean" work, important work. As such, it feeds her yearning, her desire, for a way out of the "working-class" life she has known (Steedman, 1986). It is precisely because education holds out this promise for women that it also poses a threat to them in their everyday lives. This is especially true for women in heterosexual relationships when their men feel threatened by the images of power (independence and success) attached to education. (p. 315)

In the feminist classroom the contradiction that women experience is compounded by the way in which feminist politics challenges the everyday lives they have learned to negotiate.

The complexities of student resistance to the intentions of schooling have been documented before, and indeed such accounts provide much of the data for the theoretical framework of critical pedagogy. Paul Willis's now classic work, *Learning to Labor* (1977), influenced by the theoretical work of Bowles and Gintis, Althusser, Bourdieu and Passeron, and Gramsci, was one of the first. Willis's study dealt exclusively with the experiences of male students. He included women only in their relations as girlfriends and mothers. In this context, it is interesting to note the irony of the title of the somewhat more recent book by Dale Spender and Elizabeth Sarah, *Learning to Lose* (1980/1988), a study of the experiences of girls in school. Willis explicates the social forms through which, for working-class "lads," schooling becomes the site of their reproduction as manual laborers not despite but precisely as a consequence of their resistance to the dominant ideology. By contrast, Spender and Sarah demonstrate that, for girls, schooling mandates that they embrace the social forms of femininity in such a way that it guarantees their social and economic disadvantage. For girls, their embracing of school knowledge becomes the medium of oppression.

In its classic form, critical pedagogy emphasizes that student resistance to the experiences of institutionalized education is forged from the contradictions perceived between the dominant discourse of school knowledge on the one hand and students' own lived experiences of subordination and violation on the other. According to resistance theory, students struggle to mark themselves off against the dominant discourse of the school through the enactment of practices that reaffirm and validate their subjectivities as specifically classed, raced, and gendered social actors.

It is my explicit intent in the classroom to raise with students issues of social relations from a critical perspective. But I am also a feminist who has worked for many years in feminist politics across a variety of sites. My family life, my involvement with grassroots community movements, and my intellectual work are informed in concrete ways by the politics of feminist analysis. By extension, the politics that informs my everyday life infuses my relations with students, generates the readings for the course, and suggests my classroom teaching style and practice. Yet my frustrations as a feminist teacher arise significantly from the extent to which critical thinking on transformative pedagogical practices fails to address the specifics of women's education as simultaneously a site of desire and threat.

Based on my own experiences, I know that a feminist perspective could offer understandings students might develop and bring to bear on their own experiences (Lather, 1988). Yet, I also realize that attending to feminist politics and cultural critique in the classroom requires difficult emotional work from them and from me. I know that new understandings are often experienced painfully, and that lives are transformed.

All of this has happened in Foundations 490. Yet, the forms through which such transformations have taken place are not those I anticipated—or perhaps hoped for. As a teacher and a feminist, I share the hope for the promise of education as a political project: that through the offer of a theoretical framework—analysis and critique—students would eagerly join in my enthusiasm to work for social change in their personal and public lives. Clearly there are times when women immediately embrace the intentions of feminist teaching because it helps them make a different sense of their experiences. But just as often, students struggle with these new understandings as they explore the space between the public, theoretical agenda of the course and the privacy of their everyday lives, where complex gender negotiations often take their most salient form.

In the academy, women find themselves inside institutions whose practices and intentions are historically designed to keep them outside its concrete and theoretical frames. For students, negotiating masculine content and context often means that they have to absorb as well as struggle to survive the violations of their subordination. My students often find more simple and therefore more powerful words through which to express my meaning. The legacy of the violations women experience in the academy are apparent in the following conversations:

> —I don't speak in class anymore. All this professor ever talked about was men, what they do, what they say, always just what's important to men. He, he, he is all I ever heard in class. He wasn't speaking my language. And whenever I tried to speak about what was important to me, whenever I tried to ask questions about how women fit into his scheme all I got was a negative response. I always felt I was speaking from inside brackets, like walls I couldn't be heard past. I got tired of not being heard so I stopped speaking altogether.

> —I often tried to bring up examples of famous women in class because I thought it was important that people should acknowledge that women had done some things too. But no one ever knew who I was talking about. There was this assumption that if someone was a woman she couldn't possibly have done anything famous. The most important thing that happened to me in high school was that one of my history teachers had a picture of Agnes Mcphail pinned above the blackboard in the classroom. We never talked about it directly but for me that became a symbol of a woman. Sometimes I got really disgusted in some of my classes, but I would think of that picture in that history class and that helped me to feel less alienated.

> —In history we never talked about what women did; in geography it was always what was important to men. The same in our English class, we hardly ever studied women authors. I won't even talk about math and science. I always felt that I didn't belong. Sometimes the boys would make jokes about girls doing science experiments. They always thought they were going to do it better, and it made me really nervous. Sometimes I didn't even try to do an experiment because I knew they would laugh if I got it wrong. Now I just

*deaden* myself against it, so I don't hear it anymore. But I feel really alienated. My experience now is one of total silence. Sometimes I even wish I didn't know what I know.

For me, as a feminist teacher, such statements are not only painful but revealing. The remarks suggest that the politics of my teaching should focus not on teaching women what we already know, but on finding ways of helping all of us articulate the knowledge we gain from our experience.

As a beginning point I agree with the claim of Giroux and Simon (1988):

> we are not concerned with simply motivating students to learn, but rather *establishing the conditions of learning* that enable them to locate themselves in history and to interrogate the adequacy of that location as both a pedagogical and political question. (p. 3, emphasis added)

Yet a feminist pedagogy cannot stop here. For women, the cultural, political, and ultimately historical discourse of the everyday, the present, and the immediate are conditions of learning marked by the varied forms of patriarchic violence (Brookes, 1992; Belenky, Clinchy, Goldberger, and Tarule, 1986; McMahon, 1986). Pedagogy, even radical pedagogy, does not easily translate into an education that includes women if we do not address the threat to women's survival and livelihood that a critique of patriarchy in its varied manifestations confronts.

When students engage a feminist analysis, the dynamics of the classroom present the most challenging aspects of feminist teaching. In what follows I explore the psychological, social, and sexual aspects of this context.

## PSYCHOLOGICAL DYNAMICS
## IN THE FEMINIST CLASSROOM

For women, tension in the feminist classroom is often organized around our historically produced nurturing capacity as a feature of our psychologically internalized role as caretakers. The following example is a case in point. Recently, when referring to a set of class readings dealing with peace education, I spoke about the connections between patriarchy, violence, and political economy. As I finished, one of the first students to speak was a young woman. She said, "As you were speaking I was wondering and worrying about how the men in the room were feeling. What you said made sense to me, but I felt uncomfortable about how the men took it." A couple of other women nodded their agreement. Such a protective posture on the part of women on behalf of men is a common drama played out in many classrooms.

Writing about her experience of courses in her sociology program a senior student observed the following:

> I began to compare those two theory courses and their readings to a course I was enrolled in at that point; a class entitled the "Sociology of Education," . . . [one] . . . that was clearly being taught from a feminist perspective. I commented on the reader friendliness of the books and articles written from a feminist perspective. When I read these I found them so much easier to understand because I could place myself into the article. When women write we are not only sharing our experiences with other women, we are also uniting together in support with other women to acknowledge that our experiences are not idiosyncratic, but rather the result of a web of social practices that marginalize us.
>
> I will use one of the readings from that particular course to clearly illustrate some of these thoughts. In her article "Taking Women Students Seriously" Adrienne Rich states: "Look at a classroom: look at the many kinds of women's faces, postures, expressions. Listen to the women's voices. Listen to the silences, the unasked questions, the blanks. Listen to the small, soft voices, often courageously trying to speak up, voices of women taught early that tones of confidence, challenge, anger, or assertiveness, are strident and unfeminine" (Rich, 1978, p. 243). I am one of those women who sits in silence because I am too afraid to say what is on my mind. I am one of those women whose voice quivers when I finally get up the courage to speak in class. I am one of those women whose postures and expressions distinctly show my confusion, frustration, and disinterestedness. I am one of those women who has been taught that "if you don't have anything interesting and worthwhile to say, don't say anything at all." I am one of those women who has been brought up under the prescription that it is much easier and more feminine to sit in silence than to challenge a point with confidence, anger, and assertiveness. I am one of those women about whom Adrienne Rich is speaking.
>
> It was exciting for me to actually understand and enjoy something I was required by one of my professors to read. And it felt even better to have both the courage and opportunity to say something about it in class. However, my excitement was soon stifled by an ironic situation that followed during our discussion of this article. One of the three men in the class announced to the rest of us that he did not fully understand the article. My first reaction was one of shock. "How could he not understand it?" The article was so clear to me and to most of the other women in the class.
>
> I am almost embarrassed to admit that my second reaction was one of sympathy. I felt sorry for him not only because he did not understand the article, but also because he was alone in a room full of women. He was a man in a classroom surrounded almost entirely by women, being taught by a female professor from a feminist perspective, and reading books and articles written by women.
>
> The alienation he must have been experiencing is a feeling that overtakes

my life every time I sit in a classroom surrounded by male classmates, every time I am lectured to by a male professor on topics of interest only to him, and every time I read a book or article written by a man. However, he still had enough courage to put up his hand and admit his confusion; something I could never do when the situation is reversed. (Schilling, 1992, pp. 36–37)

Similar responses to feminist critique are not specific to mixed-gender classrooms. The absence of men in the classroom does not significantly diminish the psychological investment women are required to make in the emotional well-being of men— an investment that goes well beyond the classroom into the private spaces of women's lives, and one which cannot easily be left at the classroom door.

The response women bring to feminist politics/analyses arises from women's social/political location within patriarchic forms, which requires that men be the focus of women's attentions. Examples range from general claims that men are also isolated and contained by patriarchy in what is required of them by the terms of masculinity to more specific references to personal family relations aimed at exempting intimate male relations from the general population of men. The sharing of household duties is often used as an example, although the articulation of the details of this shared housework is often vague. Young women growing up in physically violent and sexually violating homes know a more brutal side of the caretaking imperative (McDonald, personal communication, 1991).

Whether or not men are physically present in the classroom, women carry the parameters of patriarchic meaning making as a frame from within which we struggle to articulate our own interests. How women live this experience is not specific to mixed-gender classrooms. It is my observation that while the practice of a woman-as-caretaker ideology is more obvious in the presence of men, as long as women believe their interests to be served by maintaining existing relations of unequal power and privilege, this ideology holds sway whether or not men are present.

This formulation is not intended to subsume the experiences of all women and men under seamless, hegemonic constructs articulated through dominant expressions of femininity/masculinity. I use Alison Jaggar's (1983) formulation of Gramsci's notion of hegemony as a concept:

> designed to explain how a dominant class maintains control by projecting its own particular way of seeing social reality so successfully that its view is accepted as common sense and as part of the natural order by those who in fact are subordinated to it. (p. 151)

In this respect hegemony is accomplished through an ongoing struggle over meaning not only against, but for the maintenance of, power. Lesbians and gay men experience the social constructs of femininity/masculinity differently than women and men whose emotional and psychic investment is in heterosexual relationships. However, especially in professional schools, where students' aspirations for future employment often govern their willingness to challenge the status quo, pressures to conform to the dominant social text are shared by lesbians and heterosexual women alike (Khayatt, 1992). Because lesbians and gay men often remain voiceless within classroom dynamics, the relations between the women and men in the classroom remains a site that supports only practices that construct women's social acceptability as caretakers of men within the ideology of heterosexuality.

In the mixed-gender classroom much of the caretaking takes the form of hard-to-describe body language displayed as a barely perceptible "moving toward"; a not-quite-visible extending of the hand; a protective stance accomplished through eye contact. However, as the young woman's question of concern has shown, just as often it is explicitly articulated. In the feminist classroom such caretaking responses on the part of women toward men are ones that, as feminist teachers, we easily recognize and anticipate. We know we must choose words carefully and negotiate our analyses with the women students in ways that will not turn them away from the knowledge they carry in their experiences.

Following the young woman's comments, many of the men seemed to feel that what she said vindicated their feelings of discomfort with the way in which I was formulating the issues. Some of the men expressed this through verbal support of the woman's concern over their emotional well-being. They showed a strong inclination to redirect the discussion toward notions of world violence as a *human* and not a gendered problem. By doing so, the men attempted to reappropriate a speaking space for themselves, one they saw to be threatened by my analysis. Even more troublesome for me was the pleasure some of the men seemed to take in encouraging women to take up caretaking on their behalf, and in how the women seemed to be brought up against one another in the debate that followed. Rather than engaging an investigation of the substance of social forms that generate particular practices—in this case the dynamics and political economy of world violence—the question of whether or not feminist critique constitutes a confrontational stance by women against men was the substance of the debate between the women and the men and among the women. Some of the men offered verbal support for women who agreed with them and rebuttal of those who did not. However, there were more subtle forms of pleasure-taking as well. These are difficult to describe. We do not have language that can adequately express the social meaning of the practice of relaxing back into one's chair, with a barely-there smile on one's face while eyes are fixed on the object of negation. One of the reasons feminist films are a source of exceptionally powerful critique is because they can display how violation works at the level of the nonverbal. Yet such practices are unmistakable in their intent. The nonverbal is a social language that women—and all culturally marginal groups—have learned to read well and that does its sad work on women's emotions.

That such a dynamic should develop among the students was not a surprise. I know that, within the terms of patriarchy, women have had no choice but to care about the feelings of men. Women know that, historically, not caring has cost us our lives: intellectually, emotionally, socially, psychologically, and physically. I see this played out over and over again in my classes, and in every case it makes women recoil from saying what they really want to say and simultaneously leaves men reassured about their right to speak on behalf of us all.

For me, this dynamic presented a pedagogical dilemma. How could I question the particularities of our present social organization, which requires women to work as caretakers of men not only in economic/material relations, but in emotional/psychological ones as well? Furthermore, how was I to do this in ways that did not reproduce the women's strong inclination to protect the men for what was *felt* to be an indictment of men in general and the men in the classroom in particular? Specifically, how could I help them focus on social organizational practices, rather than on the men sitting next to them in the classroom?

I asked them to think of instances when we might expect men to reciprocate for women the kind of caretaking practices and ego support that women are expected to extend on behalf of men. Most specifically, I asked the women if they had ever been in the company of a male friend/partner/family member/stranger who, upon seeing our discomfort at the common public display of misogyny in such examples as billboards, had ever offered support for how uncomfortable and violated such displays must make us feel. By asking students to focus on the personal, I felt that it might be possible to relocate the women and men in a social configuration that did not take a gendered hierarchy and its attendant practices for granted. Not only the women, but the men as well, admitted that they had never had such an experience. More to the point, there was general agreement that the possibility had never even occurred to them.

Through our discussion, it became clear that as a collective social practice, for men, attentiveness to someone other than one's self is largely a matter of choice, whereas for women, it has been a socially and historically mandated condition of our acceptability as women. In a situation of inequality, acts of oppression and violation are always possible for those in power. This makes non-violation an act of choice and therefore an act of charity. Those who claim exemption from their position of power without working to alter the terms of social inequality—economic, political, and social relations—reproduce inequality as much as those who embrace their privilege unproblematically. This understanding provided, for some of the students in the class, a moment of critical reflection and transformation. It also offered a framework within which to envision a set of social relations not based fundamentally on inequality. For men such transformation often appears as a willingness to listen. Less eager to talk, they sometimes acknowledge that they can see themselves on the privileged side of the gender divide and admit that they had not previously given it a lot of thought. These acknowledgments are often fairly brief and to the point: "I had never thought of it that way" is a common response.

I want to note that male students do not escape the tensions created by a course agenda organized around our attempts at understanding the issues of gender as a fundamental social category and the pedagogical significance of this reality. As is so well demonstrated by Judith Williamson (1981/1982), women and men experience these tensions quite differently. In presenting the weekly readings, my agenda in the class was to provide the theoretical frame within which students could locate their experiences. However, located as they are on the advantaged side of the gender divide, male students often cannot name their own positions of privilege as part of the equation of gender inequality. They perceive their experiences to be irrelevant to the experiences of the women, often viewing the content of the course as irrelevant to their own lives. They far more often take recourse in notions of "society" or some disembodied "they" as a way of explaining the "personal difficulties" the women name as their experiences. While many male students concede the issues and problems of women's subordination about which "something needs to be done" (thoughts about who and how are vague and hypothetical), they often do not see that their own privilege is part of this dynamic. They continue to resist the notion that being "gendered" is not just a condition of women but that of men as well and that to talk about women's subordination in a sexist culture is simultaneously to talk about male privilege. Because they do not experience their cultural context apart from themselves it often escapes their critical analysis—often escapes their attention altogether. For this reason male students often have significant difficulty with the feminist theoretical concepts.

Sometimes they attempt to cope with their difficulties by seeking to be exempted from fulfilling the course requirements of a final paper which requires them to take up the theoretical concepts we had used during the term. They say things like: "I am not very good with words"; "I don't understand the words and when I get to the end of the article I don't know what they've said"; or even more pointedly "these are not very good authors because the language they are using doesn't make sense to me, it's like they're not speaking English."

It is interesting that the language with which male students often articulate their anxiety with feminist material echoes almost exactly the language women students often use to make known their struggles with the vast majority of theoretical material which subsumes women's specificity under the rubric of gender neutrality. The content of feminist course material directly challenges both the naturalness of the dominant interests and the comfortable indignation which dominant groups can choose, precisely because they are privileged, to bring to an examination of their own privilege. Thus feminist material often leaves male students, as Susan Aiken and her colleagues found in the context of an in-service feminist curriculum integration project, "forced to think about themselves (as individuals) in disquieting ways" (Aiken et al, 1988, p. 144).

Yet as Aiken, Anderson, Dinnerstein, Lensink, and MacCorquodale (1988) go on to demonstrate, for men in a feminist classroom, the requirement that they think about themselves in these ways is still an option rather than a requirement. This is a possibility that can never be available for women; our notions of ourselves and how we have viewed our possibilities are dislodged at their very root when we recognize the constraints on our possibilities as we have lived them.

In this sense then, Judith Williamson (1981/82) is right to focus on the contradictions which dominant discourse constructs between ideology and interest. However, given that our culture is not free of gender inequalities and differential power relations, I don't think her analysis goes far enough in demonstrating how this is a different experience for women than for men. While in general I agree with Williamson that "people don't learn in the abstract, nor through moral purpose—like when some boys try to be feminist" (p. 85) I am also deeply troubled by the implication that we can expect support from men regarding issues of justice, freedom, and possibility only when it serves their material interests to do so. I don't think that merely bringing male students to a point of "trauma" by demonstrating that "everything they took for granted is in fact relative, that everything they thought was natural is constructed, that everything they *are* can be deconstructed" (p. 85) is sufficient ground for them to change their privileged practices without requiring a moral commitment to bringing about a just and free community. Terry Eagleton (1991) is suggestive:

> One can understand well enough how human beings may struggle and murder for good material reasons—reasons connected, for instance, with their physical survival. It is much harder to grasp how they may come to do so in the name of something as apparently abstract as ideas. Yet, ideas are what men and women live by, and will occasionally die for. (p. xiii)

I offer the following example in order to demonstrate this point. Recently in an undergraduate sociology course, during a discussion of the experiences of women in math and science, several of the women students spoke—in some cases by their own account for the first time ever—of the brutalizations they had experienced in high school math and science classes. The women's words trembled into our collective space where they hung seeking both confirmation and relief. While confirmation was readily available as more and more women related similar experiences, the relief they sought was vastly more elusive caught in the mire of lost opportunities and dreams of what might have been. The male students sat transfixed, their silence deepening into the wordless realization that here they had nothing to say. Finally, as the discussion drew to a close, one of the men spoke. His simple words signalled not the trauma of contradictory experience, but the potential basis of a moral commitment to social change. He said: "I have never had such experiences. I am training to be a high school math teacher and I hope I will remember what I heard here today." While as a pedagogical possibility such moments are rare, often offset by resistances and denials, they are clearly not impossible.

These tensions pose the most significant difficulties in mixed-gender classrooms. They also provide the most salient opportunities for the creation of those shared meanings between women and men necessary to achieve the fundamental social changes for which we are looking. Listening may be the most revolutionary project men can begin to undertake.

Whether or not men carry their new understanding into their public and private lives outside the classroom is unclear. If they do, they have not shared it with me. For women, transformation often means a more active process. At times, younger women have asked to bring male friends to the class with them. More frequently, students have reported that they have asked their male friends or partners to read some of the course material (students regularly report their mothers' interest in the course readings). And some women have reported major changes in their family life, either in terms of renegotiated practices—mostly pertaining to household responsibilities—or in a decision to end a relationship. I do not want to suggest that every student in every class experiences these transformations. Progress is slow and often tentative as students struggle with the implications of their new understandings.

By shifting our focus from the topic of discussion and refocusing on the dynamics in the classroom at that moment, we made it possible to ask what cultural/political forms might articulate caretaking as a reciprocal process between women and men. This teaching strategy is central to my pedagogical agenda: identifying the moment when students might be most receptive to uncovering how they are invested in their own meaning making practice.

## SOCIAL DYNAMICS IN THE FEMINIST CLASSROOM

For many students, the social context of the feminist classroom is another sphere of tension. For the women students, the negotiation of the content and processes of feminist curricula and teaching is complicated by the presence of men on whose legitimation depends their sense of social acceptability and self-worth. It is for this reason that the processes and outcomes of consciousness-raising are problematic and threatening to those who hold social/economic power. There is a long history to the fear of women coming together and, in that space, sharing the personal stories that become the metaphorical bases for generating theories of women's subordination (Daly, 1978). The dominant forms of discourse are aimed hegemonically at preventing women from engaging in discussions that lead toward consciousness-raising; the threat of social sanctions defuse the vitality of storytelling. Telling our stories of violation and subordination in the presence of those whose advantages are highlighted and challenged by such sharing, or doing so in the presence of those who hold the discursive power to subvert the act of consciousness-raising as a feminist method, is for many women a contradictory outcome of their experiences in the feminist classroom.

I believe the following exchange demonstrates this point well. Recently, a student was making a class presentation on the topic of violence against women. A few minutes after she began her presentation, a frustrated young man demanded to know why we had to talk about women and men all the time, and why the presenter did not offer "the other side of the story." This example confirms other experiences indicating that students, particularly those who benefit from the present social arrangements, often find it difficult to engage in the self-reflection required to question the unequal and violent social relations in which we ourselves are social actors.

As a feature of classroom dynamics, the unpacking and uncovering of deeply submerged social practices of domination/entitlement experienced by the "Other" as subordination/oppression, can itself become another source for experiences of oppression. Alternately such experiences of oppression can foster a powerful desire for change, or they can become a deeply destructive experience ultimately resulting in reactionary responses from men *as well as* from women.

For women, as for other subordinate groups, it is the fact of "knowing" that is seen to be an act of insubordination. Exposing that knowledge, speaking it in a public space, claiming language with which to articulate our knowledge, and refusing to believe that the dominant discourse speaks for all—even as it speaks on behalf of patriarchic interests—is used as the justification for continued violation.

In part, patriarchy disempowers women by marginalizing our experiences of violation in an ongoing discourse that legitimates only those ways of making sense and the telling of only those kinds of stories that do not make men "look bad" (MacKinnon, 1987, p. 154). The use of language, for example, which exchanges "wife-beating" with "family violence" as a way to redirect our focus away from masculine practices is a case in point.

One way male students sometimes wish to displace the sense women make of our experience is to refocus the discussion in directions that are less disquieting for them. Power, as an embodied practice in relations of inequality, means being entitled to choose between a variety of meanings and further being entitled to decide when to hear and when not to hear the meanings articulated by another. In *The Politics of Reality*, Marilyn Frye (1983) claims that:

> it is an aspect of race (gender, social class) privilege to have a choice—
> a choice between the options of hearing and not hearing. That is part of
> what being white (male, economically advantaged) gets you. (p. 111)

Those who have access to such meaning making also have the prerogative to "strategically" forget crucial moments of oppression and violation in the lives of the powerless. Thereby they render those moments insignificant in the further construction and articulation of how we understand our history and therefore our present situation and future possibilities. This is a kind of forgetting that is never possible for the powerless to achieve precisely because the very experience of powerlessness repositions them such that they view social, political, and economic relations from a different vantage point.

History is filled with such repositionings and attempted forgettings. The history of black Americans, of visible minorities, of indigenous peoples in most countries, of the Jewish people worldwide, and of women in every culture show on a grand scale what it means to have or not to have the luxury of "forgetting" crucial moments of violation by those in power. Nor is this amnesia confined to large cultural groups and major historical events. The personal, daily lives of individuals are simultaneously and equally marked by the naming of experience that attempts to define out of existence the experiences of the powerless. To "forget" is the final and powerful negation of the experience of the oppressed by the oppressor.

The powerless, however, precisely because their experience does not accommodate "forgetting," are able to see the inadequacy of the naming from their position of disentitlement. This ability comes from living these contradictions in a way that those in the center, whose experiences and naming of those experiences coincide, can never live them. Hence for the powerless the naming is never complete and uncontested, but always in the process of negotiation; always tempered by contestation.

In the instance mentioned above, I understood the young man's demand—the tone of his voice left no doubt that it was a demand—to tell the other side of the story, to be an attempt to redirect the discussion away from his own social identity as a male who, whether he acknowledges it or not, benefits from the culturally, legally, and politically encoded social relations of patriarchy (MacKinnon, 1987). Yet men can no more deny the embodiment of their masculine privilege than any of us can deny the embodiment of our entitlement if we are white, economically advantaged, heterosexual, able-bodied, and carrying the valued assets of the privilege of Euro-American culture. As is suggested by Biddy Martin and Chandra Mohanty (1986):

> the claim to a lack of identity or positionality is itself based on privilege, on a refusal to accept responsibility for one's implication in actual historical or social relations, on a denial that positionalities exist or that they matter, the denial of one's own personal history and the claim to a total separation from it. (p. 208)

Furthermore, to the extent that sexism, racism, and social class inequalities represent social systems within which we either appropriate or struggle against particular personal relations, those who embody positions of privilege are often not attracted to self-reflective practices that might require them to acknowledge their self-serving interests.

On this occasion, I judged that, by providing for the possibility of self-reflexive critique, I might avert the tendency of such debates to degenerate into expressions of guilt and victimization which would destroy the creative potential of a feminist political discourse that speaks not only to women but to men as well. I also felt that how I presented my response was crucial. Whatever my response was, it had to be possible for women to see it as a model for how they might also take up similar challenges to their own meaning making in ways other than to demand their right to do so—precisely the point of debate. My challenge was to create the possibility for students to be self-reflexive.

The young man's demand for the "other side" of the story about men's violence against women created the space I was looking for. In classrooms, as in other social/political spaces, women and men come together unequally. In such a context, a pedagogical approach that fails to acknowledge how such inequality silences serves to reinforce the powerlessness of the powerless. I knew from my own experience that, under such circumstances, asking women to "speak up" and intervene on their own behalf would have reproduced exactly that marginalization that the young man's demand was intended to create. Clearly, I needed to employ another strategy.

The power of teaching as dramatic performance cannot be discounted on this particular occasion. Following the question, I allowed a few moments of silence. In these few moments, as the question and the dynamics of the situation settled into our consciousness, the social history of the world was relived in the bodies of the women and men around the table. What is the "other side of the story" about violence against women!? What could the women say? In large part, because the schooling dynamic is premised on a particular relationship between the asking of questions and the providing of answers, students' traditional classroom experiences supported the young man in asking his question (Britzman, 1991). Students learn early in their schooling experience: that propositions put forward in the form of a question can/ should be answered within the frames of the question as asked; that teachers know the answers to questions beforehand; and that students are asked questions to which answers can be supplied. The conceptual meaningfulness of questions is assumed and, therefore, does not enter into this agenda. Consequently, as a social dynamic, it is assumed that one might struggle with an answer to a question because of individual inadequacy, not because the question does not make sense.

Faced with the demand to articulate their reality *in terms not of their own making*, the women visibly shrank into their chairs; their breathing became invisible (Rockhill, 1987b). In contrast, whether I imagined it or not, it seemed to me that the men sat more upright and "leaned into" the response that began to formulate in my head. It seemed clear to me that the young man's objections to the woman's presentation constructed women as objects of practices which were experienced by him as unproblematic; the threat of physical violence is not one which most men experience on a daily basis. By objectifying women through his question, he reinforced his privilege to do so and male privilege more generally. I needed to find a way of repositioning us—women and men—in such a way that the young man had no options but to face his question *and* his own social location as both privileged and problematic.

The stage was set for the dramatic performance. Reassuring the young man that indeed he was right, that "other sides" of issues need to be considered whenever possible, I wondered if *he* would perhaps be the one who could tell us about the "other side" of violence against women. My memory of this moment again focuses on the breath— the men's as it escaped their bodies and the women's as it replenished theirs.

Turning the question away from the women in the class created the self-reflexive space that I believed could truly challenge the men in the class to take up not women's subordination but their own positions of privilege. Given the social realities of violence against women, the male student was no more able to answer his own question than it might have been possible for a woman to do so. At the same time, it remained for him to tell us why he couldn't answer his own question. He found himself speechless. This time, the silence that followed reversed the order of privilege to name the social realities we live. The young man's failure to find a salient way of taking up the issue he had raised made it possible for the young woman to continue with her presentation without a challenge of her fundamental right to do so.

The incident ended at this point, and the class presentation proceeded. Reflecting on my own practice in this instance, I cannot deny that my politics embraced and supported the struggle for women's autonomy and self-determination. Working with women to create the space for our voice is fundamental to this politics. Whether the young man experienced transformation or was simply intimidated into silence was something that required sorting out. I was willing to let him undertake the hard work of doing so for himself. If I had silenced him, I could only hope that perhaps the experience would provide him with a deeper understanding of an experience women encounter every day.

For many women the feminist classroom becomes a form of social critique immediately applicable to their own lives. As the relations in a mixed-gender classroom begin to change very quickly, work/career options, family relations/forms, and forms of self-representation also come into question. Sometimes the results are difficult and painful; other times they embody displays of joy and liberation. That the incident was experienced by the women in ways that signalled a moment of possibility for them is captured by the reaction of one young woman. After the long three-hour class, she came over to where I was distractedly picking up my papers and lightened the load of my exhaustion with the announcement that she wanted to be a sociologist and a feminist and would I tell her "how to become it." Both her naivete and mine embarrassed us into shared laughter; but such fleeting moments of embrace are sometimes all we have, it seems to me, to collect ourselves and move on. Such experiences reveal the feminist classroom as profoundly relevant to women's lives.

## SEXUAL DYNAMICS IN THE FEMINIST CLASSROOM

Finally, the sexual dynamics of mixed-gender classrooms are complex and often contradictory. Particularly for younger women, at times still caught in the glare of sexual exploration and identification, the feminist classroom can feel threatening. The following example is a case in point.

Recently, during the introductory lecture I use as a way of framing the seminar session, I was addressing the educational concerns about the low number of women in mathematics and science programs. On this occasion, trying to concretize the issues for the students, I asked them to indicate, by a show of hands, which of them were preparing to be math and science teachers. A number of students raised their hands. As might be expected, many of those who raised their hands were men. However, a number of women also raised their hands. A "guffawed" and embarrassed laughter rose from the back corner of the room after a young man whispered a comment to a young woman who had raise her hand.

I do not generally make use of, or support, embarrassment as a pedagogical strategy. In this instance, however, while I had not heard the comment I felt certain that I knew what the laughter was about and wanted to capture the moment as a concrete example of exactly the issues I was raising. I requested that the young man tell us what he had said. He resisted; I insisted. The use of institutional power, I believe, should not always be viewed as counterproductive to our politics. Feminism is a politics that is both historical and contingent on existing social relations. I had no problem justifying the use of my institutional power to create the possibility for privilege to face itself and own its violation publicly. Using power to subjugate is quite different from using power to liberate. The young man complied. He told us that he had whispered to the young women that perhaps she had had a sex change.

The assumed prerogative to pass such commentary on women's choices of career and life possibilities, not to mention sexuality, is not, of course new to any of us. However, in the feminist classroom, such commentary and attendant laughter become overtly political issues that can be taken up as instances of gender politics. I used the incident as an example of the kind of academic environment created for women when such interactions are not treated as problematic. In doing so, I was aware that both the women and the men experienced various degrees of discomfort. Many of the men and some of the women insisted that I was making too much of an innocent joke, while many of the women and none of the men, as far as I could tell, sat quietly with faces flushed. In thinking about how I approach my teaching, I can recall the salient details of this example to understand how gender politics can be transformed into sexual dynamics in the classroom. Not only gender, but sexuality, is a deeply present organizing principle in the classroom, and one which enters into the dynamics of how we come together as women and men in pursuit of shared meanings.

The production of shared meanings is one of the ways we experience deeply felt moments of psycho-sexual pleasure, whether across or within gender. Yet, in a patriarchic culture, women and men can find the articulation of shared meanings profoundly elusive, and can feel the desire for pleasure to be in conflict with mutual understandings.

While women have always found support in separate women's communities, education cells, political movements, work, and so on, these sites of solidarity have usually existed outside of the dominant male culture—a culture of which, we cannot forget, women are also an integral part. Social, political, and economic relations are articulated through the personal and collective experiences we have of the world. Feminist politics insist on using these experiences as the lens through which to look at the barely perceptible, yet tenacious, threads that hold social forms and forces in place. For women who refuse subordination, who refuse to pretend that we don't know, standing against these social forces has not only economic and political consequences but psycho-sexual ones as well. bell hooks (1989) comments:

> Sexism is unique. It is unlike other forms of domination—racism or classism—where the exploited and oppressed do not live in large numbers intimately with their oppressors or develop their primary love relationships (familial and/or economic) with the individuals who oppress and dominate or share in the privileges attained by domination. . . . [For women] the context of these intimate relationships is also the site of domination and oppression. (p. 130)

This dynamic is seldom, if ever, talked about in the feminist classroom, and, yet, it explains the conflicting emotional and analytic responses women have to the content of these courses.

Exploring the sexual parameters of the conditions under which women are required to undertake their intellectual work is crucial. Finding examples is not hard; relating them is. It is with difficulty that I cite specific examples, and then only briefly, because of my own complex emotions associated with writing these words and having them stand starkly, darkly on the page to be read and reread knowing that stories of violation violate at each retelling. In sharing these stories with me, students do not tell them lightly; nor do I receive them easily; they are often related in the privacy and safety of my office. One woman's books disappeared (an event reminiscent of the one related in Janice Radway's *Reading the Romance*, (1984)); another, alerted by the words, "maybe you should be reading this instead" had a copy of a pornographic magazine flung at her as she sat reading her course material; and yet another was told, as a "joke" at a social gathering, that to "celebrate" the completion of the course she would be "rewarded" by being "raped" so she could "get it out of her system" and return to her "old self." The monitoring and banning of what women read is shown in these examples to be closely associated with demands for women to conform to a particular version of male-defined sexuality. While the above may represent especially harsh examples, the antagonistic relationship drawn between women's desire for knowledge and our embodiment as sexually desirable human beings is an issue that lies always just below the surface in the classroom.

For many women, a feminist worldview is deeply incorporated at the level of everyday practice. Yet, we need to be aware that by requiring women to challenge masculine constructs—as I did in the classroom example cited above—we also require them to break with the dominant phallocentric culture. While as feminist teachers we might believe that such a break may offer the only possibilities for the resolution of this conflict, we must be aware that for many women the concrete possibility of doing so is difficult to contemplate. As Claire Duchen, quoted in Rowbotham (1989) suggests, "the tailoring of desire to the logic of politics is not always possible or acceptable" (p. 85).

Feminist critique of phallocentric culture is at once fundamentally necessary for and profoundly disruptive of the possibilities for shared meaning across gender, leaving women vulnerable to what Sheila Radford-Hill (1986) has analyzed as the potential "betrayal" and "psychosexual rejection" of women by men (pp. 168-169), attended by more or less severe economic and political consequences. None of this dynamic escapes women's awareness. "The personal is political" is not just a useful organizing concept, it is also a set of material enactments that display and reflect back how the political is personal.

As Susan Griffin (1981) suggests, a woman knows that "over and over again culture tells her that men abandon women who speak too loudly, or who are too *present*" (p. 211). Coupled with the strong cultural message that "her survival in the world depends on her being able to find a man to marry" (p. 211), many young women in the feminist classroom find themselves caught in the double bind of needing to speak and to remain silent at the same time in order to guarantee some measure of intellectual and emotional survival. While the salience of this politics is more immediately obvious in the case of heterosexual women, woman-identified (Rich, 1986 b, p. 57) women who do not comply, at least minimally, with acceptable forms of sexual self-presentation do not escape the consequences of marginalization and exclusion. For all women in professional schools specifically, compliance with particular displays of femininity can mean the difference between having or not having a job (Britzman, 1991; Khayatt, 1992).

As women and men struggle over establishing and articulating shared meanings, we need to notice the reality that, for many women, such struggles often take place in the context of deeply felt commitments reverberating with emotional psycho-sexual chords and attended by the material conditions of unequal power. While perhaps these relations are lived most deeply not in the classroom itself, but in those private spaces lived out between women and men beyond the classroom, for women, course content can be instrumental in raising questions about these relations.

The following is an example of how one woman took up these struggles in her private life. After a particular encounter in the classroom regarding the issue of voice/discourse, discussed in the context of who has the right to name whether or not a joke is funny, she wrote me the following note in her weekly critical reflective writing:

> The articles at this point in the course . . . have plunged me into the next phase of my feminist awareness, which is characterized by anger and a pervading sense of injustice. . . . The "feminist" anger that I feel is self-perpetuating. I get angry at the discrimination and stereotyping I run up against so I blame the patriarchal society I live in, in particular, and men in general. Then I think about women who feel that feminism is unnecessary or obsolete and I get angry at that subset of women. Then I think about the good guys like Mike and Cam and I get angry because the patriarchal society biases the way I think about these men, simply because they're members of a particular gender (sex class?). Then I think about men who stereotype and discriminate against women and criticize us for being "overly sensitive" when we get uptight or even just point out or suggest humanistic egalitarian changes that are good and smart and I get REALLY angry because I realize that they're all a bunch of (expletives deleted) [sic]. . . . One of the most difficult aspects of this anger is that I become frustrated and impatient with people who can't see the problems or don't see the urgent need for solu-

tions. (I am writing) a lot during this time because I often can't communicate orally with people who don't at least respect my feminist views. (quoted with permission)

hooks (1989) states that:

feminist works that focus on strategies women can use to speak to males about male domination and change are not readily available, if they exist at all. Yet women have a deep longing to share feminist consciousness with the men in their lives [the "good guys"], and together work at transforming their relationships. (p. 130)

She goes on to point out that:

concern for this basic struggle should motivate feminist thinkers to talk and write more about how we relate to men and how we change and transform relationships with men characterized by domination. (p. 130)

Yet despite their desire to genuinely share the meanings they have drawn from their experiences, for young women in the feminist classrooms, phallocentric myth-making often collides with the theoretical agenda of the course. Phallocentric myths are those beliefs that continue to marginalize women through the process of naturalizing politically created gender inequalities. The following are statements I hear often in response to concern over women's poor social and economic position: "Women are not in positions of decision and policy-making because they don't want to be"; "Everybody has equal opportunity to become school principal. Women choose not to be because they like teaching better"; "If abused and battered women don't leave their partners it is because they have deviant personalities, or because they like it"; "Women who are raped did something wrong"; "Boys are better at math, girls are better at reading, and that's just the way it is, it's natural"; "Women who do math are not really women"; "If women don't like (sexist) jokes, it's because they don't have a sense of humor"; "There are no women in history because they didn't do anything"; "Women like staying home with children"; "Men share equally in housework"; and so on. I have heard some version of all of these statements in the classroom. While the men might express a comfortable indignation at such beliefs, they don't often understand what practices are required of them to change how they live their lives. For example, one man recently told the class that he supports his wife's career by "baby-sitting" the children while she goes to work. It is precisely this imbalance of power that constructs the women's silence, suppressed behind embarrassed laughter.

The pedagogical implications of such gender relations in the feminist class-room must be taken seriously if we are to understand how and why women students might wish both to appropriate and yet resist feminist theoretical and political positions that aim to uncover the roots of our deeply misogynist culture and give legitimacy to women's desires and dreams of possibility. As feminist teachers we need to look closely at the psycho-sexual context within which we propose the feminist alternative and consider the substance of why women may genuinely wish to turn away from the possibilities feminism offers.

Women know through experience that the threat to our sexuality is a way of controlling our political activities. In her review of Spender (1982), Pierson (1983) points out that there is a long history to the process of displacing women's legitimate political and intellectual critique and struggles into distorted evaluations of women's sexuality as a form of social control hammered into place by the material conditions of women's lives. The meaning that patriarchy has assigned to the term "lesbian" has resulted in its use as a pejorative term to undermine the serious political work in which women as women have been engaged in resistance to a set of social relations marked by patriarchic domination. The misogyny of such a designation violates all women at all points of the heterosexual/lesbian continuum (Rich, 1986b). Clearly "the regulation of speaking and silence" (Walkerdine, 1985a) is not just achieved through concrete regulatory practices, but also through the emotional, psychic, and sexual sphere—articulated through the practices of patriarchic myth making—that combine in our hearts and heads to silence us from within. Given the terms of such social conditions, it would be a surprise, indeed, if women did not feel the constraints of contradictory choices and conflicting interests.

The power of patriarchic social controls on women's sexuality does not escape even (or perhaps especially) very young women. For example, within a recent three-week period, two separate groups of elementary and high school students were invited to participate in different events sponsored by the faculty where I teach. The first was a forum on women and education, attended by 150 students, at which the guest speaker, Dale Spender, presented an address entitled "Young Women in Education: What Happens to Girls in Classrooms." Three weeks later, a dramatic presentation by a feminist acting group, The Company of Sirens, presented an upbeat production called *The Working People's Picture Show* dealing with such issues as women in the work force, day care, unionism, and sexual harassment.

The question period that followed each event was telling. In each case the young women's concerns were well demonstrated by the almost identically phrased questions aimed at the program presenters, individuals who were seen as the embodiment of feminist critique: "Are you married and do you have children?" I don't believe this was a theoretical or a benign question. For many young women the concern about the compatibility of feminist politics with marriage and family is the concrete realization that making public what our feminist consciousness reveals about women's experiences of patriarchy can result in potential limits on desire. The extent to which women who display autonomy and independent personhood is seen as a threat to male power and therefore subjected to male violence was reaffirmed by the massacre at the Université de Montréal. Such events are not lost on young women.

My response to the sexual dynamics in the classroom is to create a context that offers "space" and "safety," particularly to women students. Men in the feminist classroom often state that the course readings and class discussion feel threatening and that they experience various degrees of discomfort. I would like to understand more about these feelings of threat and discomfort. What do they find discomforting? What is the basis of their dis-ease? What do they fear? I am concerned that all students—women and men—have access to the analyses we take up in the class. I am also concerned that all students feel equally validated in doing the hard work toward a transformed consciousness. However, this work is different for women than it is for men. Women need space and safety so that they are free to speak in order to better understand and act against the violations they experience in a social/cultural setting that subordinates them in hurtful and violent ways. The consciousness around which men need to do hard work is the pain of their complicity in benefitting from the rewards of this same culture. I support men in doing this hard work. Personally, I would like to see more of them try. Those who have are good and welcome allies.

The language of "space" and "safety" is not new to discussions of feminist teaching. However, I believe that it is not always clear what practices attend these abstractions. I believe, first, that women don't need to be taught what we already know: fundamentally, that women are exempted from a culture to which our productive and reproductive labor is essential. Nor do women need to be taught the language with which to speak what we know.

Rather, the challenge of feminist teaching is in finding ways to make speakable and legitimate the personal/political *investments* we all make in the meanings we ascribe to our historically contingent experiences. In this context, I address with students the contradictory reality of women's lives, wherein one's interests, at the level of practice, lie both with the dominant group and against it. Through such discussion emerges the deeply paradoxical nature of the conditions of the subordinate in a hierarchical culture marked by the inequalities of gender, class, race, and sexual desire. Approaching women's lives from this perspective means that practices previously understood by students to be a function of choice can be seen as the result of a need to secure some measure of emotional, intellectual, and quite often physical survival (Wolfe, 1986, p. 58).

Pedagogy that is grounded in simple notions of false consciousness and that articulates teaching as mediation or, worse, as a charitable act, does not support knowledge invested with the meanings students ascribe to their own experiences. This not only buries the complexity of human choices in an unproblematized notion of self-interest, but, further, can only offer validating and supplementary educational options without transforming the conditions under which we learn. By fusing women's emotional and concrete lives through feminist critique, it is possible to make problematic the conditions under which women learn, and perhaps to make a feminist political agenda viable in women's own lives wherein they can transcend the split between personal experience and social form.

## CONCLUSION

What are the possibilities of doing feminist politics/pedagogy in the classroom? In answering this question, I want to examine the potential for a feminist teaching that does more than address the concerns of the already initiated. For me, the urgency of this issue arises from my own teaching. On one hand, the often chilling stories women students share with me and each other in the context of classroom relations point to their clear understanding of the politics of gender subordination. Within the confines of traditional academic practices, the politics of personal experience are often seen to be irrelevant. In contrast, the feminist classroom can be a deeply emotional experience for many women, offering the opportunity to claim relevance for the lives they live as the source of legitimate knowledge.

On the other hand, I also hear the young women who speak to me in anger, who deride me for being the bearer of "bad news," and who want to believe that our oppression/subordination is something we create in our own heads. Given the context of violence within which students are being asked to embrace feminist politics, their concerns about their emotional, intellectual, and quite obviously, physical safety have to be recognized as crucial. For women, overt acts of violence, like the one that occurred at the Université de Montréal, are merely an extension of their daily experiences in the psychological/social/sexual spaces of the academy. Resistance to the emancipatory potential of a liberating politics indicates the extent of women's subordination. Thus, we cannot expect that students will readily appropriate a political stance that is truly counter-hegemonic, unless we also acknowledge the ways in which our feminist practice/politics *creates*, rather than ameliorates, a feeling of threat: the threat of abandonment; the threat of having to struggle within unequal power relations; the threat of psychological/social/sexual as well as economic and political marginality; the threat of retributive violence—each a threat lived in concrete embodied ways. Is it any wonder that many women desire to disassociate from "those" women whose critique of our social/cultural world seems to focus and condense male violence?

For me, the challenge of feminist teaching lies in the specifics of how I approach the classroom. By reflecting on my own teaching, I fuse content and practice, politicizing them both through feminist theory and living them both concretely rather than treating them abstractly. To elaborate: as I reflect on my teaching, it is clear from the detailing of the examples I experience in my own classrooms that feminist teaching practices cannot be separated from the content of the curriculum. Specific political moments arise exactly because of the content of the course. As is suggested by Gayle MacDonald:

> the process by which teaching occurs in a feminist classroom is one which is very different from technique/pedagogy used in other settings. (1989, p.147)

I want to extend this idea by suggesting that the difference MacDonald identifies in the feminist classroom is that, as students articulate their interests and investments through particular social practices, a dialectic develops between students and the curriculum in such a way that the classroom dynamics created by the topic of discussion reflect the social organization of gender inequality. Indeed, the irony is that feminist critique of social relations reproduces exactly the practices we are critiquing. When these practices are reproduced, so are the attendant violations, marginalizations, struggles, and transformations which again lend themselves to be revisited by a feminist critique.

An interesting case in point is the experience I have had on various occasions when I have presented some version of this argument at academic conferences. On each occasion, in responding to my presentation, some members of the audience tended to reproduce to some extent the practices that I take such great pains to critique in the text. The caretaking practices, the concern that men not feel unfairly marginalized or attacked, the willingness of men in the audience to speak unproblematically on behalf of women, and the dynamics of sexual marginalization have all played a part in the reception of my chapter-in-progress. My purpose here is not to suggest that every instance of critique of feminist social/cultural analysis is a display of phallocentric power or male privilege. Indeed, as feminist scholars we put our work forward in good faith and both invite and welcome articulate and substantive engagement of it (Ellsworth, 1989). My point is, rather, that responses to feminist critique often take forms that reproduce the gendered practices that I have described in this chapter.

The strategies I have employed in the classroom have been directed toward politicizing not only what we take up in the class as course content, but also the classroom dynamics that are generated by our topic and subsequent discussion. These practices included: shifting our focus from larger social issues to the dynamics in the classroom so that we might explore the relationship between the two; legitimating the meanings women bring to their experiences by turning challenges to these articulated meanings back on the questioner, thereby requiring the questioner to make different meanings sensible; disrupting the order of hierarchy regarding who can speak and on whose behalf; requiring that men in the class own their social location by exploring the parameters of their own privilege, rather than the limits on women of their oppression; providing opportunities for self-reflexive critique of unequal power relations; staying attentive to the political context of women's lives— those seemingly unconnected experiences made to seem livable by the tumble of daily life—in order to offer a vision of a future that women might embrace; attending to the ways in which women have been required historically to invest in particular and often contradictory practices in order to secure their own survival; and, finally, treating women's resistance to feminism as an active discourse of struggle derived from a complex set of meanings in which women's practices are invested.

The above suggestions are intended to be neither exhaustive nor prescriptive. Pedagogical moments arise in specific contexts: the social location of the teacher and students; the geographic and historical location of the institution in which they come together; the political climate within which they work; the personalities and personal profiles of the individuals in the classroom; the readings selected for the course; and the academic background of the students all come together in ways that create the specifics of the moment. It is not appropriate to think of what I have presented here as a "model" for feminist teaching. "Models" can only be restrictive and reductive because they cannot predict and thus cannot take into account the complexity of contingent and material realities. My intent, rather, has been to articulate how, at particular moments in my teaching, I made sense of those classroom dynamics that seemed to divide women and men across their inequalities in ways that reaffirmed women's subordination, and how making sense of those moments as politically rich allowed me to develop an interpretive framework for creating a counter-hegemonic teaching practice. My hope is that through such shared struggles in the classroom women might embrace for themselves the politics of autonomy and self-determination rather than reject it as a liability.

# 7 | AFTER THE WORDS

I . . . know that the foundations are fragile. I know that it doesn't take women nearly as long to learn that males are *not* superior, as it does to learn that they are. I know that thirty years of learning patriarchal values can be undermined in thirty seconds, and that the world never looks the same again. I know that women have been victims of an enormous hoax—and that it won't work twice. I know that women can be autonomous and that we are becoming so. I know that this can happen in schools. I do not think we should cease to be *outsiders* in the terms that Virginia Woolf used, but I think that we should become so strong and our concerns so central, that the term *outsider* is no longer appropriate.

—Spender,
*Invisible Women: The Schooling Scandal*

As the summer draws to a close so does the need to finish this book. There is for me, now, an urgency to complete these words that have been so much a part of my learning and teaching over the months and years of their formulation. Even more than this: these words have been a heavy load on top of children growing up, jobs begun, ended, and begun again, and households packed and unpacked. The resulting shifting and jostling of priorities and desires marked by the inevitability of experience has been made meaningful by insight and longing for the self.

Because I believe that we only ever end with beginnings, it is on these beginnings that I want to reflect as I come near to completion of this work.

On December 6, 1989, I was preparing for the last class of a graduate course I was teaching identified as Educ. 857: Seminar on Feminist Theories in Education. The class began in the early evening.

I like to teach evening courses because of the possibilities they afford for inter-action between part-time and full-time graduate students. I believe this to be important because despite the rhetoric of the need for the applicability of ideas to the concrete moments of our everyday lives—which most of my stu-dents live out in schools and other educational institutions—the academy is not always attentive to connecting what we think with what we do. It was my hope that this course could potentially afford such a possibility. And, in par-ticular, it was my belief that by teaching it in the evening I might create possibilities for dialogue between theory and practice—the necessary prereq-uisite to political action.

Educ. 857 is one of my favorite courses. The students who take the course bring with them a variety of backgrounds, diverse interests, and a wide range of prior knowledge of feminist theory. This often makes for energetic and engaged discussion. Because it also suggests possibilities for action in both the private and the professional lives of the members of the seminar, students also see it as a course that touches their lives directly. I am always moved and ener-gized—even though sometimes worn out—by the great exuberance with which the students in Educ. 857 engage the course material. This round of the course was no different.

However, we could not have imagined the irony of the juxtaposed events that were to mark this particular coming together in such a way that the details of that class would forever be burnt into our memory. No dramatist could have created a more poignant moment as was created for us on that dreary evening late in the year.

Over my years of teaching the seminar it has become my general practice to find a quiet hour or so before our class meeting. This is a time I use to reflect on what I want to do in class, to go over the assigned readings one more time, to assemble the scattered bits of information I had been gathering in my head and on my desk during the days between our weekly meetings. It is a quiet time which I value highly and guard with rigor. The image of being cocooned in my office unavailable to, as well as uninterrupted by, the outside world might capture the effect of these quiet moments. For me the late after-noon of December 6, 1989, was no exception.

Similarly, having just left classrooms, children, and schoolyards, the semi-nar students also arrive at our evening sessions from their own atomized and secluded spaces. Because the university at which I teach is located in a relatively small community, it draws students from a large geographic cir-cumference. For this reason many of the graduate students I teach travel considerable distances to take courses. I imagine that, despite their being ensconced in their cars hurtling down the highway for another evening of discussion and camaraderie, the students also savor those solitary moments before class in order to reflect on their day and to prepare for the evening. It was from these places that we arrived that evening on December 6, 1989, unaware of the world beyond the texts we were about to take up and the discussion we were about to share.

The class proceeded as usual. It had been a good term. It had also been difficult. However, in courses like Educ. 857 "good" and "difficult" are neither left unproblematized nor are they undone by each other. Achieving clarity often has the effect of seeing more; yet acting concretely on the terms of our new vision is not always easy. We had all done hard intellectual *and* personal work over the course of the term. And whether we looked toward or away from ourselves, we were not always pleased with what we saw. The "invisible" conditions that create the possibilities for gender apartheid as a feature of world culture began to make themselves apparent in our collective understandings. We knew that all was not well with the world.

In these final hours before the course and the term ended one of the women asked me if I thought there was any hope for change . . . hope for a better world. In response I spoke about the laugh of the Medusa (Cixous, in Marks and de Courtivron, 1981), about the power of voice, and about the feminist utopian vision which embraces not some static images of "the good life" but the potential of human struggle for a transformed social world. I remember vividly how encouragingly I had spoken. I also remember that I did not feel my words to be vacuous or shaded with cynicism: the energy I had shared with this class gave me hope, made possibilities visible, and gave meaning to the ongoing struggle which marks the politics I embrace. Had I known then what I knew only a short couple of hours later I might have said very different things. However, I did not know. None of us could have imagined!

What we could not have known is that this student's question came only moments after a young man entered the Engineering Building of the Université de Montréal with a rapid fire machine gun, stalked the halls and cafeteria where he selectively shot and killed a number of women, entered one of the classrooms, divided the women from the men, ordered the men to leave the room, and with the accusation that they were "just a bunch of feminists" gunned the women down. While in Educ. 857 we were celebrating the possibilities for hope, fourteen women were assassinated at the Université de Montréal.

Throughout this book it has been my concern to show how in education we do not come together equally. I ask myself here: What role does schooling and education play in creating the possibilities for such horror? What aspects of the school curriculum and schooling practice create knowledge that so systematically makes less of the many and gives power to the few?

I am continually astonished how many women carry the legacy of our educational history even into graduate school. Women's still marginal and only reluctantly given place in the academy often results in self-evaluations of inadequacy that contort and confine what we believe ourselves to be capable of. For many women, the belief that we are not capable of thinking intelligently or that what we have to say is not important often makes us wish to flee the academic halls we have struggled for centuries to enter.

It wasn't so long ago that women were excluded from formal education altogether. And when we were finally admitted, our place was only grudgingly offered. That this place is also often marked by an environment of emotional, intellectual, and physical violation, violence, and threat is something we know from experience.

For girls, education for "womanhood," the work of mothering and other "feminine" endeavors was added, like lace, on the edges of the serious education-for-public-life that articulated the schooling of boys. At the elementary and secondary levels, this division between the sexes was often displayed in the curriculum. And at the postsecondary level, physical barriers were added to the already strong division across subject matter. Women were often required to sit in special cordoned sections of the lecture hall, at the back, off to the side, or *behind* curtained partitions. Women were often excluded from particular programs, from common areas such as student social and recreational buildings and from libraries where it was believed we would distract or interfere with the activities of men. And when we were finally allowed to enter the programs of our choice and we worked against the odds of sexism and social and intellectual exclusion to gain admission to the professions, women, many with superior academic standing, were often denied employment.

Affirmative action is not a new idea—it just isn't called that when men assume preferential treatment because of their sex.

Today, of course, women are part of the educational scene. Elementary education is compulsory for all children; for some decades girls have graduated from high school at rates at least equal to, at times greater than, that of boys; and at the university level, women's undergraduate enrollment is equal to that of men. (Not, I hasten to add, in the socially advantageous and economically lucrative areas of mathematics, computer science, and engineering where women are still significantly underrepresented for the most part. Neither are there equivalencies held in graduate school, where women continue to be a minority in all areas except perhaps in the humanities, social sciences, and "women's" professions. Nor, significantly, have women achieved parity in faculty positions. Full- time, non-contract women instructors hover around fourteen percent of the total faculty complement, hitting a low of six percent for the highest academic rank and are almost completely nonexistent in administrative positions.)

As we approach the year 2000 we must not confuse quotas with expectations. Women comprise over fifty percent of the population. Academically, there is no indication that the intellectual performance of women/girls and men/boys differs in any significant respect one from the other. That women and men share responsibility for children whether in the home, in the school, or in the administration of the education we intend to provide for them, should not be seen as an exercise in quota meeting but rather as a sensible expectation in a society that claims to offer children a "balanced" view of the world.

Presently, balance is a rare commodity. As women we all live the results of an education that has served us poorly: we do not know our own history; we know nothing about the work women have done; and sometimes, being invited to internalize our own oppression, we ourselves come to believe that we have been, and continue to be, insignificant to the creation and organization of life on this planet. School administrative processes and curriculum content reflect interests that in large part exclude not only women but as well ethnic, aboriginal, racial, and social class interests. As students progress through their schooling, their chances of being taught by a woman decreases significantly; so much so that some can complete half of their secondary education and a four-year university degree and never encounter a female teacher or professor. The possibility that children might share in their learning with a black teacher, a teacher of color, a teacher from a visibly ethnic culture, an aboriginal teacher, a disabled teacher, or a gay or lesbian teacher living their sexual orientation without risk and fear is nonexistent.

I ask again: what does our schooling experience teach us? *If we are not men, if we are not white, if we are not economically advantaged, if we survive by the labor of our hands, if we are not heterosexual, and if we do not embody and display the valued assets of the privilege of Euro-American culture,* the school curriculum and classroom practices fling us to the margins. Nowhere in the curriculum do we see even a vague glimpse of a reflection of ourselves, of our present realities, or of our future dreams. Alison Dewar's words carry the meaning of our experience:

> Typically the stories we tell in schools, colleges and universities are ones that reflect the past, present, and future of powerful groups in society. The

> knowledge we teach in our educational system has a white, middle class, androcentric bias. More importantly, this bias is not presented as one possible version of reality, but more often is taught as the only legitimate and therefore, representative version of reality. (1987, p. 265)

While any number of studies might show this to be the case, my knowledge of it comes more directly through the body—my body—overtly contained within the academy by the ideological frames of "allowable" knowledge. I use this experience not to provide a form of catharsis but a series of metaphors that reveals for me in graphic and lived ways the relationship between education, form, and power.

The body of knowledge that is the curriculum and the body experience of being schooled—learning to be still and quiet (Corrigan, 1987a)—are not separable from each other in the processes of education. However else we understand the world—indeed however we might wish to intellectualize and thereby hide the lived effect of the realities we know we have lived—the concrete experiences of inclusion or of marginalization are the negotiated memories we carry. These experiences become the educational moments through which we come to explain the world to ourselves.

As form, education through schooling both offers and requires the consent to a contained agenda. For students marginalized through their gender, social class, ethnicity, culture, and desires of the body, questions of the relationship between education and power have substantively to do with how they are encouraged to embrace forms of schooling that systematically require them to deny who they are. Such forms measure their performance in school by how well they succeed in negating themselves and leave those parts of their lives that do not fit inside the dominant molding forms to pour and splash over the edges of what's acceptable and allowable.

I draw on my own history in order to tell this side of the schooling experience. I spent my early years as a child in the tumultuous cold war years of what was once known as East Block Europe. For my parents, as was the case for many people caught in the aftermath of a world gone crazy with destruction, their focus was directed to envisioning the best possible world for their children—a world they feared would not materialize in their own lifetime—but a world for which they longed.

Inherited as a birthright, this longing reproduced itself, as it often does, in children's games. My hopeful words, and those of my brother and childhood friends, echoed off the pavement of our urban streets still visibly scarred by the ravages of war. The sound of our voices escaped beyond the towering walls of the closely set city apartments where we lived. By turn we would proclaim, "when I go to America." (In those days, in that place, under those conditions, we made no distinction between Canada and the United States for it was a fantasy anyway—a fantastic improbability made possible in our heads only because the language of childhood imagination is irreverent of historical and political realities). "When I go to America," we chanted, "here is what I am going to be." And then we would mime to our friends our childish and sometimes impossible hopes for ourselves. For us, the impossibility of getting to the world on the other side of the Atlantic became, contradictorily, the symbol of all that was possible.

It was only halfway into the century of my childhood when the impossible became possible with the eruption of a national revolution and we were on our way to the "America" of our imagination. The dynamics of the exchange exacted by this migration is the basis of how I understand the violations of schooling.

While notions of "equality" and "diversity" have a long history in the context of our Canadian and larger North American consciousness, the meanings of these words have specific schooling outcomes. The language of education mirrors our apparent commitment to the democratic principles of equality. At the same time we cling to notions of Canada as a population marked by cultural, social, economic, and gender diversity. The metaphors through which we choose to describe ourselves in the schooling curriculum, whether of the "mosaic" or the "melting pot," celebrate identifiable difference even as we leave unexamined those practices and schooling forms which reinforce the *difference* that makes a difference.

Images that describe an explosion of texture and color abound in the language of education and that of schooling practices aimed at highlighting cultural diversity. We invite school children to share in the celebration of their heritages, to share with other children the cuisine of their ancestors, to display images of their national dress, to invite their classmates to dance to the rhythms of their native land, even as we remain silent about the historical, social, and political relations among diverse cultural groups. We invite young women to consider choosing nontraditional subjects in their preparation for taking nontraditional careers and jobs as their life's work; and we worry and consider it our failure and theirs when young women reject those courses that might take them out of the traditional ghetto of the female job market identified generally by lower pay, lower social status, more rigorous working conditions and more subject to the fluctuations of the world economy. And finally, in considering social class, we look to programs aimed at "topping up" students' cultural, social, and economic/academic "deficiencies" without problematizing the ways in which these very same programs pathologize those very same cultures and students we claim to honor.

Experience has shown us that the simple display of diversity does not guarantee the elimination of inequality. In fact, an uncritical focus on difference often results in the further marginalization and violation of those very students whose inclusion such practices are claiming to seek. For me, as a child and then as a young adult, this had particular implications. I soon learned that, for individuals, diversity across gender, race, ethnicity, social class, and desires of the body is either an asset or a liability. If liability, it would be the basis for inequality, isolation, violation, and social, cultural, and economic marginalization. Specifically I learned that the self-embraced project of my education required the abandonment of the cultural/social practices I had carried with me across two continents to this new place I was to call home.

Along with a new language, I learned to pack a lunch that I no longer needed to sneak unseen out of a brown paper bag for fear of being associated with the cultural oddities of taste and cuisine that it carried. One of the legacies of my education is, for the most part, the loss of this culture that is no longer an identifiable aspect of who I am. Except for a slight "lilt" in my enunciation, noticed only by those with a "good ear" and often mistaken for regional exoticism, there is nothing about me that would signal the cultural shifts of perspective I was required to accomplish as a child of nine.

The familial practices that embraced, and were embraced by, the culture of my childhood were lost in this imposed yet coveted transition from Other to Acceptable. The body experience of embarrassment and humiliation worked through me to dislodge the deeply felt moments of shared caring I experienced as a child in my home. Yet, there are still words of endearment I can speak only in the language of my childhood for them to have any significance deeper than the dictionary meanings they carry.

Never acknowledged as a loss, the shedding of the skin of my ethnicity was supposed to be painless—and I told myself that it was. It was only much later that I understood that even the possibility of this self-imposed pain was made available to me only because I was white in a deeply racist culture. It was a privilege I could not have appropriated for myself had I been a black child or a child whose visible race or ethnicity makes them even more invisible in the curriculum and schooling experience than I was made.

My brother and I learned to mimic and then laugh at the culture of the children we both struggled not to be. We internalized the violation of our negation to ease the pain of our loss. I still take delight in the richness of the nuances of a language I now speak, read, and write with hesitation and uncertainty. Yet, as a child I was in a school system obsessed with the devaluation and margin-alization of multiple language speakers/multiple culture carriers—where the ability to speak more than one language/to live through more than one culture was seen to be an intellectual liability rather than a richly useful asset. My struggle to leave behind the language/culture of my childhood created in me an equal and opposite obsession to get the new language right as it simultane-ously, and I believe deliberately, alienated me from those, like my parents, who could not. Gradually my syntax and accent gave me away less and less.

Yet who I am is not only constructed by who I have become, but as well by the memory of those parts of my life that I have been asked to leave as unformed/unframed pools. These parts of my experience were uncontained as well as unaccounted for inside the forms that articulate education and schooling (Williams, 1991, pp. 181–201).

Translating experience into metaphor has enabled me to "render visible the visible" (Bersianik, 1986, p. 48). This is not an easy thing to do. To begin, I need to say that for me this telling of my own educational experiences pre-sents itself as a paradox. The social and cultural implications associated with being a female university professor implore me to keep silent by not speaking and therefore making unspeakable the realities I know I have lived. Have I not, after all, been successful in precisely those institutions which I critique with such energy? Have I not, in the end, benefitted exactly from those prac-tices that I scrutinize with such rigor? And am I not, despite myself, inside those very institutions and practices that I hold up to question? To be sure, my silence is the price extracted from me by institutions and social practices that agree to tolerate me only so long as I agree to pay the price. That I feel pressure to come to terms with these negotiated realities does not make these institutions and practices any less violating and coercive. As is the case for Judge Maxine Thomas (Williams, 1991) my schooling taught me to:

> wear all the contradictions at the same time, to wear them well and recon-cile them. [To] swallow all the stories, all the roles, [and open] wide to all the expectations. (p. 196)

I was a good student. Yet my silence does not make social inequality more livable for not being spoken. To speak our histories is the only safety net against obliteration.

By definition, social life is collective and interdependent. Historically we enter and live out social relations unequally. Whether or not we choose to acknowledge it, the knowledge we derive from our experience is a conse-quence of these social/historical realities lived in minute detail. Dominant and subordinate social, cultural, and economic groups do not agree on what counts as useful knowledge. This disagreement is not a function of the objective/subjective dichotomy, but rather of the unequal power to articulate the knowledge each group derives from its own experience. In other words, the dominant social, cultural, and economic groups are able to renege ownership of the knowledge they derive from their experience and instead call it universal and objective. This privilege speaks more about their power than about the "truths" they claim to have uncovered.

The stories I learned in school had a remarkable singularity about them—a single voicedness where debates, if they took place at all, questioned only the details without remotely touching the foundations of the basic paradigms upon which the stories were premised. Throughout the seventeen years of formal education that preceded my graduate studies, I did not study the history, culture, and political realities of women, of the laboring classes, of racial and ethnic minorities, of lesbians and gays. This is all the more remarkable when I consider that my area of study was the "great thinkers" of the Western Intellectual Tradition.

A couple of years ago, while preparing to write this book, I revisited my undergraduate philosophy texts still sitting—now somewhat sundrained—on my book shelves, only to discover to my dismay that there was not a single volume among them written by a woman. Nor had any of them been written by anyone who could be identified as an author of color. To my recollection issues of ethnic and cultural difference were never discussed. There were no voices from the labor movement. Nor, indeed, was it made remotely possible for me to learn from those texts a discourse other than the massive assumptions and prescriptions of heterosexuality.

All of this might be astonishing enough. Given the language of educational rhetoric claiming for itself ideologies and practices that embrace notions of freedom, democracy, and equality, the distinctly one-sidedness of the story I learned in school seems a curious oversight—even more so since I earned my pre-graduate education in the heady reformist days of the sixties and early seventies.

However, on looking back, there is something that seems *even more* astonishing than the limited/limiting perspectives of the books from which I was asked to absorb the knowledge of the culture which promised me equality of possibility: at the time I read these books I had not even registered the deeply exclusionary practices that they created and made to seem natural. Not to have noticed my own violation speaks of a process more deeply violating than I could have imagined at the time.

This experience is what I have since come to call the *double-cross-reversal,* that is, the privilege of the dominant to talk at great length about that which is not and to stay silent about that which is. For socially subordinate groups, this reversal means that: possibility is defined through denial; freedom is reinterpreted through constraint; violence is justified as protection; and in schools, contrary to the belief that they are places where knowledge is shared, knowledge withheld articulates the curriculum.

The stories I carry with me about my own educational experiences stand in opposition to my own locus of desire—to sing, to dance, to speak—simple acts of possibility. Yet history has shown us that such possibilities are never simple. We carry the baggage of our history and it makes us *shy:*

> and the shyness of the poor is another mystery. I myself in the midst of it can't explain it. Perhaps it is neither a form of cowardice nor of heroism. It may be lack of arrogance. (The School Boys of Barbiana, 1971, p. 4)

At one level we are made shy by our collective history of marginalization. But at another level—at a level that is lived more closely, at a level that is less easy to distance—we are made shy by our personal histories; those strands of experience that are woven into the patterns of our lives. In this, our social identities are crosscut not only by who we are but, as well, by the ceaseless reinforcement of who we are not. And in this schools play a major part.

I remember some considerable years ago arriving as a grade nine student in a new high school. As for many students, for me, the transition between elementary and high school signalled the possibility for new beginnings. I was excited at the idea of what I thought I was about to learn. And I was excited about where I believed this learning was going to take me. In looking ahead, I was determined to leave behind what as a child I had learned to live as the silencing vestiges of my ethnic/immigrant background often experienced as a deeply carried "shyness." I was unwilling to demand that I be noticed, knowing all the while that my "lack of language" and the peculiarities of my cultural capital made explicit that visibility which could not be spoken.

Entering grade nine, questions of ethnicity long since suppressed, I was ready to create new possibilities for myself. I thought entry into high school would provide the obscurity I sought (and thought I needed) to reposition myself beyond my immigrant biography, only to discover that my experience as Other was to be rearticulated across what I eventually came to learn were a new set of parameters: that of gender.

On the particular morning that I recall so well, I had been cajoled out of the stuffiness of the library into the warm sunshine of that bright September day. My arms loaded with books and my mind preoccupied, I set about to find a quiet place in which to spin my dreams about my future. I proceeded to cross what appeared to me to be a large lovely green space. Suddenly I saw a cluster of young men charging toward me. In panic and with knees weak with terror I realized I was standing in the middle of the football field. Not knowing which way I should go—and in reality having nowhere to go—I stood transfixed and bewildered. In retrospect I should have known. In most high schools (certainly any of those I went to) the only available green space was, by priority, given over to the playing of football, an activity that not only eliminated many of the young men, but all of the young women. As they mowed me down I realized I had trespassed into a space not intended for me. My presence in that space, not unnoticed by this advancing steam roller, had no effect on their will, desire, or inclination to stop short of what to me was a potential disaster. The game was all.

For well over twenty years this story has stayed with me as a metaphor not only for the situation of girls in school. It speaks as well to the condition of all marginal cultural/social groups in a society that is marked massively and unmistakably by the privileges of domination. It speaks to the condition of the world itself scored profoundly by the horrors of ceaseless military interventions and made fragile by the hostile disregard for the balances of nature. The ritualized game of exclusion, violation and obliteration of the many for the narcissistic pleasure of the few is played through the evil phallic posturing of those insane enough to have learned the lessons of their unexamined privilege well.

With this experience lodged firmly in my subconscious (because it is only recently that I have been able to understand the psychological/emotional import that that football field incident had on how I formulated the possibilities of my own schooling and future), I proceeded through the various levels of credentialization in the increasingly marginalizing world of academia. That this world was also increasingly masculinized and male-centered is not beside the point. And while I found myself again and again back in the middle of that metaphorical football field, picking myself up, looking still and again for that quiet place where I could spin my dreams, I found that increasingly the mowing down was less arbitrary and while more subtle and sophisticated, certainly more profound.

Proceeding through high school, then university, and finally graduate school, as a woman in the academy, I found myself repeatedly faced with the production of the demonstration of my knowledgability and skill with words in an environment where both what I knew and the words with which I understood this knowledge hovered on the margins, outside the pale of masculine homosociality, catching only partial and momentary glances, as bodies shift, of the fire that burns at the center of male academic practices and camaraderie. Mary Daly's (1978) remarkable exposition of social practices that rivet patriarchal power into place (witchburnings, suttees, footbinding, genital mutilation, modern gynecological practices, and the socially sanctioned and institutionalized violence against women worldwide) would suggest that the fuel for this fire is to be found in the bodies of women.

My education both offered and simultaneously withheld the promise of a future I could embrace. Moving closer, the tips of my fingers warmed. Simultaneously I caught the sideways glances that were sometimes bewildered by, sometimes hostile to, yet sometimes grateful for my presence. No longer marginalized through my ethnicity it was now as a woman that I became aware of my signification as the Other—a body that did not conform to the straight lines of the masculine body of knowledge that marks acceptable discourse and self-presentation. Bewildered by the ambiguities of my place around the warming fire, bruised by my inability to decode these contradictory discourses, my immediate inclination, almost intuitive (and what is intuition beyond a profound sensitivity to lived realities) was to pull back into a terrain that I knew. As my eyes began to focus and adjust to what the light at the center had made to appear as a black void, I caught the movement of other bodies in the shadows. Having stayed focused in this direction long enough, what had been made to appear as darkness and formlessness has begun to present itself with the clarity of a moonlit winter night.

The stories in this book have allowed me to break the code of silence enforced by the mandates of objectivity and finally speak what through my experience I had always known: *if we are not men, if we are not white, if we are not economically advantaged, if we survive by the labor of our hands, if we are not heterosexual, and if we do not embody and display the valued assets of the privilege of Euro-American culture,* schools are not the sites of possibility which the rhetoric of educational discourse wishes to portray.

What I learned in school was that successful forms of self-violation are rewarded with credentials; that the study of the accomplishments of great men simultaneously hides the life realities of those whose labor—often gratuitous—is required to reproduce a world in which some men (very specific men) can become great; and finally that educational rhetoric conforms to the mandates of the double-cross-reversal, offering a great deal of information about that which is not, and withholding information about that which is.

Now I sit on the other side of the educational divide. The stories my students tell me about their educational experiences are not unlike those

I already know all too well. Women speak of unconscionable sexism while those in power co-opt the language of the powerless. Women's struggle for equality and inclusion, as well as our attempts to gain public acknowledgment of our violation and marginalization, are countered by claims of reverse sexism, preferential treatment of women, and the silencing and intimidation of those who have never known what it means to be truly without voice, as women are, not because we cannot speak but because we are not heard and not being heard we cease to speak.

Women repeatedly tell me of their conscious decision to stop speaking in classrooms where sexism is a non-negotiable dynamic of the curriculum and classroom practice. Some women tell me of not having spoken in class for years. Economic marginality continues to limit students' access to education. The division between mental and manual labor continues to suppress what counts as acceptable knowledge. Many students who carry the weighted baggage of their racial/ethnic identity slow, and eventually step to the sidelines, in the race for academic success. And questions of sexual identity never enter the classroom even as we turn a blind eye to the violations of homophobia that hold many students physically, emotionally, and psychologically hostage to their peers.

This is not to say that there are not courageous teachers who struggle to maintain programs and create curricula against the will of those whose interests are not served by students who know too much—teachers who openly share strategies for transformation and who offer support in the struggle to uncover the deeply political nature of education. Before we can decide where we might go with what we know, we need to understand what it means to be educated against ourselves. We need to learn new skills: to see what is hidden, to hear the voices that have been silenced against their will, to create curricula out of the invisible. We need to live and teach from a place that refuses to displace dignity with efficiency. We need to believe that our collective possibilities are diminished, not enhanced, by an educational process that does not honor the history, culture, social realities, abilities, and diversity of each of us. And in the end, we need to understand why assimilation is not the road to equality and why compliance continues to violate the promise of possibility.

# BIBLIOGRAPHY

Aiken, S. H., Anderson, K., Dinnerstein, M., Lensink, J. N., and MacCorquodale, P. (Eds.). (1988). *Changing Our Minds*. New York: SUNY Press.

Aisenberg, N., and Harrington, M. (1988). *Women of Academe: Outsiders in the Sacred Grove*. Amherst: University of Massachusetts Press.

Anderson, L. (1986). At the Threshold of the Self: Women and Autobiography. In M. Monteith. (Ed.). *Women's Writing: A Challenge to Theory*. Brighton: The Harvest Press.

Armstrong, P. and Armstrong, H. (1982). *The Double Ghetto: Canadian Women and Their Segregated Work*. Toronto: McLelland and Stewart.

Assiter, Alison. (1985). Did Man Make Language? In Edgeley, Roy and Osborne, Richard. (Eds.). *Radical Philosophy Reader*. London: The Thetford Press.

Atwood, M. (1985). *The Handmaid's Tale*. Toronto: McClelland and Stewart— Bantam Books.

Bannerji, H., Carty, L., Dehli, K., Heald, S., McKenna, K. (1991). *Unsettling Relations: The University as a Site of Feminist Struggles*. Toronto: The Women's Press.

Barreno, M. I., Horta, M. T., and daCosta, M.V. (1975). *The Three Marias' New Portugese Letters*. New York: Doubleday.

Barrett, M. (1980). *Women's Oppression Today: Problems in Marxist Feminist Analysis*. London: Verso.

Bartky, S. L. (1985). Toward a Phenomenology of Feminist Consciousness. In M. Vetterling-Braggin, F. A. Elliston, and J. English. (Eds.). *Feminism and Philosophy*. Totowa: Rowman and Allanheld.

Barton, M. (1991). *A Quilted Text: A Feminist Exploration of Violence in the Lives of Women at an Adult Education Centre*. Unpublished M.Ed. Thesis. Kingston: Queen's University.

Beck, E. T. (1983). Self-Disclosure and the Commitment to Social Change. In C. Bunch, and S. Pollack. (Eds.). *Learning Our Way: Essays in Feminist Education*. Trumansburg: The Crossing Press.

Belenky, M. F., Clinchy, B. M., Goldberger, N. R., and Tarule, J. M. (1986). *Women's Ways of Knowing: The Development of Self, Voice, and Mind*. New York: Basic Books.

Bellamy, L. A., and Guppy, N. (1991). *Opportunities and Obstacles for Women in Canadian Higher Education*. In J. Gaskell and A. McLaren. (Eds.). *Women and Education: A Canadian Perspective*. Calgary: Detselig Enterprises.

Bersianik, L. (1986). Aristotle's Lantern: An Essay on Criticism. In S. Neuman, and S. Kamboureli. (Eds.). *A Mazing Space: Writing Canadian Women Writing*. Edmonton: Longspoon Press.

Brittan, A., and Maynard, M. (1984). *Sexism, Racism and Oppression*. Oxford: Basil Blackwell.

Britzman, D. (1991). *Practice Makes Practice: A Critical Study of Learning to Teach*. New York: SUNY Press.

Brodkey, L. (1987). Writing Ethnographic Narratives. *Written Communication* (January): 67–76.

Brodribb, S. (1987). Women's Studies in Canada: a History. *Resources for Feminist Research* (Special Issue): 1–3.

Brookes, A. L. (1992). *Feminist Pedagogy: An Autobiographical Approach*. Halifax: Fernwood Publishing.

Cann, J., Cunningham, J., Fowler, S., Kelso, F., Mohamdee, S., and Postma, A. (1993). *What Is Wrong With This Picture?* Video production. Kingston: Queen's Television.

Caplan, P. J. (1989). *Don't Blame Mother: Mending Mother-Daughter Relations*. New York: Harper & Row.

Chernin, K. (1987). In The House of the Flame Bearers. *Tikkun* (July/August): 55–59.

Cixous, H. (1981). Castration and Decapitation. *Signs* 7(1): 41–55

The Company of Sirens. 176 Robert Street. Toronto, Ontario, Canada. M5S 2K3

Connell, R. W., Dowsett, G. W., Kessler, S., and Ashenden, D.J. (1981). Class and Gender Dynamics in a Ruling-class School. *Interchange* 12(2/3): 102–117.

Corrigan, P. (1987a). In/Forming Schooling. In D. Livingston and Contributors. *Critical Pedagogy and Cultural Power*. Toronto: Garamond Press.

Corrigan, P. (1987b). Race/Ethnicity/Gender/Culture: Embodying Differences Educationally: An Argument. In J. Young. (Ed.). *Breaking the Mosaic: Ethnic Identities In Canadian Schooling*. Toronto: Garamond Press.

Corrigan, P. (1988). Masculinity as Right. OISE: Unpublished manuscript.

Corrigan, P., and Sayer, D. (1985). *The Great Arch*. New York: Blackwell.

Corrin, C. (1992). Magyar Women's Lives: Complexities and Contradictions. In C. Corrin. (Ed.). *Superwomen and the Double Burden*. Toronto: Second Story Press.

Culley, M. (1985). Anger and Authority in the Introductory Women's Studies Classroom. In M. Culley, and C. Portuges. (Eds.). *Gendered Subjects: The Dynamics of Feminist Teaching*. Boston: Routledge and Kegan Paul.

Daly, M. (1978). *Gyn/Ecology: The Metaethics of Radical Feminism*. Boston: The Beacon Press.

de Lauretis, T. (1984). *Alice Doesn't: Feminism, Semiotics, Cinema*. Bloomington: Indiana University Press.

de Lauretis, T. (1986). Feminist Studies/Critical Studies: Issues, Terms, and Contexts. In T. de Lauretis. (Ed.). *Feminist Studies/Critical Studies*. Bloomington: Indiana University Press.

Delphy, Christine. (1987). Protofeminism and Antifeminism. In T. Moi (Ed.). *French Feminist Thought*. Oxford: Basil Blackwell.

DeShazer, M. K. (1986). *Inspiring Women: Reimagining the Muse*. New York: Pergamon Press.

Dewar, A. (1987). Knowledge and Gender in Physical Education. In J. Gaskell and A. McLaren. (Eds.). *Women and Education: A Canadian Perspective*. Calgary: Detselig Enterprises.

Dorfman, A. (1983). *The Empire's Old Clothes: What the Lone Ranger, Babar, and Other Innocent Heroes Do To Our Minds*. New York: Pantheon Books.

DuPlessis, R. B. (1985). *Writing Beyond The Ending: Narrative Strategies of Twentieth-Century Women Writers*. Bloomington: Indiana University Press.

Duras, M. (1981). Smothered Creativity. In E. Marks, and I. de Courtivron, (Eds.). *New French Feminisms*. New York: Schocken Books.

Eagleton, (1991). *Ideology: An Introduction*. New York: Verso.

Eisenstein, H. (1983). *Contemporary Feminist Thought*. Boston: G. K. Hall and Co.

Eisner, E., and Peshkin, A. (Eds.). (1990). *Qualitative Inquiry in Education: The Continuing Debate*. New York: Teachers College Press, Columbia University.

Ellsworth, E. (1989). Why Doesn't This Feel Empowering: Working through the Repressive Myths of Critical Pedagogy. *Harvard Educational Review* 59 (August): 297–324.

Elshtain, J.B. (1981/82). Feminist Discourse and Its Discontents: Language, Power, and Meaning. In O. Keohane, M.Z. Rosaldo, and B. Gelpi, (Eds.). *Feminist Theory: A Critique of Ideology.* Chicago: University of Chicago Press.

Faludi, S. (1991). *Backlash: The Undeclared War Against American Women.* New York: Crown Publishers

Flax, J. (1980). Mother-Daughter Relationships: Psychodynamics, Politics and Philosophy. In H. Eisenstein, and A. Jardin. (Eds.). *The Future of Difference.* New Brunswick: Rutgers University Press.

Fox-Keller, E. (1985). *Reflections on Gender and Science.* New Haven: Yale University Press.

Freire, P. (1972). *Pedagogy of the Oppressed.* New York: Herder and Herder.

Frye, M. (1983). *The Politics of Reality: Essays In Feminist Theory.* Trumansburg: The Crossing Press.

Gaskell, J. (1987). Course Enrollment in the High School: The Perspective of Working-Class Females. In J. Gaskell and A. McLaren. (Eds.). *Women and Education: A Canadian Perspective.* Calgary: Detselig Enterprises.

Gaskell, J. (1991). Contesting the Meaning of Skill in Clerical Training: The 'Art' of Managing Horses, or the 'Skill' of Driving. In J. Gaskell and A. McLaren. (Eds.). *Women and Education: A Canadian Perspective.* (Second Edition). Calgary: Detselig Enterprises.

Gaskell, J. (1992). *Gender Matters from School to Work.* Milton Keynes: Open University Press.

Gaskell, J., McLaren, A. T., and Novogrodsky, M. (1989). *Claiming An Education: Feminism and Canadian Schools.* Toronto: Garamond Press.

Gayatri, C. S. (1987). *In Other Worlds: Essays in Cultural Politics.* New York: Methuen.

Gilbert, S. M., and Gubar, S. (1979). *The Madwoman in the Attic: The Woman Writer and The Nineteenth-Century Literary Imagination.* New Haven: Yale University Press.

Gilman, S. P. (1973). *The Yellow Wallpaper.* New York: The Feminist Press.

Giroux, H. and Simon, R. (1988). Critical Pedagogy and the Politics of Popular Culture. OISE: Unpublished manuscript.

Glaspell, S. (1927). *A Jury of Her Peers.* London: Ernest Benn.

Golding, W. (1962). *Lord of the Flies.* London: Faber and Faber Ltd.

Griffin, S. (1981/82). The Way of All Ideology. In N. O. Keohane, M. Z. Rosaldo, and B. C. Gelpi. (Eds.). *Feminist Theory: A Critique of Ideology.* Chicago: University of Chicago Press.

Griffin, S. (1981). *Pornography and Silence: Culture's Revenge Against Nature.* New York: Harper and Row.

Grossman, K. (1992). A Feminist Perspective on the Research Process: Theory, Practice, Barriers. Unpublished M.Ed. Thesis. Kingston: Queen's University.

Grumet, M. (1985). Curriculum As Form. Unpublished manuscript.

Grumet, M.R. (1988). *Bitter Milk: Women and Teaching.* Amherst: University of Massachusetts Press.

Guppy, N., Balson, D. and Vellutini, S. (1987). Women and Higher Education in Canadian Society. In J. Gaskell and A. McLaren. (Eds.). *Women and Education: A Canadian Perspective.* Calgary: Detselig Enterprises.

Hamilton, R. (1986). Working at Home. In R. Hamilton and M. Barrett. (Eds.). *The Politics of Diversity.* Montreal: Book Center.

Hamilton, R. (1987). Does Misogyny Matter? *Studies in Political Economy* 23 (Summer): 123–139.

Hamilton, R. (1990). Feminism and Motherhood, 1970–1990: Reinventing The Wheel? *Resources for Feminist Research* 19(December): 23–32.

Hartmann, H. (1984). The Unhappy Marriage of Marxism and Feminism: Towards a More Progressive Union. In R. Dale, G. Esland, R. Ferguson, M. McDonald. (Eds.). *Education and the State: Politics, Patriarchy, and Practice.* Vol. 2. Sussex: Falmer Press.

Haug, F. (Ed.). (1987). *Female Sexualization.* London: Verso.

Heckle, S. (1980). *A Jury of Her Peers.* Film.

Hoagland, S. L. (1988). *Lesbian Ethics: Toward New Value.* Palo Alto: Institute of Lesbian Studies.

hooks, b. (1981). *Ain't I A Woman: Black Women and Feminism.* Boston: South End Press.

hooks, b. (1984). *Feminist Theory from Margin to Center.* Boston: South End Press.

hooks, b. (1989). *Talking Back: Thinking Feminist, Thinking Black.* Boston: South End Press.

hooks, b. (1990). *Yearning: Race. Gender and Cultural Politics.* Toronto: Between the Lines.

hooks, b . (1992). *Black Looks: Race and Representation.* Toronto: Between The Lines.

Howe, F. (1983). Feminist Scholarship: The Extent of the Revolution. In C. Bunch, and S. Pollack. (Eds.). *Learning Our Way: Essays in Feminist Education.* Trumansburg: The Crossing Press.

Hull, G.T., Scott, P.B., and Smith, B. (Eds.). (1982). *All the Women are White, All the Blacks are Men, But Some of Us are Brave.* Old Westbury: The Feminist Press.

Imray, L., and Middleton, A. (1983). Public and Private: Marking the Boundaries. In E. Gamarnikow, D. Morgan, J. Purvis, and D. Taylorson, (Eds.). *The Public and the Private.* London: Heinemann.

Irigaray, L. (1985). *This Sex Which Is Not One.* Ithaca: Cornell University Press.

Jaggar, A. (19833. *Feminist Politics and Human Nature.* Sussex: The Harvest Press.

Jayawardana, K. (1986). *Feminism and Nationalism in the Third Word.* London: Zed Books.

Jenson, J. (1986). Gender and Reproduction: Or, Babies and the State. *Studies in Political Economy* (Summer): 9–46.

Johnson, S. (1987). *Going Out of Our Minds: The Metaphysics of Liberation.* Freedom: The Crossing Press

Keller, C. (1986). *From a Broken Web: Separation, Sexism, and Self.* Boston: Beacon Press.

Keller, E. F. (1985). *Reflections on Gender and Science.* New Haven: Yale University Press.

Kelly, J. (1984). *Women History and Theory.* Chicago: University of Chicago Press.

Keohane, N. O., Rosaldo, M. Z. and Gelpi, B. C. (Eds.). (1981/82). *Feminist Theory: A Critique of Ideology.* Chicago: The University of Chicago Press.

Khayatt, Didi. (1992). *Lesbian Teachers: An Invisible Presence.* Albany: SUNY Press.

Kolodny, A. (1987). A Determined Life. *The Women's Review of Books* (June): 5–7

Kristeva, J. (1986). Woman's Time. In T. Moi. (Ed.). *The Kristeva Reader.* Oxford: Basil Blackwell.

Lather, P. (1988). Feminist Perspectives on Empowering Research Methodologies. *Women's Studies International Forum* 11: 569–581.

Lee, E. (1992). Social Construction of Femininity: The Female Socialization Process. Unpublished Honors Thesis. Kingston: Queen's University.

Lees, S. (1986). *Losing Out: Sexuality and Adolescent Girls.* London: Hutchinson.

Lerner, G. (1986). *The Creation of Patriarchy.* Oxford: Oxford University Press.

Lewis, M. (1977). *Some Implications of Paulo Freire's Philosophical and Pedagogical Approach for Canadian Education.* Unpublished M.A. Thesis. Toronto: University of Toronto.

Lewis, M. (1988a). The Construction of Femininity Embraced in the Work of Caring for Children—Caught Between Aspirations and Reality. *The Journal of Educational Thought* 22 (October): 259–268.

Lewis, M. (1989). The Challenge of Feminist Pedagogy. *Queen's Quarterly* 96 (Spring): 117–130.

Lewis, M. (1990) Interrupting Patriarchy: Politics, Resistance, and Transformation in the Feminist Classroom. *Harvard Educational Review* 60 (4): 467–488.

Lewis, M. (1991) Mr. Brown's Math Class and Other Stories of Exclusion. *Women's Education des Femmes* (Summer): 28–31.

Lewis, M. (1992a). Power and Education: Who Decides the Form Schools Have Taken and Who Should Decide? In J. Kincheloe and S. Steinberg. (Eds.). *Thirteen Questions: Reframing Education's Conversations.* New York: Peter Lang.

Lewis, M. (1992b). Equality Through Diversity. *Symposium Publication.* Toronto: FWTAO.

Lewis, M. (1993). Private Spaces: The Political Economy of Women's Solitude. In D. Wear. (Ed.). *The Center of The Web: Women and Solitude.* New York: SUNY Press.

Lewis, M. (forthcoming) Solidarity Work and Feminist Practice. In P. Lather and E. Ellsworth. (Eds.). *Situated Pedagogies.*

Lewis, M. (1988b). *Without a Word: Sources and Themes for a Feminist Pedagogy.* Unpublished Doctoral Dissertation. Toronto: University of Toronto.

Lewis, M. and Simon, R. (1986). "A Discourse Not Intended for Her": Teaching and Learning Within Patriarchy. *Harvard Educational Review* 56 (November): 457–472.

Longfellow, B. (1986/87). When These Lips Speak Together. *Border/Lines.* Nov. 6, pp. 26–29.

Lorde, A. (1980). *The Cancer Journal.* San Francisco: Spinsters/Aunt Lute.

Lorde, A. (1984). *Sister Outsider.* Trumansburg: The Crossing Press.

Luke, C., and Gore, J. (Eds.). (1992). *Feminisms and Critical Pedagogy.* New York: Routledge.

MacDonald, G. (1989). Feminist Teaching Techniques for the Committed but Exhausted. *Atlantis* 15 (1): 145–152.

MacDonald, M. (1981). Schooling and the Reproduction of Class and Gender Relations. In L. Barton, R. Meighan, and S. Walker. (Eds.). *Schooling Ideology and the Curriculum.* Sussex: The Falmer Press.

MacKinnon, C. A. (1983). Feminism, Marxism, Method, and the State: An Agenda for Theory. In E. Abel, and E. K. Abel. (Eds.). *The Signs Reader: Women, Gender and Scholarship.* Chicago: University of Chicago Press.

MacKinnon, C. (1987). *Feminism Unmodified: Discourse on Life and Law.* Cambridge: Harvard University Press.

Mairs, Nancy. (1986). *Plaintext: Deciphering a Woman's Life.* New York: Harper and Row.

Malette, L. and Chalouh, M. (Eds.). (1990). *Polytechnique, 6 Decembre.* Montreal: Les editions du remue-menage.

Marcus, J. (1988). *Art and Anger: Reading Like a Woman.* Columbus: Ohio State University Press.

Marcuse, H. (1964). *One Dimensional Man.* Boston: Beacon Press.

Marks, E. and de Courtivron, I. (Eds.). (1981). *New French Feminisms: An Anthology.* New York: Schocken Books.

Martin, B., and Mohanty, C. T. (1986). Feminist Politics: What's Home Got to Do with It? In T. de Lauretis. (Ed.). *Feminist Studies/Critical Studies.* Bloomington: Indiana University Press.

McCormack, T. (1987). Feminism, Women's Studies and The New Academic Freedom. In J. Gaskell and A. T. McLaren. (Eds.). *Women and Education: A Canadian Perspective.* Calgary: Detselig Enterprises.

McDonald, B. (1990). An Exploration of Personal Knowledge: Breaking Out and Away From The God's Eye Perspective. Unpublished M.Ed. Thesis. Kingston: Queen's University.

McDonald, B. (1991). A Feminist Politics within the Community of the School: Unravelling Our Hearts/Sexualities and Identities. Paper presented at the JCT: Conference on Curriculum Theory and Classroom Practice. Dayton, Ohio.

McDonald, B. (1992). How to Raise Hell in Gentle Ways and Be Heard: The Personal is Political. Paper presented at the JCT: Conference on Curriculum Theory and Classroom Practice. Dayton, Ohio.

McDonald, B. (1993). Social Discursive Spaces of the Body: A Site of Schooling. Unpublished Manuscript. Toronto: OISE.

McMahon, M. (1986). A Circuitous Quest: Things That Haunt Me When I Write. Unpublished Manuscript. Toronto: OISE

Mies, Maria. (1986). *Patriarchy and Accumulation on a World Scale: Women in the International Division of Labor.* London: Zed Books Ltd.

Miles, A., and Finn, G. (Eds.). (1989). *Feminism in Canada: From Pressure to Politics.* Montreal: Black Rose Books.

Miller, J. L. (1990). *Creating Spaces and Finding Voices: Teachers Collaborating for Empowerment.* New York: SUNY Press.

Modleski, T. (1986). Feminism and the Power of Interpretation: Some Critical Readings. In T. de Lauretis. (Ed.). *Feminist Studies/Critical Studies.* Bloomington: Indiana University Press.

Moi, T. (1985). *Sexual/Textual Politics: Feminist Literary Theory.* London: Methuen.

Moi, T. (Ed.). (1986). *The Kristeva Reader.* Oxford: Basil Blackwell.

Moraga, C. and Anzaldua, G. (Eds.). (1981/83). *This Bridge Called My Back: Writings by Radical Women of Color.* New York: Kitchen Table Press; Women of Color Press.

Morgan, D. (1981). Men, masculinity and the process of sociological enquiry. In H. Roberts. (Ed.). *Doing Feminist Research.* London: Routledge and Kegan Paul.

Morton, M. (1988). Dividing the Wealth, Sharing the Poverty: the (Re)formation of 'family' in law in Ontario. *The Canadian Review of Sociology and Anthropology* 25 (May): 254–275.

Munich, A. (1985). Notorious Signs, Feminist Criticism and Literary Tradition. In G. Greene, and C. Kahn. (Eds.). *Making A Difference: Feminist Literary Criticism.* London: Methuen.

Murch, K. (1991). *The Chilly Climate for Women on University Campuses: Video.* London, Canada: The University of Western Ontario.

Oakley, A. (1972). *Sex, Gender and Society.* London: Temple Smith.

O'Brien, M. (1987). Fiction and Fact. *Resources for Feminist Research* 16 (June): 57–59.

O'Connell, D. (1983). Poverty: The Feminine Complaint. In J. Turner and L. Emery. (Eds.). *Perspectives on Women in the 1980's.* Winnipeg: University of Manitoba Press.

Olsen, T. (1978). *Silences.* New York: Delta/Seymour Lawrence.

Phillips, A. (1987). *Divided Loyalties: Dilemmas of Sex and Class.* London: Virago Press.

Pickard, T. (1992). An Open Letter to My Colleagues, Students, Referees and Friends. Kingston: Queen's University.

Pierson, R. R. (1983). Review of *Women of Ideas and What Men Have Done to Them. Resources for Feminist Research* 12 (July): 17–18.

Pierson, R. R. (1987). Two Marys and a Virginia: Historical Moments in the Development of a Feminist Perspective on Education. In J. Gaskell, and A. T. McLaren. (Eds.). *Women and Education: A Canadian Perspective*. Calgary: Detselig Enterprises.

Pratt, M.-B. (1991). *Rebellions: Essays 1980–1991*. New York: Firebrand Books.

Radford-Hill, S. (1986). Considering Feminism as a Model for Social Change. In T. de Lauretis (Ed.). *Feminist Studies/Critical Studies*. Bloomington: Indiana University Press.

Radway, J. (1984). *Reading the Romance: Women, Patriarchy and Popular Literature*. Chapel Hill: University of North Carolina Press.

Rich, A. (1979). *On Lies, Secrets, and Silence*. New York: W.W. Norton and Co.

Rich, A. (1986a). *Of Woman Born: Motherhood as Experience and Institution*. New York: W.W. Norton and Co.

Rich, A. (1986b). *Blood, Bread, and Poetry*. New York: W.W. Norton and Company.

Rockhill, K. (1987a). The Chaos of Subjectivity in the Ordered Halls of Academe. *Canadian Woman Studies: "Women's Psychology."* 8 (Winter): 4, 12–17

Rockhill, K. (1987b). Violence Against Wives. Unpublished manuscript. Toronto: OISE.

Rockhill, K. (1991). Literacy as threat/desire: longing to be SOMEBODY. In J. Gaskell, and A. McLaren. (Eds.). *Women and Education: A Canadian Perspective* (Second Edition). Calgary: Detselig Enterprises.

Rowbotham, S. (1973). *Woman's Consciousness, Man's World*. Harmondsworth: Penguin Books

Rowbotham, S. (1989). To be or not to be: The dilemmas of mothering. *Feminist Review* (31): 82–93.

Sawicki, J. (1991). *Disciplining Foucault: Feminism, Power, and the Body*. New York: Routledge.

Schilb, J. (1985). Pedagogy of the Oppressors? In M. Culley and C. Portuges. (Eds.). *Gendered Subjects: The Dynamics of Feminist Teaching*. Boston: Routledge and Kegan Paul.

Schilling, L. (1992). Women and Language: A Struggle with Tradition. Unpublished Honors Thesis. Kingston: Queen's University.

The School Boys of Barbiana. (1971). *Letter to a Teacher*. Trans. by N. Rossi and T. Cole. New York: Vintage Press.

Schuster, M. R. And Van Dyne, S. R. (Eds.). (1985). *Women's Place in the Academy: Transforming the Liberal Arts Curriculum*. Totowa: Rowman and Allanheld.

Showalter, E. (Ed.). (1985). *The Female Malady: Women, Madness and English Culture 1830–1980*. New York: Penguin Books.

Silman, J. (1987). *Enough Is Enough: Aboriginal Women Speak Out*. Toronto: The Women's Press.

Silvera, M. (1983). *Silenced*. Alton: Williams and Wallice.

Silvera, M. (1991). *Piece of My Heart*. Toronto: Sister Vision Press.

Silverman, K. (1984). Histoire d'O: The Construction of Female Subject. In C. Vance. (Ed.). *Pleasure and Danger: Exploring Female Sexuality*. Boston: Routledge and Kegan Paul.

Simon, R.I. (1992). *Teaching Against The Grain*. Massachusetts: Bergin and Garvey.

Simon, R.I. (1987). Work Experience. In D. Livingston and Contributors. *Critical Pedagogy and Cultural Power*. Toronto: Garamond Press.

Smith, B. (1981). *The Ladies of the Leisure Class*. Princeton: Princeton University Press.

Smith, D. (1978). A Peculiar Eclipsing: Women's Exclusion from Man's Culture. *Women's Studies International Quarterly* (1): 281–295.

Smith, D. (1979). A Sociology for Women. In J. A. Sherman and E. T. Beck. (Eds.).

*The Prism of Sex: Essays in the Sociology of Knowledge.* Madison: The University of Wisconsin Press.

Smith, D. (1987). Women's Perspective as a Radical Critique of Sociology. In S. Harding. (Ed.). *Feminism and Methodology.* Bloomington: Indiana University Press.

Smith-Rosenberg, C. (1986). Writing History: Language, Class, and Gender. In T. de Lauretis. (Ed.). *Feminist Studies/Critical Studies.* Bloomington: Indiana University Press.

Sontag, S. (Ed.). (1987). *A Barthes Reader.* New York: Hill and Wang.

Spender, D. (1980). *Manmade Language.* London: Routledge and Kegan Paul.

Spender, D. (Ed.). (1981). *Men's Studies Modified: The Impact of Feminism on the Academic Disciplines.* Oxford: Pergamon Press.

Spender, D. (1982). *Invisible Women: The Schooling Scandal.* London: Writers and Readers Publishers.

Spender, D. and Sarah, E. (Eds.). (1980/1988). *Learning To Lose: Sexism and Education.* London: The Women's Press.

Spivak, G. (1987). *In Other Worlds: Essays in Culture and Politics.* New York: Methuen.

Stanley, Autumn. (1992). Review of Gerda Lerner's *The Creation of Patriarchy. Women's Studies International Forum.* 15(3): 434–438.

Steedman, C. (1982). *The Tidy House: Little Girls Writing.* London: Virago Press.

Steedman, C. (1986). *Landscape for a Good Woman: A Story of Two Lives.* New Jersey: Rutgers University Press.

Thompson, J. (1983). *Learning Liberation: Women's Response to Men's Education.* London: Croom Helm.

Volosinov, V. N. (1973). *Marxism and The Philosophy of Language.* Trans. by L. Matejka and J. R. Titunik. New York: Seminar Press.

Walkerdine, V. (1985a). On the Regulation of Speaking and Silence: Subjectivity, Class and Gender in Contemporary Schooling. In C. Steedman, C. Urwin, and V. Walkerdine. (Eds.). *Language, Gender and Childhood.* London: Routledge and Kegan Paul.

Walkerdine, V. (1985b). The End of Hope. Unpublished Manuscript.

Wear, D. (1993). *The Center of the Web: Women and Solitude.* New York: SUNY Press.

Weedon, C. (1987). *Feminist Practice and Poststructuralist Theory.* Oxford: Basil Blackwell.

Weiler, K. (1988). *Women Teaching for Change.* South Hadley: Bergin and Garvey.

Welch, S.D. (1985). *Communities of Resistance and Solidarity: A Feminist Theology of Liberation.* Maryknoll, NY: Orbis Books.

The Whig Standard. (March 14, 1988). Woman Claims Sex Bias as Department Vetoes Her Bid to be Firefighter. Kingston, Ontario Canada.

Williams, P. J. (1991). *The Alchemy of Race and Rights: Diary of a Law Professor.* Cambridge: Harvard University Press

Williamson, J. (1981/82). How Does Girl Number 20 Understand Ideology. *Screen Education* 40 (Autumn/Winter): 80–87.

Willis, P. (1977). *Learning to Labor: How Working Class Kids Get Working Class Jobs.* New York: Columbia University Press.

Witherell, C. and Noddings, N. (Eds.). (1991). *Stories Lives Tell: Narrative and Dialogue in Education.* New York: Teachers College Press.

Wolfe, A. (1986). Inauthentic Democracy: A Critique of Public Life in Modern Liberal Society. *Studies In Political Economy* (Autumn): 57–81.

Woolf, V. ([1929] 1977). *A Room of One's Own.* London: Collins Publishing Group.

Woolf, V. ([1938] 1966). *Three Guineas.* San Diego: Harcourt Brace Jovanovich .

Young, J. (Ed.). (1987). *Breaking the Mosaic: Ethnic Identities in Canadian Schooling.* Toronto: Garamond Press.

# INDEX